Academic
Writing

Academic
Writing

working with sources
across the curriculum

Mary Lynch Kennedy

SUNY College at Cortland

Hadley M. Smith

Ithaca College

PRENTICE-HALL, INC., Englewood Cliffs, New Jersey 07632

Library of Congress Cataloging in Publication Data

Kennedy, Mary Lynch, (1943-)
  Academic writing.

  Bibliography: p.
  Includes index.
    1. English language—Rhetoric. 2. Report writing.
    3. Interdisciplinary approach in education.
  I. Smith, Hadley M., (1950-)   II. Title.
  PE1478.K39–1986   808′.042   85-6277
  ISBN 0-13-001611-X

Editorial/production supervision
  and interior design by Martha M. Masterson
Cover design by Ben Santora
Manufacturing buyer: Harry Baisley

Printed in the United States of America

10 9 8 7 6 5

ISBN 0-13-001611-X 01

PRENTICE-HALL INTERNATIONAL (UK) LIMITED, *London*
PRENTICE-HALL OF AUSTRALIA PTY. LIMITED, *Sydney*
PRENTICE-HALL CANADA INC., *Toronto*
PRENTICE-HALL HISPANOAMERICANA, S.A., *Mexico*
PRENTICE-HALL OF INDIA PRIVATE LIMITED, *New Delhi*
PRENTICE-HALL OF JAPAN, INC., *Tokyo*
PRENTICE-HALL OF SOUTHEAST ASIA PTE. LTD., *Singapore*
EDITORA PRENTICE-HALL DO BRASIL, LTDA., *Rio de Janeiro*

To Bill, Liam, and Maura

—M.L.K.

To Nancy, Colin, and Annie

—H.M.S.

Contents

chapter 13
Planning the Research Paper   199

chapter 14
Writing and Revising the Research Paper   220

Preface
To the Instructor

The purpose of *Academic Writing* is to teach freshman writers how to understand the ideas they read in college-level texts and use these ideas in academic writing tasks. The most obvious rationale for this approach is that outside the composition class, a major portion of college students' writing is related to, or based on, their reading. College professors rarely ask students to express views about personal experiences. Instead, they expect students to write about assigned readings. From the first day of class they expect freshmen to be able to deal with readings on literal and interpretive levels when performing writing tasks such as paraphrasing, summarizing, and outlining; moreover, they require students to apply the knowledge gained from reading to writing essays and research papers. Thus, typical college-level assignments draw heavily both on students' writing skills *and* on their reading skills.

Academic Writing teaches students how to read with comprehension and how to paraphrase, summarize, react to, quote, critically review, and research other writers' ideas. The format is that of a combined rhetoric and workbook. The textbook provides integrated instruction in writing and reading oriented toward the type of academic tasks that college freshmen typically face. Each chapter stresses the interrelationship between writing and reading processes and demonstrates how students can use writing and reading strategies together to approach college-level assignments, ranging from short paraphrasing tasks to complete research papers.

Throughout the book, we systematically analyze writing and reading processes so that students see how to approach academic tasks according to a structured, step-by-step plan. We make extensive use of material from college textbooks and supplemental readings covering a wide range of academic disciplines. Ilustrative examples of actual student responses to writing/reading assignments based on passages from college textbooks are included. While the examples from textbooks used in this book reflect the difficulty level that students encounter in courses across the curriculum, we present concepts at a level that is accessible to the majority of freshmen.

We make no assumptions about students' prior knowledge. For example, in the first part, Reading to Rephrase, we first give a thorough explanation of the basic units of language and then gradually move on to complicated aspects of sentence structure, to build a base for teaching paraphrasing. Knowledge of sentence structure is a significant variable influencing success in paraphrasing. Thus, a review of basic sentence structure is necessary in order for students to learn to paraphrase. As in the first part, throughout the book we explicate fundamental concepts before we present new knowledge. Thus, *Academic Writing* is organized to assure that all the necessary background information needed for basic academic writing and reading is available.

The overall organizational format of the book reflects its purpose: to help college students understand the ideas they process during reading and use them in academic writing tasks. The text contains six parts, in which we teach students the reading comprehension strategies they need for different writing purposes. The purpose in the first section is READING to REPHRASE other writers' ideas and use them in paraphrases; in the second section, READING to REDUCE other writers' ideas and use them in summaries; and in the third section, READING to REACT on paper to other writers' ideas. In the fourth section, students READ to REVIEW critically other writers' ideas. In the fifth section, they READ to REPEAT other writers' ideas in direct quotations. Finally, in the last section, they READ to RESEARCH other writers' ideas, and they use the other five Rs to incorporate the research in an extended paper. Thus, as students work through the text, they learn to *read* with comprehension while using six Rs: *rephrase, reduce, react, review, repeat,* and *research*—the operations they need to *compose* well-written academic papers.

The organizational format of each section helps students to understand the actual processes of reading and writing. Students learn how to segment academic assignments into a series of tasks. Each section begins with an introduction that explains how the academic writing strategy fits into the overall academic writing process and shows how students can use it to respond to college assignments. Then the particular writing technique covered in the section is explained in detail. The diagram shows the format for each section.

By emphasizing writing and reading processes, we provide students with a systematic plan that allows them to break down intellectual tasks into a series

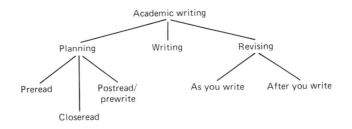

of discrete subskills that they can tackle one at a time. Thus, students see intellectual activity as a set of related strategies rather than as a set of unattainable standards of performance. Concentrating on process shifts the focus from professionally produced writing to student writing and reading. In fact, to show students how to approach academic writing/reading assignments, we use examples from actual student papers rather than from the work of recognized experts. *Academic Writing* will lead students to understand that a systematic analysis of writing and reading processes can provide the basis for success in courses across the curriculum.

The Instructor's Manual contains answers to exercises, additional writing assignments, and a bibliography of useful materials related to college reading and writing.

The planning of *Academic Writing* began six years ago. Over the past four years various portions of the text have been used in the course "College Reading and Writing" at Ithaca College, and for two years a pilot version of the manuscript served as the text for seventeen sections of this course. Thus, the instructional techniques, heuristics, exercises, and assignments have been tested thoroughly. We are greatly indebted to the people who used early versions of the text and offered their comments, suggestions for revision, and encouragement, especially our colleagues Ann O. Gebhard, Margaret Dietz Meyer, and Jeannette Miccinati, and all the students enrolled in the course.

We have informed *Academic Writing* with the ideas of a number of researchers in composition and reading. We owe much to Linda Flower, John Hayes, and Bonnie Meyer. A number of people generously helped us with the preparation of early pilot versions and the present manuscript. We owe thanks to Helen Armstrong, Katy Heine, Lary Jones, Becky Knauer, Dorothy Owens, John Paine, and Kathy Raine. We would also like to thank Liam Lynch Kennedy for his creative graphic contributions. At Prentice-Hall, we have had the privilege of working with an outstanding English editor, Phil Miller; with Robin Baliszewski; and with Karen Horton. We are indebted to our reviewers who contributed their ideas and insightful analysis: Lisa Albrecht, SUNY, Buffalo; Louis Emond, Dean Junior College; Patricia Grignon, Saddleback College; Michael J. Gustin, University of California, Los Angeles; Mary Frances Minton, Virginia

Commonwealth University; William Peirce, Prince George's Community College; and James L. Pence, Yavapai College. Finally, we want to give special thanks to Nancy Siegele and Bill Kennedy, whose help, humor, and moral support kept us smiling.

Mary Lynch Kennedy
Cortland

Hadley Smith
Ithaca

Academic Writing

Introduction

One of the most important events in Western European history occurred in Athens almost twenty-four hundred years ago when the Greek philosopher Plato founded the Academy, the forerunner of the modern college and university. As a result, students who formerly had depended on traveling lecturers for their "higher education" were able to attend a permanent school. Plato taught his students a systematic approach to study and thought that was later copied by many other educators. Thus, Plato's Academy marked the beginning of a long tradition of set *academic* procedures and standards that have developed in higher education over the centuries. Your college professors will expect you to understand and use the present-day *academic* approaches to study, especially those that involve writing and reading. The purpose of *Academic Writing* is to introduce you to the most important academic approaches and give you a set of strategies for responding to academic writing assignments in an intelligent, scholarly way.

ACADEMIC WRITING ASSIGNMENTS

Throughout your years in college you will encounter many different classroom situations that require writing. Each writing task will make you show your knowledge of an assigned *topic* to a particular *audience*. Often your professor will give you the topic, but sometimes you will have to choose, define, and limit the topic yourself. The audience who will read your paper are usually the course professor and your classmates. As an academic writer you form the link between the information on the topic and your audience. However, your role is not limited to passing on information just as you find it in books and articles. As you work on an academic writing assignment, you must make a series of decisions. For example, you must decide what sources of information you will use, what these sources mean, how you will organize the ideas, and what words you will use to explain the ideas. By making these decisions, you make the paper your own work rather than just a list of other people's thoughts. *Academic writing strategies* give you guidelines for making these decisions. All academic writing involves using certain standard strategies to communicate information on a given topic to a particular audience.

Knowledge of Academic Writing Topics

Your success with college writing assignments will be greatly affected by your knowledge of the topics. College professors will seldom assign topics based only on your past experiences such as, "Describe your home town," or "Compare high school and college." Even when you already have some knowledge of the assigned topic, your professor will expect you to learn more about the topic from academic sources, such as the professor's lectures, class discussions, films, and experiments. The *main source of your knowledge* for most topics, however, will be your assigned *reading* in the course textbook and in library articles and books that your professor has recommended or placed on reserve. Because reading is the main way of learning about academic subjects, *Academic Writing* will focus on *academic reading sources*.

Knowledge of the Academic Audience

Your audience is the person or people who will read your paper. As we have pointed out, for the majority of your college papers, your audience will be your professors and classmates. However, you may get assignments that ask you to write for other audiences. For example, an accounting student writing a practice financial report might be required to target the report for top company executives, for company stockholders, for the general public, or for other accountants. The way the student writes the report will depend upon the audience for which it is meant. It is important to remember that writing is not one-way communication. Even though your readers are not staring you in the eye as you write, they are very real, and you have to take their needs into account.

When you compose academic papers in which you use ideas you have read in articles and books, do not assume that your audience is familiar with the same background material or sources that you have read. You have to give your readers background information about your ideas and mention the reading source where you found them. You also have to be careful to indicate the difference between your own ideas about a topic and the ideas you have learned from your reading. For example, if you are writing a paper about the causes of World War I, you have to let your readers know when you are giving your own interpretation of the causes of the war and when you are presenting the views of an author whose book you have read. Throughout *Academic Writing* we will help you adapt your writing to your audience.

Knowledge of Academic Writing Strategies

Once you have knowledge about your topic and have thought about your audience's needs, you are ready to plan your paper. Sometimes your professors will tell you the academic writing strategy or plan they want you to use. For example, your assignment might be to *summarize* and *react* to Freud's theory of personality. The italicized words describe the writing plans you would need to use to complete the assignment. More often the instructor will not suggest a plan, and you will have to decide which strategy is best for the particular assignment. *Academic Writing* will provide you with specific plans for presenting and using reading materials in your compositions. You will learn how to *rephrase* (paraphrase), *reduce* (summarize), *react* to, critically *review*, *repeat* (quote), and *research* the material that you read. Knowledge of these six Rs, *rephrase, reduce, react, review, repeat,* and *research,* will enable you to respond to academic assignments in a mature, scholarly way.

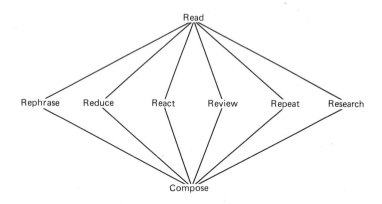

You will use the six Rs singly at times, but more often you will combine them to respond to academic assignments. As an example of how these strategies are integrated, imagine that you are taking an introductory course in political science, and your professor has assigned the following paper topic:

As a leader of India's struggle to gain freedom from England, Mahatma Gandhi encouraged his followers to "fight" against British authority and military strength without using any violence. This strategy grew in part out of Gandhi's belief that any violence was morally wrong even if the goal of the violence was to end injustice. In a 750-word essay, answer each of the following questions. Base your answers on the three reserve readings on Gandhi and on your own thoughts.

1. How did Gandhi see nonviolence as a political weapon?
2. How well would Gandhi's nonviolent strategies work if applied to current political conflicts?
3. What is your reaction to Gandhi's insistence that political strategies should be based on strong ethical principles?

Now let's see how a student might use all of the six Rs in writing a response to this question.

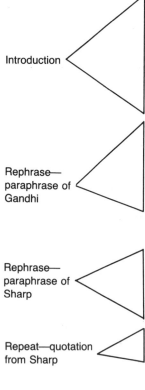

Introduction

Rephrase—paraphrase of Gandhi

Rephrase—paraphrase of Sharp

Repeat—quotation from Sharp

The popular image of Mahatma Gandhi as a prophet of nonviolence tends to underestimate his skill as a political strategist. In fact, Gandhi saw his principle of nonviolent resistance, which he called satyagraha, both as a moral code and as a political weapon. Unfortunately, satyagraha would work successfully only in a limited range of current political situations. But Gandhi's insistence on using only ethical means to achieve political ends deserves close attention today.

Although satyagraha was a moral principle, its goal was to achieve a real-world victory as well as maintain the moral integrity of the individual. Indeed, Gandhi chose the word *satyagraha,* a combination of the Sanskrit words for *truth* and *firmness,* because he felt it indicated a strength or force to support the truth (Gandhi 87). Clearly, Gandhi was willing to use this force to achieve political goals. Although Gandhi was a devout Hindu, his commitment to nonviolent political struggle came from his own thought rather than from religious doctrine. Sharp explains that many other Hindus felt people should avoid getting involved with the struggle between good and evil and instead rise above it spiritually; however, Gandhi felt one had a duty to directly oppose injustice (8). As Sharp points out, "The heart of satyagraha as an ethical principle is a technique of social action which has been used as a means of struggle for humanitarian goals and for basic change" (62). Thus, satyagraha was well suited to serve as a philosophical basis for Gandhi's campaigns for political goals.

From a practical point of view, satyagraha was the perfect political weapon for the Indians in their struggle for independence. Gandhi explained that since brute force was the only method of opposition Western powers recognized, India either

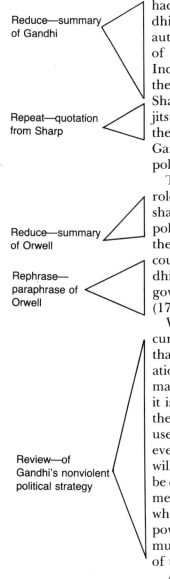

Reduce—summary of Gandhi

Repeat—quotation from Sharp

Reduce—summary of Orwell

Rephrase—paraphrase of Orwell

Review—of Gandhi's nonviolent political strategy

had to oppose Britain with war or with "non-cooperation." Gandhi went on to say that nonviolent resistance struck at the British authorities' true vulnerability, their inability to control millions of Indians by military strength alone. He stated that if most Indians refused to either cooperate with or rely upon the British, then England would no longer be able to rule India (157–58). Sharp describes Gandhi's technique as "a kind of political jiu-jitsu which generated the maximum Indian strength while using the British strength to their own disadvantage" (11). Clearly, Gandhi saw nonviolent resistance as a source of tremendous political strength for the Indian people.

There seems little question that satyagraha played a major role in achieving Indian independence. Even one of Gandhi's sharpest critics, George Orwell, readily admitted that Gandhi's political strategies worked in India (Orwell 179–80). However, there is considerable debate as to whether or not satyagraha could work in other political situations. Orwell stated that Gandhi's nonviolent strategies would be useless against a totalitarian government that quietly disposes of even the mildest opponents (178).

When we think of satyagraha as a possible tool to resolve current political conflicts, we must understand as did Gandhi that nonviolent resistance will work in some but not in all situations. Under certain conditions, nonviolent resistance can make matters so difficult for the oppressors that they may decide that it is not diplomatically or economically worthwhile to maintain their control. For example, American blacks have successfully used nonviolent resistance in the civil rights movement. However, in cases where oppressors are ruthless and completely unwilling or unable to compromise, nonviolent resistance will not be effective. In South Africa, a black nonviolent resistance movement would be unlikely to succeed since the extremely repressive white government does not feel it can afford to give up any power. Thus, the success of nonviolent resistance depends very much today, as it did in Gandhi's time, upon the characteristics of the situation in which it is used.

Although Gandhi was unquestionably an effective political leader, his unwillingness to resort to unethical or immoral means to achieve a political victory makes him unique among twentieth-century politicans. As I watched the Richard Attenborough film *Gandhi,* I was particularly struck by the scene in which Gandhi fasted almost to death to stop Indians from using violence against the British. I realized that no American politician would make a similar sacrifice for moral or ethical principles. In fact, we take

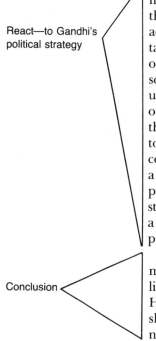

React—to Gandhi's political strategy

for granted that our politicians' statements of principles are often mere rhetoric that they use to help themselves get elected and then largely ignore once they are in office. We have become accustomed to the news stories of politicians who are "on the take." We expect politics to be "dirty." As an example, I think of my family discussion of the Watergate incident, a political scandal that revealed President Nixon and his staff members' unethical political strategies. My father maintained that Nixon's only mistake was getting caught. I disagreed with my father at the time, and I still do today. I feel our political system places too much emphasis on winning elections and not enough on commitment to basic principles such as honesty and justice. At a time when many of us accept unethical behavior as a necessary part of politics, we would do well to study Gandhi's political strategies more closely. Gandhi demonstrates that one can achieve a major and difficult political victory without compromising one's principles.

Conclusion

Gandhi developed the concept of nonviolent action as both a moral principle and an effective political tool. Clearly, there are limits to the situations in which nonviolent resistance will work. However, Gandhi's commitment to ethical behavior in politics should serve as a model to us as we attempt to improve the nature of our political institutions.

Works Cited

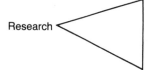

Research

Gandhi, Mohandas K. <u>The Essential Gandhi.</u> Ed. Louis Fisher. New York: Vintage Books, 1962.
Orwell, George. "Reflections on Gandhi." In <u>A Collection of Essays by George Orwell.</u> New York: Harcourt, Brace, Jovanovich, 1946.
Sharp, Gene. <u>Gandhi as a Political Strategist.</u> Boston: Porter Sargent Publishers, 1979.

This example shows you how you can use the academic writing strategies we teach in this book—paraphrase, summarize, react, quote, review, and research—to respond to an actual academic assignment. Throughout the book, we will continue to emphasize how the strategies work together in academic writing. We will teach you how to learn about assigned topics from reading materials, how to analyze your academic audience's needs, and how to use appropriate academic writing plans. Writing academic papers will never be as effortless as writing a thank-you note. However, after you work through the exercises and cases in this book, you will be able to approach academic assignments with increased confidence and expertise.

THE PROCESS OF ACADEMIC READING AND WRITING

We have just discussed a way of thinking about academic reading and writing that can help you to cope with college level work. Overall, the academic writing process is the same process you use for any type of writing: (1) you collect your ideas and *plan* what you are going to write about; (2) you *write* to get your ideas down on paper; (3) you *revise* your writing to make your ideas more understandable to your reader and to make them conform to the conventions of standard written English (grammar, punctuation, mechanics).

Planning

As we pointed out earlier, the central difference between academic and nonacademic writing occurs in the planning stage of the writing process. Because academic assignments require you to write about other people's ideas as well as your own views on the topic, you often have to comprehend, analyze, and combine ideas from various reading materials and summarize and paraphrase them as well as quote directly from them.

Many students do not realize the importance of careful, purposeful reading. They approach academic reading materials the same way that they approach popular novels and magazine articles. Good readers, however, know how to read for different purposes. They adapt their techniques to the particular purpose of the reading; consequently, they use very different strategies for academic work than for leisure reading.

When students read academic material, comprehension does not come naturally. It is the result of thinking about the reading material in very specific ways. Throughout *Academic Writing* we will propose reading methods that involve three sets of activities: (1) *prereading* (2) *close reading,* and (3) *postreading/prewriting.* As you work through these three procedures, you will increase your understanding of the important ideas in academic sources and will work to explain these ideas to someone else. Prereading, close reading, and postreading/prewriting are essential parts of the academic writing process.

Writing

Writing is taking your own ideas and the ideas you got from reading, organizing them in sentences and paragraphs, and communicating them to your audience. Most likely, your planning-stage notes will be sketchy and disconnected. In the first draft of your paper, you will shape the planning notes into various patterns and structures and logically arrange your ideas in a way that will help the reader of your paper follow your train of thought.

Revising

Writers revise *as* they compose and *after* they complete a draft. As you write your papers, you will find yourself stopping frequently to reread a few words or sentences and cross out or add information. After you complete a paper, you will read it over to make further revisions. In *Academic Writing* we provide you with *checklists for revision*. These checklists allow you to evaluate realistically the various assignments that you write.

You will notice that each section of this book is patterned after the *plan, write, revise* reading/writing process. You will learn specific reading and writing techniques, but more important, you will acquire a general method for approaching academic assignments. Always keep in mind how each technique that you learn fits into the overall academic writing process.

Throughout *Academic Writing* we present a number of *cases in point*—opportunities for you to apply the strategies you are learning to actual college assignments. As you work through these cases, you will come to understand how you operate as both a writer and a reader in college. The aim of this book is to help you improve your ability to write about the ideas you encounter in college reading sources. In a sense the best measure of how well you use the strategies for academic writing and reading will not be your performance on the cases in point in this book but rather your success on the papers required for your other courses.

Reading To Rephrase

WHAT IS PARAPHRASING?

How many times have you read something you were sure you understood and then found that you were totally unable to explain the material to someone else? Many students experience the frustration of feeling that they know something but are unable to show they understand it. The problem is that there are different levels of understanding. Reading a chapter in a textbook without becoming confused is one level of understanding. However, reading a chapter and being able to express the ideas in the chapter in your own words is a higher level of understanding. The process of translating someone else's ideas into your own words is called *paraphrasing*. Unfortunately, the process of paraphrasing is not often taught as a separate skill even though much of the work assigned in college assumes that students will be able to paraphrase complicated academic writing. In the next three chapters, we will involve ourselves in the paraphrasing process.

The following definition describes the unique characteristics of academic paraphrases:

When you paraphrase a piece of academic writing, you write a passage that has *exactly* the same meaning as the original piece of writing but is different enough in both the choice of words and the arrangement of ideas to be considered your own work. You must *always* accompany a paraphrase by a clear statement that identifies the piece of writing on which the paraphrase is based.

This definition makes several important points about an academic paraphrase:

1. The paraphrase must have exactly the same meaning as the original. You must put *all* the original information in it, but you should not put in information that is not in the original. This extreme precision is an *absolute* essential for any academic paraphrase.
2. The paraphrase must be different enough from the original to be considered your own work. You may ask, "How different is different enough?" You will learn the answer to this question in the next three chapters.
3. The paraphrase must always include a reference to the original source.

Paraphrasing vs. Summarizing

Failure to distinguish between paraphrasing and summarizing can cause you serious problems. A paraphrase contains *all* the information in the original source. *No part of the original is left out.* A summary contains only the *most important* information in the original. The following example gives both a paraphrase and a summary of the same piece of writing.

Original piece of writing: Urban renewal is the term used to describe the efforts of cities to accomplish the three major objectives of slum prevention through neighborhood conservation and housing code enforcement, rehabilitation of structures and neighborhoods, and clearance and redevelopment of structures and neighborhoods.

Blair, George. *American Local Government.* New York: Harper & Row, 1964. 88.

Paraphrase: Cities often attempt to prevent slums by enforcing housing codes and conserving, rehabilitating, clearing, and redeveloping buildings and neighborhoods. This process is referred to as urban renewal. *Summary:* Measures cities take to prevent slums are called urban renewal.

Notice that the summary contains the original passage's main idea but not all the details. Now look at the paraphrase. It contains each piece of information in the original only in different words. Clearly, a paraphrase is useful when you want to record precisely the original's total meaning, and the summary is useful when you need only the original's main idea. We will discuss summaries in depth in the next section.

Paraphrasing vs. Quoting

Quoting is writing the *exact* words and word order of the original source. *When you quote a source always put quotation marks around the words that you borrow and tell exactly where they come from.* This process of acknowledging the source is called *documentation*. We will discuss quoting and documentation in detail in Chapter 12.

Some freshmen quote directly every time they use information from an outside source. This is usually a mistake. Direct quotations are necessary only when you have reason to use the precise wording of the original. For example, if you were writing a paper on a certain Supreme Court decision, you might want to quote directly from the part of the U.S. Constitution that the Supreme Court was asked to interpret in the case. Usually you can express other writers' ideas without quoting their exact words. But remember you still have to document the source because you are paraphrasing someone else's ideas. Forgetting to document either a quotation or a paraphrase is considered a form of plagiarism, a very serious academic offense that can lead to failure or even expulsion. In the academic world, writers' ideas and words are their personal property, and students can use these ideas only if they properly acknowledge the original writers. If you have *any* questions concerning the general issue of plagiarism, or if you are unsure whether or not you are plagiarizing when you write, make sure that you consult your instructor.

SUMMARY

What paraphrasing is:

1. A method of preserving the meaning of an information source in your own words
2. A writing tool that helps avoid using too many quotations
3. A study tool that helps you put ideas in a form that will be easier to study and remember
4. A writing tool that helps you clarify ideas taken from an outside source
5. A reading technique that helps you unlock the meaning of difficult textbook passages

What paraphrasing is not:

1. Summarizing only the main points of a source
2. Quoting directly from a source
3. Copying a source using only slightly different words and sentence structure
4. Including your own ideas with those from the source
5. Altering the content of the original in any way

In order to paraphrase an academic source, you must locate the sentence or passage that best serves your purpose and then capture its meaning in your own words.

HOW PARAPHRASING FITS INTO THE ACADEMIC WRITING PROCESS

Planning
  Prereading
    1. Clarify assignment and topic.
    2. Consider your audience's needs.
    3. Preview the academic source.
    4. Set goals for reading.
      a. What do you expect to learn from the source?
      b. What clues will help you find the information you want?
      c. What part of the source will you read closely?
  Close Reading
    1. As you encounter difficult sentences, ask
      a. What do any unfamiliar words mean?
      b. What is (are) the sentence kernel(s)?
      c. How is (are) the sentence kernel(s) expanded?
      d. What is the main idea of the sentence?
    2. Make notes on the content of the source.
  Postreading/Prewriting
    1. Decide what you will paraphrase.
    2. Write a loose paraphrase.
    3. Reconsider topic and audience.
Writing
    1. Substitute synonyms for words in the original source.
    2. Use varied sentence patterns.
    3. Change the order of ideas.
    4. Break down long sentences into shorter ones.
    5. Make abstract ideas more concrete.
Revising
  As You Write
    1. Compare paraphrase with original sentence and with loose paraphrase.
    2. Consider paraphrasing pitfalls.
    3. Evaluate paraphrase in terms of topic and assignment.
    4. Evaluate paraphrase in terms of audience needs.
  After You Write
    1. Compare paraphrase to overall plan.

chapter 1

Planning
the Paraphrase

Often students think of paraphrasing as just a minor part of the writing process. In fact, some students wait until they are writing the final drafts of their papers to begin putting the ideas from sources into their own words. However, to paraphrase effectively, you must start at the planning stage. Waiting until the end of the writing process to think about paraphrasing can lead to weak paraphrases and inappropriate choice of source material.

PREREADING

Clarifying the Assignment and the Topic

There is no point in worrying about translating an author's ideas into your own words until you have located material that is appropriate for your assignment. Too often students assemble a vast array of sources and work to paraphrase them only to find that none of them are relevant to the assigned topic. Asking yourself the following questions about your assignment will help ensure that you locate sources appropriate for your paper and will begin to prepare you for paraphrasing these sources.

Do you understand the meaning of the assignment?

Many students begin to write before they fully understand what they are supposed to accomplish in their papers. Before you do anything else, spend some time thinking about what the assignment asks for. Can you relate the assignment to what you have been studying in the course? Do you understand all the ideas and terminology in the assignment? Does the assignment have different parts that must be answered separately? Make sure you consult the instructor if you are unable to answer any of these questions.

Does the assignment ask you to use academic sources?

Some assignments may ask for your own reactions and specifically state that you should not include other people's ideas. Other assignments will require that you use the information from academic sources in your paper. Before you look to academic sources for ideas, make sure that this approach will be appropriate for your assignment.

If you need to locate your own sources, what will you look for?

The assignment should serve as a guide in selecting sources. You should make a list, based on the assignment, of topics and key terms that you will look for in the titles of academic sources as you do the research. If you can make this list very specific, you will save time in research and avoid using inappropriate sources in your paper.

Is the assignment open-ended? If so, how will you limit it?

Many assignments allow you to choose your own topic either entirely or in part. You should try to decide on a specific topic before you begin to do research. In some cases, you may need to do a certain amount of reading to get an idea of topic possibilities. However, you should begin your reading with as specific a focus as possible. You can always change your topic if there are too few sources for your original choice.

Can you rewrite the topic in your own words as it might eventually appear in your introduction?

Paraphrasing the assigned topic not only helps clarify the assignment but also gives you a head start on writing your paper. The first thing you will need to do in your paper is explain the topic you are writing on. You can record the result of the work you did to understand the topic at the prereading stage and thus begin to write your introduction.

EXERCISE 1

Carefully read the following operations.

1. Underline any vocabulary words you do not understand.
2. Enumerate the different parts of the assignment.
3. Indicate whether the assignment calls for (a) reaction, (b) academic sources, or (c) reaction and academic sources.

4. List the topics and key terms you would look for in the titles of academic sources as you do research.

5. Rewrite the assignment topic in your own words.

6. Underline statements that offer clues to the writer's plan.

Now use the operations to analyze the following assignment.

1. *(for a biology class)* Read the two articles on reserve in the library on contamination of American waters. In a two-page essay, answer the following question: What are the effects of oil spills on the fish population near the Atlantic and Pacific coasts?

2. *(for an art history course)* Give your impression of the Pop Art movement and explain how it evolved.

3. *(for a political science class)* Restate Marx's definition of communism for the students in this class.

4. *(for a psychology class)* Compare and contrast the theories of Freud, Jung, and Horney. Summarize the theories and explain how psychotherapists use them today.

5. *(for a literature class)* Write a brief (200–250-word) paper in which you describe what it is like to be a pilgrim en route to Canterbury in Chaucer's time.

Considering Your Audience's Needs

When you paraphrase, you express the ideas in an academic source in a form that your audience can readily understand *without having read the original source*. Even when you are writing for a professor, someone who has read widely in your topic area, you cannot assume that the professor will be familiar with every source you find. Although you may be writing on assigned readings, most professors prefer that you write as if your audience is unfamiliar with the source. Many students make the mistake of writing as if their audience has already read the source, and thus they produce a paper that is extremely difficult to understand. Paraphrases of particular sentences or passages from a source make little sense unless your audience has some notion of the background into which this information fits. *You must think about your audience even before you begin to read the sources for your paper because the intended audience will affect the amount and type of information you choose to paraphrase.* Asking the following questions will help you prepare to paraphrase for a particular audience.

How much general background information will your audience have on the topic? How much of this background will you need to provide?

When you select information from sources to paraphrase and include in your paper, you should not ignore the general background information that helps your audience understand the parts of text that speak specifically to your topic. If you do not record this background information as you read, you may be unable to provide your audience with the context that will make the ideas you paraphrase understandable.

Will your audience be familiar with any vocabulary specific to the field of study?

As you read through a source that uses a specialized vocabulary, you usually begin to think about the subject in terms of these words. However, if you are reading with the intention of eventually paraphrasing the source, you must begin to think of the words that will help you to communicate the ideas in the source to your audience. Remember that your audience is not necessarily familiar with the original source and thus may not know the specialized vocabulary you learned from the source.

Previewing the Academic Source

When you first look at a source that you have been instructed to use or have located through your own research, you should first preview the source to get a general notion of what it is about. Previewing helps in two ways: First, it helps guide you to sources that will be appropriate for your topic and thus eliminates unnecessary reading. Second, it forms a basis for understanding the source as you move on to a careful reading. The detail that you come across in your close reading will be more meaningful to you if you first have a general notion of what the source is about. As a result, you will be better able to decide what parts of the text you should select for paraphrasing. Asking the following questions will help you preview an academic source.

What is the title of the source?

The title is the most obvious clue to the general content of an academic source. When you do research, you will often use titles as the basis for deciding which sources seem potentially useful. Read the titles carefully and try to project what the sources will be about.

Who is (are) the author(s)?

Sometimes you use the author rather than the title to guide you to the material relevant to your topic.

What are the subdivisions of the source?

If you are working with a book, look through the table of contents to locate chapters that seem relevant to your topic. Then look at the subsections of these chapters to find the parts that will be most useful. For an article look at the section headings. Pay close attention to any parts of the source that seem to summarize main ideas.

What do the text study aids tell you about the content of the source?

Many books and articles are organized specifically to help you preview the source before your close reading. Outlines, introductions, abstracts, summaries, conclusions, review questions, and other study aids all help you understand what sources are about and direct you to the pages that cover specific topics.

Can you make connections between the topic and the ideas in the source?

Before you read carefully, you should use previewing to help you think of how the information in the source will fit into your paper. *Write down these connections as preliminary notes* before you begin your close reading. If you can't make a connection, then you may decide not to bother reading the source.

EXERCISE 2

Preview the article on pages 250–252 in Appendix B. Answer each of the following questions based on your preview.

1. What is the title of the source?
2. Who is (are) the author(s)?
3. What are the subdivisions of the source?
4. What do the text study aids tell you about the content of the source?

Setting Goals for Reading

Based on your knowledge of the topic and audience and on your preview of the source, you should decide what you want to accomplish as you read.

What do you expect to learn from the source?

You should think of what information related to your topic you hope to have when you finish reading the source. A good method is to actually write out questions that you want to answer as you read. Recording the answers to these questions as you read is an effective way to begin paraphrasing the source.

What clues will help you find the information you want?

Note any key words or phrases that will help you know when you have found the information you are looking for.

What part of the source will you read closely?

Instructors generally assume that you will read all assigned readings. If a paper topic is based on particular sources that the instructor has chosen, then you will want to read all the sources carefully. However, when you are trying to locate sources on your own, you may find in your preview that only certain parts of the sources are useful to you. In these cases, you would carefully read only the relevant sections. Previewing can help you locate the sections that need to be read completely. Also, you can scan sources, looking for key words or phrases that point to the sentences you may want to paraphrase.

CASE IN POINT 1

Assume you are enrolled in an introductory course in communications. Your professor has assigned different paper topics to each of six discussion groups in the class. This is your assignment:

> Words are not our only means of communication. Write a two-page, five-paragraph essay, in which you explain the role of different types of nonverbal communication in daily life. You will find useful information for your essay in Mehrabian's article "Communication Without Words," which is on reserve in the library. Be prepared to share your written essay with your classmates in discussion groups.

> You may find it useful to use the following organization for your essay.

> 1. In the first, introductory paragraph, define nonverbal communication, mention different types of nonverbal communication, and point out what a person's nonverbal behavior communicates.
> 2. In each of the three body paragraphs, present one of the types of nonverbal communication you mentioned in the introduction. Explain what the specific type of communication conveys.
> 3. In your last, concluding paragraph, sum up the role that the different types of communication you discussed in your essay play in everyday life.

The article "Communication Without Words" can be found in Appendix B. Before you read the article, use the four prereading strategies in order to

1. Clarify the assignment and topic.
2. Consider your audience's needs.
3. Preview the academic source.
4. Set your goals for reading.

Stop here, unless your instructor tells you otherwise. You will have a chance to come back to this assignment later.

CLOSE READING

Figuring Out the Meaning of Difficult Sentences

As you read through academic sources, you will come across sentences that you have difficulty understanding. How frequently this happens depends upon the complexity of the subject matter and the author's style of writing. If an academic source has relatively few of these difficult sentences, you may be able to understand the message even if you skip over them. However, if the key ideas are expressed in difficult sentences, or the difficult sentences occur frequently, you will have to make sure that you comprehend these sentences as you come across them.

You can increase your understanding of difficult sentences by asking yourself the following sequence of questions.

What are the meanings of any unfamiliar words?
What is (are) the sentence kernel(s)?
How is the sentence kernel expanded?
What is the sentence's main idea?

What are the meanings of any unfamiliar words?

As you read, you will sometimes have to stop and either look up or figure out the meanings of unfamiliar words. Frequently the meaning of an entire sentence will depend upon a single word. In such cases, you must understand the crucial word before you can arrive at the meaning of the sentence.

An important part of learning a subject is becoming familiar with the special vocabulary of that field of study. Thus, especially in introductory courses, you should make sure that you look up any words that you do not know. Textbooks often contain *glossaries,* lists of important terms along with their definitions, to help you learn the special vocabulary of a particular subject. You can also compile your own vocabulary list for each course. Such lists can serve as a quick reference when you need to look up words and are also helpful when you are reviewing for exams.

What is (are) the sentence kernel(s)?

Almost all sentences in academic writing have subject/verb units. We call these units *sentence kernels* because the meanings of sentences develop from them just as plants sprout from seeds or kernels. It is important to locate the sentence kernel when you read a complicated sentence because the kernel provides the key to the organization of the writer's thoughts. Once you find the sentence kernel, you can unlock the meaning of the sentence and paraphrase it.

The following example illustrates the importance of locating the sentence kernel.

By virtue of its connection to many other societal ills such as drug addiction, crime, and disease, poverty can be considered a very basic social problem.

Although this sentence is not hard to read, many students do not completely understand it because they get the impression that its main idea concerns social problems in general. However, identifying the sentence kernel helps focus in on the true main idea:

By virtue of its connection to many other societal ills such as drug addiction, crime, and disease, <u>poverty</u> <u>can be considered</u> a very basic social problem.

The sentence kernel shows that the sentence is about poverty in particular rather than about social problems in general. Readers who are sensitive to the sentence kernel achieve a fuller understanding of the sentence. The key to unlocking meaning often hinges on finding the kernel, especially with more complicated sentences.

Up to this point we have limited our discussions to sentences built around a single sentence kernel. However, the sentences that you paraphrase will often contain more than one sentence kernel. Consider the following example:

The combined sentence contains all the information from each one-kernel sentence. Since the one-kernel sentences have the same verb, it makes sense to form a single sentence by joining the two subjects with *and*. Below are other ways a writer can combine one-kernel sentences in a single sentence.

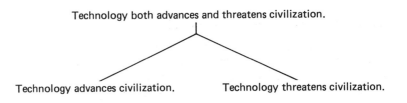

The combined sentence is built from one-kernel sentences that have the same subject but different verbs.

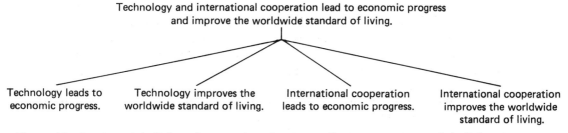

Technology and international cooperation lead to economic progress and improve the worldwide standard of living.

| Technology leads to economic progress. | Technology improves the worldwide standard of living. | International cooperation leads to economic progress. | International cooperation improves the worldwide standard of living. |

The combined sentence is built from four one - kernel sentences. Sentences are commonly built from even more than four one - kernel sentences.

These examples show some ways writers combine one-kernel sentences into long sentences. *Notice that the basic technique for locating one-kernel sentences within a complicated sentence is to look for subject/verb units.* Remember that every sentence kernel is organized around a subject/verb combination. *Understanding and paraphrasing a complex sentence often involves unpacking the one-kernel sentences that make up the larger sentence.* This process helps you locate the individual ideas that combine to form the full meaning of the sentence and thus makes the sentence easier to read.

How is the sentence kernel expanded?

We have pointed out the importance of locating the sentence kernel parts: the subject and the verb. But almost every sentence contains more than just the kernel. In fact, if we keep only the sentence kernel and throw away the rest of the sentence, we may destroy the meaning of the sentence. Consider the following sentence:

> The marvelous technology of mechanizing an ever increasing number of functions too hazardous, too laborious, too dangerous, or too complex for direct control by humans almost certainly promises tremendous improvements in the nature of work in our society.

Sentence Kernel: <u>Technology</u> <u>promises.</u>

Notice that the sentence kernel by itself does not make much sense. The words surrounding the kernel give us the added information we need to get the meaning. Of course, the sentence kernel plays an extremely important role because it forms the most basic unit of both sentence structure and meaning. However, other sentence parts may also help determine what the sentence means. Notice what happens when we replace some of the sentence's original words while keeping the same kernel:

> The horrifying <u>technology</u> of modern nuclear weapons definitely <u>promises</u> the complete destruction of human civilization.

Clearly the meaning of the second sentence has little in common with that of the original sentence even though both sentences contain the same kernel. In fact, combining a given sentence kernel with various words can make sentences that have many different meanings. In order to paraphrase a sentence, you should understand the way that the words outside of the sentence kernel may affect the meaning.

We call the process of adding words to a sentence kernel *expanding* the sentence kernel. The meaning of the sentence kernel is, of course, expanded by the words that are added to it. Often the expansions involve describing the subject and/or verb in more detail. The two previous sample sentences are both expansions of the same kernel. You can better understand and paraphrase a sentence by first locating the sentence kernel and then figuring out how the author has expanded this kernel to develop the idea more fully.

What is the main idea of the sentence?

Looking up unfamiliar words, locating sentence kernels, separating out sentence kernels that are combined, and seeing how the kernels are expanded will help you figure out the main idea of sentences that are difficult to understand. Meaning is embodied in words and the way that they are arranged into sentences. These strategies help you use knowledge of words and sentence structure to draw this meaning out. As we will see in the next chapter, understanding the structure of a sentence makes it easier for you to put the idea from this sentence into your own words.

Make Notes on the Content of the Source

As you work through a difficult academic source, you should make sure to write down the central ideas that you get from your reading. This is especially important for sentences that you need to pause over and study carefully to get the main idea. After you work to understand a difficult and significant sentence, you should make notes to preserve the meaning in your own words. In your own books, you can make these notes in the margin. Separate jottings in a notebook will be necessary for library materials. It is essential that you make some record of the understanding that you work to achieve. Do not trust your memory. You will forget many ideas you get from your close reading unless you write them down in your own words as you read. These notes can form the basis for the paraphrasing you will do later.

CASE IN POINT 2

Reread Case in Point 1 and reconsider your goals for reading. Now you are ready to return to Mehrabian's article for a *close reading*. As you read, use the close-reading strategies from this chapter. Be sure to take notes on the content. Check that you have answered the questions for figuring out the meaning of the difficult passages we have underlined in the article. For each of the under-lined passages, ask the following questions:

1. What are the meanings of unfamiliar words?
2. What is the sentence kernel?
3. How is the sentence kernel expanded?
4. What is the main idea of the sentence?

Be sure to take notes on the main ideas.

Stop here, unless your instructor tells you otherwise. You will have a chance to come back to this assignment later.

POSTREADING/PREWRITING

Deciding What You Will Paraphrase

As you look over the parts of the source that you made notes on or marked as potentially useful, you may see that some parts no longer seem important, some repeat ideas that appear elsewhere in the source, and some still remain relevant for your topic. Note the sections that you still think you might want to paraphrase.

Writing a Loose Paraphrase

In your own words, quickly write down the idea in the sentence or passage that you will want to paraphrase. This preliminary paraphrase could be written in the margin of your textbook, in your reading notes, or on the three-by-five-inch reference cards you are compiling for your paper. At this stage don't try to polish the paraphrase. Merely get down the main idea.

There are two reasons for coming up with loose paraphrases at this prewriting stage. First, loose paraphrasing forces you to write your notes in your own words. Second, just after you have finished reading, you will have good recall of the source and thus will be able to preserve the meaning you got from reading it. Over time, you may forget parts of the source and confuse different sources with each other. Make sure you record the title and author along with the loose paraphrase. Don't lose track of where the information came from.

Reconsidering Topic and Audience

After you write down each loose paraphrase, reread the assignment and take a moment to think again about your topic and audience. In particular, you should consider the following questions:

Is the information in the source relevant to the topic?

It is not too early in the writing process to begin to edit your notes and eliminate information that looked promising at first but on closer consideration doesn't seem to fit with your topic. Also begin to think of how and where you will use particular information in your paper, and record these thoughts in your notes next to the loose paraphrase.

Will your audience be able to understand the paraphrase if it stands alone? Will you need to include more information from the source so that the paraphrase makes sense?

When you have just finished reading a source and go back to consider a particular passage, you still remember the ideas that came before and after the passage; you know the *context* in which the passage appeared in the original source. Sometimes the passage will not make sense to someone who is not familiar with this context. You must make sure your audience will be able to understand your loose paraphrase if it stands alone.

What other revisions of the paraphrase will you have to make to suit your audience?

Although you should not take the time to perfect your paraphrase at this point, it is worthwhile to note quickly any changes you will need to make so that your paraphrase will suit your audience better. You should note, for later correction, any sections of the loose paraphrase that might confuse your audience.

CASE IN POINT 3

Review cases in point 1 and 2 and the Mehrabian article in Appendix B. They represent all the work you have done on the assignment up to this point. Now you are at the postreading/prewriting stage during which you will (1) decide on the parts of the text that need to be paraphrased, (2) come up with loose paraphrases, and (3) reconsider the topic and audience. The next step is to write loose paraphrases of the passages that are underlined in the Mehrabian article.

Stop here, unless your instructor tells you otherwise. You will have a chance to come back to this assignment later.

chapter 2

Writing
the Paraphrase

Although putting the meaning of an original source into your own words may not sound too complicated, it is often hard to paraphrase complex academic materials. To paraphrase complicated material, students need to approach the process systematically. In this chapter we discuss five basic strategies that will help you write paraphrases effectively.

USING SYNONYMS

When two words have approximately the same meaning, we say that they are *synonyms*. For example, the words *last* and *endure* are synonyms since their meanings are very similar. In our discussion we will include not only single-word synonyms but also certain phrases containing several words. For example, the phrase *continue as before* is a synonym for *last* just as *endure* is. It is often difficult to find a single word that has exactly the same meaning as a word in the academic vocabulary.

Finding Synonyms for Words You Already Know

Even when you are paraphrasing familiar words, you may have trouble finding synonyms for them. Many students who encounter this difficulty consult a dictionary or thesaurus and copy synonyms without considering how these words fit into the general sense of the sentence. This is usually a mistake. Paraphrases filled with synonyms taken indiscriminately from a dictionary or thesaurus are awkward and confusing. Strive to come up with your own synonyms that you can use with confidence rather than synonyms you have taken from a reference book. Following is a step-by-step procedure for finding synonyms for familiar words.

1. Come up with a word or phrase from your vocabulary that comes as close as possible to the meaning of the original word.
2. Read the original sentence substituting your synonym for the original word. Reread the sentence to see if it makes sense. If the new word changes the meaning, come up with another synonym and try the substitution again.
3. Compare the dictionary definitions of the original word and your synonym. If the definitions do not correspond, come up with another synonym and try the substitution again.

Finding Synonyms for Unfamiliar Words

Using Context Clues. When you are trying to paraphrase a passage that contains a word you don't understand, you may feel a strong urge to check a dictionary or a thesaurus for a synonym. Before you consult a reference book, try to figure out the approximate meaning of the unfamiliar word based on its relationship to the words you already know in the sentence. We call this procedure using *contextual clues* to discover a meaning. See if you can use contextual clues to figure out a synonym for each italicized word in the sentences below.

> After meeting someone for the first time, we often retain a *gestalt* of what that person is like but cannot remember specific details such as eye color.
> This particular *matrix* has four rows and five columns and thus can hold a total of twenty data values.

In the first sentence, the meaning of *gestalt* is shown to be something other than a memory of specific details, so a gestalt may mean an overall impression. The second sentence by describing a specific matrix suggests some of the general defining characteristics of a matrix. We could guess that a matrix is a gridwork having definite length and width that can be used to store numbers. Check each of these words in the dictionary and see how close the definitions derived from context are to the actual definitions.

Contextual clues will not give you a complete definition of an unknown word, but they will help you unlock enough of the meaning to know what synonym to substitute for it. Always check a synonym you figure out from contextual clues by substituting it for the word it replaces in the original sentence.

If you are not sure the synonym fits, you should consult a dictionary to check your understanding of the original word. Also, check your synonym against those listed in a dictionary or thesaurus.

Using a Dictionary and a Thesaurus.   The only strategy many students use for finding synonyms consists of looking up the original words and searching for synonyms in a dictionary or thesaurus. Actually, this should be the *last* of a series of steps. As we mentioned before, if you copy a synonym or a definition from a reference book without examining its fit in the original sentence, your paraphrase may not sound right or may not mean the same as the original. If you use the dictionary to find a substitute for an unknown word, try the following procedure.

1. Read *all* the definitions for the word. (Do not read the synonyms.)
2. When the dictionary lists more than one definition, reread the original sentence and see which definition works best in the context.
3. Try to come up with your own synonym based on the definition.
4. Replace the original word with your synonym. Does the sentence still have its original meaning?
5. If the dictionary gives synonyms for the original word, compare them to your synonym. Do they mean the same thing?

Repeating Key Words

You do not have to find a substitute for every word in the sentence you are paraphrasing. In many cases, some words from the original *must* be repeated in the paraphrase. For example, suppose you are paraphrasing the following definition of photosynthesis from your biology textbook:

> Photosynthesis refers to a biochemical process by which green plants make their own food using light as a source of energy.

Even though the word *photosynthesis* appears in the textbook definition, you must include it in your paraphrase to identify the process you are writing about. In such cases, repeat words that are essential to the meaning of the sentence, but make the other words and the sentence structure different enough from the original to avoid plagiarism. You may also have to repeat words that have no simple synonyms. As a rule of thumb, don't repeat more than three words in a row from the original.

EXERCISE 3

Read carefully the following paragraph from James Monaco's book, *How to Read a Film*. Rewrite the paragraph, substituting synonyms for the

underlined words and phrases. Words that are single-underlined should be familiar to you. Remember to use the step-by-step procedure for finding synonyms for familiar words (p. 26) for these single-underlined words. Words that may be unfamiliar to you are double-underlined. If contextual clues do not unlock the meaning, consult your dictionary and use the step-by-step procedure for finding synonyms for unfamiliar words (p. 27).

The theoretical interrelationship between painting and film continues to this day. The Italian Futurist movement produced obvious parodies of the motion picture; contemporary photographic hyperrealism continues to comment on the ramifications of the camera esthetic. But the connection between the two arts has never again been as sharp and clear as it was during the Cubist Period. The primary response of painting to the challenge of film has been the conceptualism that Cubism first liberated and that is not common to all the arts. The work of mimesis has been left, in the main, to the recording arts. The arts of representation and artifact have moved on to a new, more abstract sphere. The strong challenge film presented to the pictorial arts was certainly a function of its mimetic capabilities, but it was also due to the one factor that made film radically different from painting: film moved.

Monaco, James. *How to Read a Film.* New York: Oxford University Press, 1977. 25.

USING VARIED SENTENCE PATTERNS

In the first section, we discussed how to expand sentence kernels. We stressed the ways that expanding a sentence kernel can alter or modify sentence meaning. However, we can change an expanded sentence kernel without altering meaning. We can take the basic units of the sentence and switch their order in the sentence without affecting the ideas they represent. In this process, we change the pattern of the sentence, but we do not alter its meaning. Varying sentence pattern is *extremely* important in paraphrasing since the goal is to repeat an idea with different sentence structure as well as with different words.

Let's look at an example of how the pattern of a sentence might be altered:

Original sentence: Technology can cause a disaster.
Altered sentence: A technological disaster is possible.

In this example we altered the sentence pattern by changing the subject from *technology* to *disaster*. Of course, there are many other ways to shift basic sentence parts without changing meaning. When several variations of an original sentence pattern occur to you, you may wonder which one you should choose for your paraphrase. Several options may be equally good, but you can sort out the good from the bad choices by considering the following points:

1. Does the altered sentence mean *exactly* the same as the original, and is this meaning clear to someone who reads the altered sentence without seeing the original?
2. Does the altered sentence read smoothly?

To see how these guidelines are applied, consider the following alteration of the sentence we worked with earlier:

> *Original sentence:* <u>Technology</u> <u>can cause</u> a disaster.
> *Altered sentence:* <u>Causing</u> a disaster <u>can be</u> a result of technology.

As in the previous examples, we obtained the altered sentence by shifting the basic parts of the original sentence. But is the meaning of the new sentence absolutely clear? With this word arrangement, we cannot easily distinguish between the cause and the effect in the sentence pattern. Also, the new sentence sounds terribly awkward. Thus we would not use this altered sentence as a paraphrase of the original.

Changing sentence patterns is a crucial and extremely powerful paraphrasing strategy. When you master this strategy, you will find that complex sentences can be paraphrased with much greater ease and understanding.

EXERCISE 4

Switch the order of sentence units to vary the pattern of each of the following short sentences. Be prepared to explain how you reordered the basic units of the original sentence.

Example:

Original sentence: Dependence is a product of parental overprotection.
Altered sentence: Parental overprotection produces dependence.

1. The total energy in an atom equals the mass times the speed of light squared.
2. The stockmarket often changes in response to international political events.
3. Napoleon was defeated by the combined forces of England and Germany at the Battle of Waterloo.
4. Adolescence begins with various changes in the body, including an increase in sex hormones.

5. The invention of the snowmobile has markedly changed the lives of Eskimos.

6. The interlocking triangles of the geodesic dome form a surprisingly strong self-supporting structure.

CHANGING THE ORDER OF IDEAS

Very often a sentence will be difficult to understand and thus to paraphrase because it contains several different ideas. In the last chapter, we discussed sentences that were a combination of closely related sentence kernels. These sentence kernels shared either a subject or a verb, so they could be easily written together as a single idea. However, other sentences contain two or more kernels that do not have subjects or verbs in common. When you read sentences of this type, you will recognize that they contain more than one idea since each sentence kernel usually expresses a separate idea.

> <u>Technology</u> <u>can improve</u> the quality of life if <u>we</u> <u>plan</u> carefully for the future.

This sentence contains two entirely separate sentence kernels as shown below.

Expanded sentence kernel 1: <u>Technology</u> <u>can improve</u> the quality of life
Connecting word: if
Expanded sentence kernel 2: <u>we</u> <u>plan</u> carefully for the future

The term *clause* refers to a sentence kernel and the words that serve to expand it. Thus the two expanded sentence kernels above are the two clauses in the sentence. *Every clause must contain a sentence kernel and thus must have a subject and a verb.* You may notice that the word *if* hangs between the two expanded sentence kernels in our example. We will discuss words such as *if* in detail later, but for the moment we will say that they are part of the clause that they are directly in front of. *If* comes at the beginning of the second clause, so it is part of this clause. Thus, we would identify the two clauses in the sentence we have been discussing as follows:

> *Clause 1:* <u>Technology</u> <u>can improve</u> the quality of life
> *Clause 2:* if <u>we</u> <u>plan</u> carefully for the future

An important paraphrasing strategy is to change the order of ideas in the sentence by reordering the clauses. Thus, we might begin to paraphrase the sentence in the earlier example by putting the clauses in reverse order.

Original sentence: Technology can improve the quality of life if we plan carefully for the future.

Reordered sentence: If we plan carefully for the future, technology can improve the quality of life.

This technique is similar to changing the sentence structure of a one-kernel sentence, as we discussed on page 28. However, when we reorder clauses, we are shifting around much larger units of meaning. We would, of course, have to change the vocabulary to complete our sample paraphrase.

EXERCISE 5

Rewrite each of the following sentences so that the clauses are in reverse order.

Example:

When Boris Pasternak was awarded the Nobel Prize for his novel *Doctor Zhivago,* Soviet authorities pressured him to reject the prize.

Soviet authorities pressured Boris Pasternak to reject the Nobel Prize when he was awarded it for his novel *Doctor Zhivago.*

1. As the Industrial Revolution progressed, exploitation of child labor became a serious social problem.
2. Although there are currently several theories concerning the origin of the universe, the Big Bang theory is the one most widely held.
3. Just as a heated gas will expand, a cooled gas will contract.
4. Despite the common belief that the brush is the primary tool of the painter, many well-known paintings were created entirely with pallet knives.
5. For someone who undergoes major surgery, it is extremely important to begin walking as soon as possible after the operation to avoid developing lung infections.
6. Before you invest your money, you should invest fifteen minutes of your time in reading the *Wall Street Journal* each day.
7. If there were any chance of surviving a nuclear war at all, we would not be giving our wholehearted support to complete disarmament.
8. Even though the secretary of defense disagreed with the president's plan to send troops to the Middle East, he did not resign from office.

BREAKING LONG SENTENCES INTO SHORTER ONES

We have already observed that certain sentences are difficult to understand because they contain a number of different ideas. These complicated sentences almost inevitably contain more than one clause and are difficult to follow. When trying to understand and paraphrase long sentences that have more than one clause, it often helps to break up the sentence into two or more shorter sentences, each organized around a clause. Presenting the ideas in several sentences allows your reader to deal with the ideas one at a time. When approaching academic material that is difficult to understand, it is often helpful to look carefully at the individual ideas that are tied together in sentences.

The following long sentence needs to be broken down. It has four clauses. See if you can locate them.

Mental disorder is undoubtedly a serious problem in our society, and as a result, dozens of different psychotherapeutic procedures have been developed over the past few decades, but to date these procedures rarely lead to a complete cure, so psychologists continue to search for new theories concerning the origin of mental problems and to look for new techniques for eliminating the distress of mental patients.

Below we have underlined the subjects and verbs in each clause.

Mental <u>disorder</u> <u>is</u> undoubtedly a serious problem in our society, and as a result, <u>dozens</u> of different psychotherapeutic procedures <u>have been developed</u> over the past few decades, but to date these <u>procedures</u> rarely <u>lead</u> to a complete cure, so <u>psychologists</u> <u>continue</u> to search for new theories concerning the origin of mental problems and to look for new techniques for eliminating the distress of mental patients.

Once we have located the individual clauses, the procedure for creating the shorter sentence is really quite simple. First, we divide up the original sentence where the clauses join. Second, we make sure that the shorter sentences have the proper logical connectors to preserve the original sentence meaning.

Mental disorder is undoubtedly a serious problem in our society. As a result, dozens of different psychotherapeutic procedures have been developed over the past few decades. However, to date these procedures rarely lead to a complete cure. Consequently, psychologists continue to search for new theories concerning the origin of mental problems and to look for new techniques for eliminating the distress of mental patients.

Breaking down the original sentence into shorter sentences is the first step in the paraphrasing process. Next, write each short sentence in your own words. You might also change the order of the shorter sentences to get farther away from the pattern of the original sentence.

When you are paraphrasing, it is often useful to break up a long sentence into shorter sentences even when the long sentence contains only one clause. Sometimes even sentences with one clause contain so much information that they are difficult to understand.

EXERCISE 6

Read carefully each of the long sentences below and underline the clause(s). Then write several shorter sentences with the same meaning as the original long sentence. The number of short sentences you should use is suggested after each long sentence. Make sure you provide logical connections between the short sentences.

Example:

Albert Einstein's theory of relativity was originally considered so controversial that it was not included in Einstein's list of accomplishments when he was awarded the Nobel Prize. [Use two shorter sentences.]

1. Albert Einstein's theory of relativity was originally considered very controversial.
2. Therefore, it was not included in Einstein's list of accomplishments when he was awarded the Nobel Prize.

1. Economics is the study of how people and society end up choosing, with or without the use of money, to employ scarce productive resources that could have alternative uses, to produce various commodities and distribute them, now or in the future, among various persons and groups in a society. [Use two shorter sentences.]

Samuelson, Paul A. *Economics*. 10th ed. New York: McGraw-Hill, 1976. 3.

2. Like all matter, the human body is composed of atoms and molecules, and in its moment-to-moment functioning depends upon the millions of interactions occurring between the various atoms and molecules it contains. [Use two sentences.]

Vander, Arthur J., James H. Sherman, and Dorothy S. Luciano. *Human Physiology: The Mechanisms of Body Function*. 2nd ed. New York: McGraw-Hill, 1975. 6.

3. After listening to a late baroque piece carefully all the way through, we may be surprised to realize how soon all the basic material is set forth and then, after that, how regular and repetitious the music is. [Use two sentences.]

Kerman, Joseph. *Listen*. 2nd ed. New York: Worth Publishers, 1976. 85.

4. Since the history of Western civilization has been one of invasion and conquest, the languages of various European peoples have intermingled for thousands of years; thus, it is difficult for modern linguists to determine the exact characteristics of the very early European languages. [Use three shorter sentences.]

5. Calculus, the mathematical technique that revolutionized the study of physics, was invented separately by both the British scientist Sir Isaac Newton and the German mathematician Wilhelm Leibniz, and although Newton's name is most commonly associated with the technique, Leibniz's notation is the one in common use today. [Use four shorter sentences.]

MAKING ABSTRACT IDEAS MORE CONCRETE

Most writing contains both *concrete* and *abstract* words. In general, concrete words describe or represent things that we can see, hear, touch, smell, or taste, whereas abstract words describe or represent things that we can think of but do not sense directly. Concrete words give us a sensory image. They often help us *see* in our minds a scene or an action. Abstract words give us ideas that speak to our judgment and reason rather than to our senses. For example, in a series of words describing a flower, the word *red* is concrete since it calls up a sensory image of a color. In the same series, *lovely* is an abstract word, requiring a judgment, since two people may disagree on whether or not a flower is lovely. Concrete words make us respond with our five senses, and abstract words make us use our minds to go beyond our senses.

Both concrete and abstract words are necessary in writing. However, concrete words are usually easier to understand than abstract words because they require less interpretation. Sentences that contain a lot of abstract words can be hard to read. When you are paraphrasing sentences that have many abstract words, you can make the meaning clearer by substituting concrete words for the abstract words.

The following sentence contains a number of abstract words:

The <u>creation</u> of an overall design for a complete computer system <u>is</u> the responsibility of a systems analyst whereas the <u>implementation</u> of the design plan <u>is</u> often the duty of a computer programmer.

We have underlined the subjects and verbs in the two clauses in this sentence. Notice that the subjects and verbs are abstract words. We cannot see an image of *creation* or *implementation* in our minds. The verb *be* does not describe a situation for which we have a visual picture. Now we will change the sentence so that the subjects and verbs are concrete.

The <u>systems analyst</u> <u>designs</u> the entire computer system, and the <u>computer programmer</u> <u>makes</u> the proposed system work.

The second sentence is easier to understand not only because it contains simpler words but also because we can visualize in our minds what the sentence says. The subjects are specific types of people, and the verbs are actions. When paraphrasing complicated sentences that contain abstract words, it is especially important to substitute concrete words for the original subject and verb. If these basic sentence-kernel parts are concrete words, the overall meaning of the sentence will be much easier to understand.

EXERCISE 7
Rephrase the passages below, using the following strategies:

1. Substitute synonyms.
2. Vary sentence pattern.
3. Change the order of ideas.
4. Break long sentences into shorter ones.
5. Make abstract ideas more concrete.

Write your paraphrases in your notebook.

1. When the division of labor has been once thoroughly established, it is but a very small part of a man's wants which the produce of his labor can supply. He supplies the far greater part of them by exchanging that surplus part of the produce of his own labor, which is over and above his own consumption, for such parts of the produce of other men's labor as he has occasion for. Every man thus lives by exhanging, or becomes in some measure a merchant, and the society itself grows to be what is properly called a commercial society.

   —Adam Smith, *The Wealth of Nations*

2. Yes, my friend; for the truth is that you can have a well-governed society only if you can discover for your future rulers a better way of life than being in office; then only will power be in the hands of men who are rich, not in gold, but in the wealth that brings happiness, a good and wise life. All goes wrong when, starved for lack of anything good in their own lives, men turn to public affairs hoping to snatch from thence the happiness they hunger for. They set about fighting for power, and this internecine conflict ruins them and their country. The life of true philosophy is the only one that looks down upon offices of state; and access to power must be confined to men who are not in love with it; otherwise

rivals will start fighting. So whom else can you compel to undertake the guardianship of the commonwealth, if not those who, besides understanding best the principles of government, enjoy a nobler life than the politician's and look for rewards of a different kind?

—Plato, *The Republic*

3. Indeed, we learn the manner in which mental intuition should be used, by comparing it with vision. For he who wishes to look at many objects at a time with one and the same glance, sees none of them distinctly; and similarly he who is used to attending to many objects at the same time in a single act of thought, is confused in mind. But those artisans who practise delicate operations, and are accustomed to direct the force of their eyes attentively to single points, acquire by use the ability to distinguish perfectly things as tiny and subtle as may be. In the same way, likewise, those who never disperse their thought among different objects at one time, but always occupy all its attention in considering the simplest and easiest matters, become perspicacious.

—Descartes, *Rules for the Direction of the Understanding*

CASE IN POINT 4

Case in point 4 is a continuation of cases 1, 2, and 3. It is in three parts:

Part I. Reread cases in point 1, 2, and 3. Look over all your responses to these cases.

Part II. Use the five paraphrasing strategies explained in Chapter 2 to paraphrase the reading excerpts that are underlined in the text. As you paraphrase, be sure to

1. Substitute synonyms.
2. Vary sentence patterns.
3. Change the order of ideas.
4. Break long sentences into shorter ones.
5. Make abstract ideas more concrete.

Part III. Use the outline presented in the assignment (Case 2) to write the two-page essay. Incorporate three of the seven paraphrases from part II at the places you think each fits most appropriately.

Stop here, unless your instructor tells you otherwise. You will have a chance to come back to this assignment later.

chapter 3

Revising the Paraphrase

As we mentioned in the introduction to this book, revising is not just a process of looking over a completed paper for errors. Writers revise as they write as well as after they have completed a draft of a paper. You revise paraphrases just as you revise the other parts of your paper.

REVISING PARAPHRASES AS YOU WRITE

In the case of paraphrasing, the most significant revisions will take place as you write. The reason is that as you write, you need to look at both your notes and the original source in order to decide whether or not your paraphrase is adequate. It would be awkward and time consuming to check each source when you are trying to read through and revise the entire paper. Thus, you should carefully revise each paraphrase as you write the first draft of your paper.

Comparing the Paraphrase with the Original and with Your Loose Paraphrase

When you have finished writing a paraphrase during the writing stage, you should immediately compare it to the original and to the loose paraphrase you jotted down in your notes or in the text margin. Even when you apply the five paraphrasing strategies, you may occasionally get away from the meaning of the original, or you may remain too close to the original wording or sentence structure. You need to compare your paraphrase to the original to see if these problems have occurred. Since your loose paraphrase is a record of your initial understanding of the original source as you read it, comparing your final paraphrase to the loose paraphrase helps you check to see that you have preserved the original meaning.

The eight *paraphrasing pitfalls* should serve as a guide when you compare your final paraphrase to the original and to your loose paraphrase:

1. Misreading the original
2. Including too much of the original
3. Leaving out important information
4. Adding your opinion
5. Summarizing rather than paraphrasing
6. Substituting inappropriate synonyms
7. Expanding or narrowing the meaning
8. Forgetting to document

Now let's discuss how you can detect and remedy these paraphrasing pitfalls.

The Pitfall of Misreading the Original

Clearly, it is important to understand the meaning of the original sentence before you complete a paraphrase. However, you can certainly begin the process of paraphrasing before you have a complete understanding of the original sentence. Remember that some of the procedures during the planning and writing stages will increase your understanding of the sentence. Coming up with a loose initial paraphrase and then refining it will help you to stay close to the original sentence meaning. Remember that the sentence kernel is the sentence's most basic unit of meaning. Always take time to figure out the sentence kernel(s) when you are having trouble figuring out the meaning.

The Pitfall of Including Too Much of the Original

Chapter 2 gives detailed instructions on how to change vocabulary and sentence structure. Use these strategies and you will avoid the pitfall of following the pattern of the original sentence too closely when you paraphrase. As a rule of thumb, you should never repeat more than three words in a row from the original sentence.

The Pitfall of Leaving Out Important Information

You can guard against leaving out important ideas if you make sure that your paraphrase captures the central idea of each clause in the original. Remember that the number of clauses in the original is, in a sense, the number of separate thoughts. Although your paraphrase does not have to correspond to the original clause for clause, it has to include all of the information contained in each of the clauses in the original sentence.

The Pitfall of Adding Your Own Thoughts

Often students include in paraphrases their own interpretations of authors' ideas. Since these interpretations are not parts of the original sources, they cannot appear in paraphrases. To avoid this pitfall, be sure you understand what the sentence means before you finish your paraphrase.

The Pitfall of Summarizing Rather Than Paraphrasing

A summary is less precise than the original. Details that could be important to a reader are left out. A summary clearly will not do in situations where the meaning of the original must be represented completely.

The Pitfall of Substituting Inappropriate Synonyms

You should always use the procedure suggested earlier for finding synonyms rather than simply relying on the dictionary and using a word-by-word substitution process. An essential feature of that procedure is checking to make sure that the original meaning is preserved. When you work with a complicated sentence, it is especially important that you get a sense of the meaning of the entire sentence before you begin to substitute synonyms for the original words.

The Pitfall of Expanding or Restricting Meaning

Make sure that your paraphrase includes the same number of examples or situations as the original sentence does. Pay close attention to the scope of the original. Expanding or limiting the meaning may make an important difference in the ideas people will get from the sentence.

The Pitfall of Forgetting to Document

Remember that in an academic paper you must give the source of information that you paraphrase just as you must give the source of a direct quotation. *Failing to document a paraphrase is plagiarism.* Chapter 12, which covers the use of direct quotations, describes the proper format to use for documentation. You should make sure that your first draft clearly indicates what ideas are paraphrased from sources and what ideas are your own.

Although we have discussed each of the paraphrasing pitfalls separately, a poor paraphrase will often have several of these problems. Correcting one pitfall can actually cause a new difficulty. Thus, you should check the final version of your paraphrase for *all* of the potential pitfalls, even if you have already written several versions.

EXERCISE 8

Below are two sentences from textbooks along with sample student paraphrases. Analyze each paraphrase to see if the student writer has had problems with any of the eight paraphrasing pitfalls. If you locate pitfalls, give the student advice on how to remedy the problem and improve the paraphrase.

> *Original Sentence:* Astronomy is concerned primarily with an aspiration of mankind, which is fully as impelling as the quest for survival and material welfare, namely, the desire to know about the universe around us and our relation to it.
>
> Baker, Robert H. *Astronomy.* 7th ed. New York: D. Van Nostrand, 1959. 1.

Student Paraphrases:

(a) Astronomy deals with what man is all about, and it tells us what man is trying to do in life with the main goal of knowing the universe and how man functions in it.

(b) People don't like to be in the dark about their future. They want an understanding of the universe so they can deal with life.

(c) Astronomy is concerned basically with an aspiration of mankind which is as impelling as the quest for survival and material welfare, namely the desire to know about the universe and our relationship to it.

(d) Astronomy is concerned basically with a desire of mankind. This is completely as driving as the pursuit for survival and material welfare. It is basically the request to have information about the universe around us and our relation to it.

(e) Man's most aspiring desire in astronomy is to know as much about the universe as possible and our relation to it.

> *Original Sentence:* Somatic cells, while tiny compact worlds within themselves, nevertheless do not exist in isolation; instead, cells bond together, according to their special function, and thereby form definite units or structures called tissues.
>
> Luckman, Joan, and Karen C. Sorensen. *Medical-Surgical Nursing.* Philadelphia: W. B. Saunders, 1974. 138.

Student Paraphrases:

(a) A tissue is formed by the bonding of different somatic cells according to their common functions.

(b) Tissues that are definite units or structures are formed by cells that bond together. They bond according to the special functions they have. Somatic cells are an example of small cells that bond together to form a tissue instead of remaining separate.

(c) Somatic cells, like any other cells, do not live alone. They join together with other cells depending on their specific functions and form a substance called tissue.

(d) Tissues are formed when somatic cells collide outside their small worlds. In order for these cells to be bonded, they must match in a certain way.

(e) Tissues are formed by the bonding together of somatic cells according to their special functions.

EXERCISE 9

Reread the paraphrases you wrote for Exercise 7. Analyze carefully each paraphrase to check for pitfalls. If you locate any of these pitfalls, use the suggestions in this chapter to revise your paraphrase.

Evaluating the Paraphrase in Terms of the Topic

As you write the first draft of your paper, you decide what ideas and facts you will include, and you may even decide in the midst of writing to make a major change in emphasis or organization. Thus, by the time you start writing a particular paraphrase you may have departed from your original plan, and the information you are paraphrasing may not fit into the new direction that your paper is taking. If you have changed your writing plan, you must make sure the paraphrase still helps develop your topic.

Evaluating the Paraphrase in Terms of Audience Needs

When you are paraphrasing, your primary concern with your audience is that the content of the original source comes through clearly. In the process of checking for the paraphrasing pitfalls, you have made sure that the content of your paraphrase matched the content of the source. Now you must make sure that your audience will be able to understand your paraphrase. At the planning stage you assessed your audience's needs by asking two questions about the original source. You must now ask variations of the same questions to see whether or not your paraphrase is appropriate.

1. By reading the paper up to the point where the paraphrase is included, will your audience acquire enough background information to understand the paraphrase?

2. Will your audience be familiar with all the vocabulary in the paraphrase?

REVISING AFTER THE FIRST DRAFT IS COMPLETE

After you have finished the first draft of the paper, you will come back to edit your work and to write future complete drafts of the paper. At this stage your paraphrases should be accurate representations of the original sources, and thus you should not have to refer back to the original sources again. However, you still must consider how well the paraphrases accomplish your goals for writing your paper. You also must make sure that the paraphrases are written according to the accepted standards for written English.

Seeing How Your Paraphrase Fits Into Your Overall Plan

As you read through a completed draft of a paper, you should pay attention to how your paraphrases work together with your own ideas and with the paraphrases based on other sources. Many student papers seem like patched-together pieces of unrelated information. By carefully considering how well each paraphrase fits into the rest of your paper, you can avoid this impression.

Grouping Related Paraphrases Together.   As you revise, you may find that paraphrases need to be moved around to different parts of the paper so that they are grouped with similar information. Make sure that all the information you have on a particular aspect of your topic is grouped together. *Discuss one idea at a time, not one source at a time.* Later in this book we will explain specific ways to blend ideas from various sources.

Organizing each paragraph around a *topic sentence*—a sentence that includes the central idea of the paragraph—will help you to keep control of the information from academic sources. Decide what idea you want to develop in each paragraph and write your *own* topic sentence. Do not use a paraphrase for your topic sentence, as that would take control out of your hands and pass it to the author of the academic source. When you have a clear topic sentence, bring in paraphrases of relevant information to support the idea in the topic sentence.

The following checklist will help you evaluate your first rough draft of a paper before you go on to produce a second or final draft.

CHECKLIST FOR REVISION

A. Essay organization
  1. Does your paper have clear organizational divisions?
      a. Introduction?
      b. Body?
      c. Conclusion?
  2. Does each of your paragraphs include the necessary elements?
      a. A clearly stated topic sentence?
      b. Supporting sentences?
      c. Transitional and unifying devices?

B. Paraphrases used in the essay
   1. Is your paraphrase preceded by background information for your audience?
      a. Author and title of source?
      b. Proper documentation?
   2. Does your paraphrase blend in logically and smoothly with the material that surrounds it?
   3. Are related paraphrases grouped together?
   4. Do all paraphrases contribute to the paper as a whole?
   5. Is the content of each paraphrase easy to understand?
C. Consider the paraphrasing pitfalls. Have you:
   1. Misread the original?
   2. Included too much of the original?
   3. Left out important information?
   4. Added your own opinion?
   5. Summarized rather than paraphrased?
   6. Substituted inappropriate synonyms?
   7. Expanded or narrowed the meaning?
   8. Forgotten to document?
D. Editing—for grammar, usage, and mechanics

CASE IN POINT 5

Reread the essay you wrote in response to Case in point 4. Check that none of your paraphrases contain any paraphrasing pitfalls. Then compare your paraphrases to the topic and to your audience's needs. Check that you have grouped related paraphrases together. Finally, edit your essay for grammar, usage, and mechanics. Now produce a final draft of your essay.

WRAP-UP EXERCISE FOR REPHRASING

The following exercise gives practice in maintaining the meaning of an original sentence and locating paraphrasing pitfalls.

1. Divide the class into groups of three.

2. Number the members of your group #1, #2, and #3. Sit in a triangle facing each other.

3. Read the sentence *from the list below* that has the same number as your number in the group. Do *not* read either of the other sentences.

4. Write a paraphrase of the sentence that you read. Close the book when you are done without reading the other sentences. Label your paraphrase *a*.

5. When all your group members are finished with their paraphrases, pass your paper to the person on your left and take the paper from the person on your right.

6. Write a paraphrase of the *student paper* that you now have. Label your new paraphrase *b*.

7. Set all the *a* paraphrases aside. Exchange the *b* paraphrases by again passing papers to the left as in step 5.

8. Write a paraphrase of the student paper that you have just received. Label this paper *c.*

9. Your group should now have *a, b,* and *c* paraphrases of each of the three sentences. Group the paraphrases based on the same sentences together.

10. Open the book and, working together as a group, compare the *c* paraphrase of sentence #1 with the original sentence. If the two do not have the same meaning, back track through the three versions to locate the place(s) where the meaning changed. Come to an agreement on why the meaning was lost. Follow the same procedure for sentences #2 and #3.

1. Light is a complex phenomenon since it seems to behave as a wave, a particle, or both simultaneously depending on how it is studied.

2. Unfortunately, very little Old English poetry has been preserved for modern scholars, and the majority of the manuscripts that have come down to us are fragmentary, with large sections missing or damaged.

3. The treatment of the Indians by the white settlers of North America exemplifies the general principle that advanced cultures often destroy the more primitive groups they come in contact with.

Reading to Reduce

WHAT IS SUMMARIZING?

The process of reducing a longer work to shorter form is called *summarizing*. Recall the summaries you have worked with in the past:

> When you recalled the main points of a story
>
> When you read a brief condensation that gave the general idea of a book, film, or play
>
> When you read an abridgement of a magazine article or book

Can you think of examples of other types of summaries?

Summarizing is a technique you will use often in college. You will be asked to write different types of summaries for different purposes, but your primary goal will always be the same: *to make the original shorter without changing its meaning.* Some typical academic situations that call for summarizing are the following:

> To *recapitulate*—go over and repeat to yourself—the main ideas (headings and substance) of textbook chapters and lecture notes while you are studying.
>
> To write a *synopsis* or brief summary of the plot of a novel, film, or play
>
> To restate briefly in *notes* the main points of a textbook chapter

To write a *precis,* a shortened version that retains the organization and structure of the original article or book

To write an *abstract* of your own or another writer's essay

To write a summation of studies or experiments in a *review of the literature*

Can you think of other types of summaries you are called upon to write in college?

Later in your college career you may need to read *briefs,* which are summaries of leading legal cases, or *abstracts,* which are summary descriptions of the contents of articles in professional journals.

> *Definition:* When you summarize a piece of academic writing, you *reduce the original material without changing its meaning.* You retain main ideas and leave out details and minor examples. You must *always* accompany a summary with a clear statement that identifies the original piece of writing.

This definition makes several important points about an academic summary:

1. The summary must be shorter than the original. The length of your summary will vary from assignment to assignment. Depending on your purpose for summarizing, you may reduce a source to one-half, one-third, or even one-eighth its original length.
2. The summary should have the same meaning as the original. In your summary you should retain *the main ideas* in the original source and leave out details and examples. Never add information that is not in the original.
3. The summary must always include a reference to the original source. In Chapter 12 we will discuss the importance of this reference and the details of correct referencing.

Summarizing vs. Paraphrasing

The main difference between a summary and a paraphrase is the degree of completeness. A *paraphrase* contains all the information in the original. It is a translation of the original; nothing is left out. A summary focuses on the most important ideas in the original. It is a reduction of the original; secondary or minor points are left out. Notice the difference between the paraphrase and the summary in the following example.

Original sentence: The cowbird, as well as other species of birds, lays its eggs in another bird's nest and thus avoids hatching and raising its own young.

Paraphrase: Certain birds, including the cowbird, do not hatch and raise their own offspring but rather pass on these responsibilities by laying their eggs in other birds' nests.

Summary: Cowbirds do not hatch or raise their own young.

It is important to note that when you summarize you may employ some of the same strategies you use for paraphrasing. For example, after you read the original, you *locate* and *emphasize* the *main idea.* Then as you combine various ideas into sentences and paragraphs, you may *substitute synonyms* or *change sentence structure.* In effect, your summary may contain brief paraphrases of parts of the original work. Notice that in the above example, the original wording, "avoids hatching and raising," is paraphrased as "do not hatch or raise." Thus paraphrasing strategies are an important part of the summarizing process.

Summarizing vs. Quoting

Just as your summary can contain brief paraphrases, it can also include brief quotations from the original work. However, if you include more than three consecutive words from the original, remember to use quotation marks. The following example shows how a quotation might be included in a summary.

Original Sentence: Women from ages sixteen to twenty-five pay less for automobile insurance because they have fewer serious accidents, especially accidents involving driving while intoxicated, and their driving records, like those of women of all ages, are 23 percent better than those of men.

Summary with Quotation: Because women have fewer accidents and driving records "23 percent better than those of men," they pay less for car insurance.

SUMMARY

What summarizing is:

1. A method of reducing an information source to its main ideas
2. A writing tool that enables you to give your reader the gist of an information source
3. A study tool that helps you recapitulate the main points of material you have to learn

4. A reading technique that helps you to differentiate primary ideas from details and examples

What summarizing is not:

1. Paraphrasing or providing a word-for-word translation of a source
2. Including your own ideas with those in the source

In order to summarize an academic source, locate the sentences or passages that best serve your purpose and then reduce them to their essential meaning.

HOW REDUCING FITS INTO THE ACADEMIC WRITING PROCESS

Planning
  Prereading
    1. Clarify assignment and topic.
    2. Consider audience needs.
    3. Use a systematic approach for previewing the reading source.
    4. Set goals for reading.
  Close Reading
    1. As you encounter difficult sentences you wish to summarize, locate and emphasize the important ideas by asking:
       (a) What is the sentence kernel?
       (b) What is the sentence gist?
    2. As you encounter paragraphs you wish to summarize, locate and emphasize the main ideas by asking:
       (a) What is the topic sentence?
       (b) What is the writer's plan?
       (c) What is the gist of the paragraph?
    3. As you encounter longer passages or articles you wish to summarize, locate and emphasize the most important ideas by asking:
       (a) What is the author's organizational format?
       (b) What is the author's thesis?
       (c) What is the gist of each paragraph?
  Postreading/Prewriting
    1. Reread your assignment and decide what you will summarize.
    2. Reconsider your audience.
Writing
    1. Combine the ideas in the reduced information to produce synthesis sentences.
    2. Use outlining and organizational signals to write a precis.
Revising
  When You Revise the Summary as You Write:
    1. Compare the summary to the original source and search for pitfalls.
    2. Compare the summary to the topic.
    3. Compare the summary to audience needs.
  When You Revise the Summary after You Write:
    1. See how your summary fits into your overall plan.

chapter 4

Planning
the Summary, Part I

Before you write the first draft of your summary, you will engage in a number of planning activities. Most important, determine whether your summary will be a part of a larger paper that includes paraphrasing, direct quoting, and other academic writing forms or whether the summary will stand by itself.

PREREADING

Clarify the Assignment and the Topic

When you receive an assignment that calls for summarizing academic sources, study it carefully and do not proceed to read the sources or to write until you answer two crucial questions:

How much reduction of the original source is necessary?
What type of summary does the assignment require?

There are two different kinds of summaries: *freestanding summaries* that satisfy the total assignment and *component summaries* that are only part of a larger paper. When instructors assign freestanding summaries, sometimes they word the assignment generally, for instance, Give the substance of the reserve reading, or Summarize textbook Chapter 3. Other times they specify the form the summary should take; for example, Write a precis or an abstract of the article, or Give a synopsis of the film you saw in class. If you do not understand the terminology your professor uses, be sure to consult him or her before you begin to read and write.

Component summaries are usually shorter than freestanding types because they become part of a longer paper. Sometimes your instructor will remind you to summarize. For example, an assignment may state: Write a critical review of the reserve article that includes a brief statement of its chief points. More often you will have to decide how much of the paper (if any) should be a summary of the sources. Later chapters in this book will help you to make this decision.

Consider Your Audience's Needs

When you summarize, you reduce an academic source so that your audience reads only the main ideas or the gist. Asking the same questions that we posed in our discussion of paraphrasing will help you prepare to summarize for different purposes:

> How much general background information will your audience have on the topic? How much of this background will you need to provide?
>
> Will your audience be familiar with any vocabulary specific to the field of study?
>
> How much reduction of the original is necessary?

EXERCISE 10

Decide whether the following summaries are audience based or writer based. As you read each summary, ask yourself:

> Does the writer assume that his or her audience has read the original?
>
> Does the writer fail to provide his or her audience with sufficient background information about the topic?

If the answer to either question is yes, the summary is writer based rather than reader based. In that case, decide what advice you can give the writer about attending to the audience's needs.

1. The story describes a young boy who had known a priest who died. Most of the story gives the boy's own thoughts and memories of Father Flynn and the remarks other people make about the priest. The boy had learned a lot from the priest and is contemptuous of the remarks the other people make about the dead priest. Joyce indicates that the priest had been losing his mind because he broke a sacred chalice used for Mass.

2. As human beings, we tend to think of ourselves as infinitely superior to all other creatures, thus forgetting that we too are animals. In his book *The Naked Ape,* Desmond Morris presents a study of human beings as animals. He takes the analytic tools that zoologists typically use to study animals and applies them to the study of humans. Morris's main objective is to make the reader see human beings from a new perspective by objectively analyzing human behavior as one would that of another species.

3. Gillis describes how the White Russians and the Red Russians battled for control. In particular, he concentrates on the influence of forces outside Russia on this struggle. He mentions that the Allies intervened on the side of the White Russian Army. But their efforts failed to tip the balance of power and were largely ineffective. The White Russians were never able to mount a serious challenge to the power of the Red Russians in the major population centers.

4. In Shakespeare's *Hamlet,* Rosencrantz and Guildenstern are relatively minor characters who are killed as an offshoot of the struggle between Hamlet and his stepfather Claudius. However, in the play *Rosencrantz and Guildenstern Are Dead,* playwright Tom Stoppard makes the plight of these two characters the focus of the drama. Stoppard points out the tragedy of two unimportant men caught up in events that they neither understand nor control.

5. The study involved attitudes toward old people. They found that old people are generally thought of as less mentally able despite evidence to the contrary. This is clearly unfair. Some old people are just as sharp as they were when they were young. My grandfather, who is still a practicing lawyer, is a good example.

Previewing the Academic Source

When you are looking for sources that are appropriate for your topic, ask yourself the same questions we discussed with regard to paraphrasing in Chapter 1:

1. What is the title of the source?
2. Who is (are) the author(s)?
3. What are the subdivisions of the source?
4. What do the study aids tell you about the content of the source?
5. Can you make connections between the topic and the ideas in the source?

Once you have located a source or your professor has assigned a particular source for summarizing, in addition to the above questions, ask yourself about the organizational plan of the source:

6. What are the major organizational signals?
7. What are the smaller organizational signals?
8. What do you expect to learn from the source?
9. What clues will help you to find the information you want?
10. Will you read all or only part of the source?

CASE IN POINT 6

Let's establish once again the setting we described in cases 1 through 5. You are a student in Introduction to Communications. For homework, your professor gives the following assignment:

> Select one of the four articles on library reserve and write a concise, abridged version of it in 150–200 words. You will present your precis to other members of the class.

The four reserve articles appear in Appendix B. Assume you have chosen to work with John F. Wilson and Carroll C. Arnold's passage, "Human Communication." Before you read closely, be sure you have performed the following prereading activities:

1. Study the assignment to determine the type of summary and the amount of summary it requires.
2. Consider your audience's needs.
3. Preview the passage, asking the preview questions, and record your answers.
4. Set your goals for reading.

Remember to take notes and mark the passage.

Stop here, unless your instructor tells you otherwise. You will have a chance to come back to this assignment later.

CLOSE READING

Locate and Emphasize the Most Important Ideas in Sentences

What is the sentence kernel?

In order to locate the most important ideas in a sentence you want to summarize, ask yourself the same questions you posed when you paraphrased. First, *what are the words that tell in a very general way what the sentence is about?* These words are the *subject* and *verb* of the sentence. They comprise the *sentence kernel.* Underline the sentence kernel in the following sentence.

> Schools in large cities, such as New York, Boston, and Philadelphia, have been criticized for passing students from grade to grade for demonstrated effort, regular attendance, and good citizenship rather than for adequate academic performance.

Did you underline *schools* and *have been criticized?* The subject (schools) and the verb (have been criticized) are the sentence kernel. Look for the sentence kernel when you read difficult sentences in sources you are trying to summarize, for the sentence kernel contains the primary information in the sentence.

What is the *gist* of the sentence?

The second question to ask yourself when you are trying to locate the most important ideas in a sentence is, *What is the phrase or brief sentence that expresses more specifically the large subject area of the sentence kernel?* We call this the *gist* of the sentence. In order to determine the gist, try to figure out the additional information about the sentence kernel that the author presents. In our sample sentence above, the sentence kernel tells us "schools have been criticized." Furthermore, the author points out which schools have been criticized—"Schools in large cities such as New York, Boston, and Philadelphia"—and explains why they have been criticized—"for passing students from grade to grade for demonstrated effort, regular attendance, and good citizenship rather than for adequate academic performance."

The next step is to take the additional information and try to reduce it. First, examine the remaining information and the author's *purpose* for presenting it. In order to determine the author's purpose, ask: Is the writer giving an explanation, a description, or a narration? In our sample sentence, the first part supplies the reader with a *description* of the *setting* of the school, and the remaining information, "for passing students from grade to grade for demonstrated effort, regular attendance, and good citizenship rather than for adequate academic performance," gives the reader an *explanation* for the criticism of the schools. Jot the author's purpose in the margin.

DESCRIPTION:
(setting)

EXPLANATION:
(reasons for criticism)

Schools in large cities, such as New York, Boston, and Philadelphia, have been criticized for passing students from grade to grade for demonstrated effort, regular attendance, and good citizenship rather than for adequate academic performance.

Second, weigh the importance of the remaining information and perform four operations: (1) eliminate details, (2) categorize ideas, (3) rearrange words, and

(4) substitute synonyms. Actively work on the sentence, underlining, annotating, scratching out unnecessary words, and inserting new words.

You will probably decide that the examples of particular large cities are unimportant. Eliminate the examples by drawing a line through them. You are left with *large cities*. For *large cities* you can substitute the single adjective *urban*. Now rearrange the words, and you have *urban schools*.

urban

<u>Schools</u> in large cities, ~~such as New York, Boston, and Philadelphia,~~ <u>have been criticized</u> for passing students from grade to grade for demonstrated effort, regular attendance, and good citizenship rather than for adequate academic performance.

Although the examples of the particular cities were unimportant, the specific reasons why the urban schools have been criticized are significant. Once again, use the operations of eliminating details, substituting synonyms, rearranging words, and categorizing ideas to reduce these "reasons" to fewer words. Work on the sentence, underlining, annotating, and scratching out unnecessary words.

promoted

passing students from grade to grade for ~~demonstrated~~ effort, ~~regular~~ attendance, and ~~good~~ citizenship rather than ~~for adequate~~ academic performance.

Notice that we can substitute the single synonym *promoted* for *passing from grade to grade* and eliminate the unnecessary adjectives. Thus for the main-idea sentence we are left with the following information:

Urban schools have been criticized for promoting students for effort, attendance, and citizenship rather than academic performance.

RECAPITULATION

As you encounter sentences you wish to summarize, follow these five steps:

1. Read the sentence.
2. Reread the sentence and underline the *sentence kernel* (the subject and the verb).
3. Examine the remaining information in order to determine the author's *purpose* for presenting it.
4. Weigh the importance of the remaining information and condense it.
   (a) Eliminate details.

(b) Categorize ideas.

(c) Rearrange words.

(d) Substitute synonyms.

5. Write out the revised version of the sentence.

EXERCISE 11

Follow the five steps given above in order to summarize the following sentences. Be sure to underline and annotate the sentence.

1. Silicon-based integrated microcircuits, better known to the public as "chips," form the heart of modern computers and calculators.

2. Abstract art is often seen as more than just an ornament; it is seen, in fact, as a representation of a general attitude toward life or culture.

3. Rattlesnakes are able to locate their prey and strike accurately by using not only information from their eyes but also information from their "pits," which are sense organs that can detect the heat emitted by warm-blooded animals.

4. In the modern agricultural process referred to as *drilling*, seeds, fertilizers, pesticides, and herbicides are often simultaneously injected into the ground thus eliminating the necessity of performing many separate operations on the same field.

5. In October of 1934, Mao Tse-Tung along with an army of over 85,000 Communist soldiers began the Long March, one of the most famous military maneuvers of the twentieth century, which ended one year and 5,000 miles later with only 30,000 survivors.

Locate and Emphasize the Most Important Ideas in Paragraphs

Good readers have a clear sense of what constitutes a paragraph. A *paragraph* is a group of sentences that develop one main idea. A paragraph is easy to identify because the first word is indented. In a long passage, the indentation signals the reader that the author is shifting focus or beginning to talk about a new idea. Paragraphs may differ in function and structure, and they also vary in length. But regardless of its length, a good paragraph pursues one central idea.

What is the topic sentence?

Read the following paragraph carefully:

Depending on needs, resources, and awareness, smart savers put a portion of their total assets in four investment categories: cash, insurance, income, and equity. They put the part of their disposable salaries that they need to have readily available in cash in savings and checking accounts at the local bank. Another chunk of their paychecks is earmarked for insurance, such as life, health, disability, automotive, and home. After cash and insurance needs are taken care of, they buy short- and long-term bonds, money-market funds, or certificates of deposit, investments that will generate a steady income because they have a fixed rate of return. Lastly, if they are adventurous and have any money left, they speculate in equities: real estate, stocks, and collectibles, such as silver and gold.

Now reread the paragraph and pose the same questions you ask to locate the main idea of a sentence: (1) What are the words that tell in a very general way what the whole paragraph is about? and (2) What specific parts of the kernel idea does the author discuss throughout the paragraph? In answer to the first question, did you underline "smart savers put a portion of their total assets in four investment categories"? These words form the kernel of the paragraph just as the subject and the verb form the kernel of a sentence. Usually, *the kernel idea of a paragraph will be longer and more detailed than the kernel of a sentence.* To answer the second question, reread the paragraph and try to reduce important secondary information to a single main-idea sentence. In the rest of the paragraph, the writer discusses each of the four types of investments: cash, insurance, income, and equities. Therefore, the main idea is contained word for word in the first sentence of the paragraph:

> Smart savers put a portion of their total assets in four investment categories: cash, insurance, income, and equities.

The information that expresses the main, all-encompassing idea that the complete paragraph develops is sometimes, as in the example paragraph above, communicated to the reader in the form of a sentence. This sentence is called the *topic sentence* of the paragraph. The topic sentence may appear at the beginning of the paragraph as it does in the above example, or it may come at the end of the paragraph. However, the topic sentence may also appear in the middle of the paragraph. Consider the following example:

> Decentralized retail establishments, whether clustered at a focal point or located separately from other retail stores, are not an exclusive phenomenon of North American cities. This decentralizing trend is also apparent in European and Asian cities. But the planned shopping center, located in an outlying sector of the city, is more or less distinctive of cities in North America. Such centers are customarily planned by privately owned and managed land-development corporations, but subject to varying degrees of regulation by the municipality in which they are located. The usual procedure is for the corporation to acquire the land,

erect the structures, and lease them to companies or individuals for business or related purposes. As we have noted, such centers are functional for the automobile age.

Gist, Noel, and Sylvia Fava. *Urban Society.* 6th ed. New York: Thomas Y. Crowell Co., 1974. 244.

The topic of this paragraph—the planned shopping center—is introduced in the third sentence toward the middle of the paragraph. The first two sentences, which discuss the general concept of decentralized retail establishments, lead into this topic sentence. The remaining three sentences focus on the planned shopping center.

It is important to remember that authors do not always use topic sentences to communicate the gist. Sometimes the readers have to figure it out for themselves. Consider the following example:

Buddha is said to have achieved spiritual enlightenment through meditation and fasting. Similar procedures, however, are used to prepare for divine inspiration in religions the world over. This fact has implications for how one might view the development of religion in various cultures. Indeed, this aspect of the religious experience may be a direct response to man's universal physiological characteristics. People the world over share common experiences as a consequence of being members of the same species. It seems reasonable that they might interpret these experiences the same way.

The first sentence of the paragraph tells how Buddha acquired spiritual enlightenment. The remaining sentences, however, suggest that Buddha is used merely as an example because they discuss a larger population—religious people throughout the world. The final sentence contains part of the main idea of the paragraph: people everywhere have the same interpretation of certain experiences. We combine these ideas to arrive at the following summary:

Human beings everywhere share certain experiences that they interpret as having religious significance.

EXERCISE 12

Read each of the following paragraphs and underline the topic sentence if there is one. Decide whether or not the topic sentence is (a) at the beginning of the paragraph, (b) at the end of the paragraph, (c) in the middle of the paragraph, (d) at both the end and the beginning of the paragraph, or (e) unstated.

1. In the attempt to confine a cluster of symptoms that have distinguished schizophrenia from other emotional disturbances, Eugene Bleuler's classical "four A's" denoting the fundamental symptoms are generally observed. These symptoms are ambivalence, association disturbances, autism, and affective impairment. The signs of perceptual disturbance such as ideas of reference, delusions and hallucinations, and illusions can also be experienced in the psychotic situation. The defense mechanisms of denial and projection are prominent. Negativistic behavior may also be a sign of the syndrome.

   Burgess, Ann W., and Aaron Lazare. *Psychiatric Nursing in the Hospital and Community.* 2nd ed. Englewood Cliffs: Prentice-Hall, 1976. 261.

2. Life insurance policies are written by more than 1,800 different companies that own assets of approximately $252 billion and employ 1,575,000 people. In the United States there are 145,000,000 policyholders whose lives are insured for $1,778 billion and who, in a recent year, paid $33 billion in premiums. Benefit payments to policyholders and to the beneficiaries of policyholders who died were in excess of $20 billion. The life insurance industry is truly gigantic in all dimensions.

   Glos, Raymond, Richard Steade, and James Lowry. *Business: Its Nature and Environment.* 8th ed. Cincinnati: South-Western Publishing Co., 1976. 420.

3. The Thirty Years War (1618–48) brought to a climax a number of forces which had been building up in the sixteenth century. The German people, who bore the brunt of the fighting and suffered the most from it, called it the Great War. Actually it was a series of wars rather than a single conflict. Either name for it is somewhat artificial, for between 1450 and 1660 there were only four years (1548, 1549, 1550, and 1610) in which organized fighting did not occur in Europe. Nonetheless, the Thirty Years War, in its phases and results, had a certain unity. It originated as part of the continuing struggle of Catholic and Protestant forces for the religious control of the West. But in its later stages the character of the war shifted from religious to political. At the same time the war itself shifted Europe's balance of power westward from Germany to France.

   Judd, Gerrit P. *A History of Civilization.* New York: MacMillan, 1966. 376.

4. What makes a program successful? Certainly a lot depends on such major production elements as the performers, the camera shots, the audio, and the direction. But there are many other elements, not all as obvious perhaps but nevertheless important, which contribute to a production. One of these is the use of television graphics—the various titles, photographs, lettering, illustrations, and diagrams that appear in virtually every television program. Graphics generally serve a very utilitarian function; to convey information to the viewer. Yet when graphics are

carefully designed and imaginatively used in a production, they are capable of doing much more.

Wurtzel, Alan. *Television Production*. New York: McGraw-Hill, 1979. 251.

5. The ultimate step in this evolution of writing would have been the complete separation of the alphabetic from the non-alphabetic characters and the exclusive use of the former in written communication. The Egyptians were reluctant to take this step. Their traditions of conservatism impelled them to follow old habits. Although they made frequent use of the consonant signs, they did not commonly employ them as an independent system of writing. It was left for the Phoenicians to do this some 1500 years later. Nevertheless, the Egyptians must be credited with the invention of the principle of the alphabet. It was they who first perceived the value of single symbols for the individual sounds of the human voice. The Phoenicians merely copied this principle, based their own system of writing upon it, and diffused the idea among neighboring nations. In the ultimate sense it is therefore true that the Egyptian alphabet was the parent of every other that has ever been used in the Western World.

Burns, Edward M., *Western Civilizations: Their History and Their Culture*. 7th ed. New York: W. W. Norton, 1968. 48.

chapter 5

Planning the Summary, Part II

FURTHER CLOSE READING

In the last chapter we began to discuss strategies that will help you to summarize an author's ideas as you read closely. We worked with two close-reading strategies, locate and emphasize the most important ideas in sentences and locate and emphasize the most important ideas in paragraphs. In this chapter we will continue our discussion of the second of the two strategies, and we will introduce a third strategy, locate and emphasize the most important ideas in long passages. We will first consider how you can determine the organizational principles in paragraphs.

Locate and Emphasize the Most Important Ideas in Paragraphs

What is the author's plan?

After you have located the author's topic sentence or decided on the main idea, the next step in the paragraph-summarizing process is to identify the *author's plan*—the way the author organizes primary (superordinate) and secondary (subordinate) ideas on a topic.* Authors use five types of plans:

*Meyer, Bonnie J. F. "Reading Research and the Composition Teacher: The Importance of Plans." *College Composition and Communication* 33(1982): 37–49. Meyer's thesis on the basic writing plans that affect reading comprehension governs our methods for teaching summarizing.

1. Antecedent/consequent
2. Comparison
3. Description
4. Response
5. Time order

Let us discuss these plans and examine how authors use them to develop paragraphs.

Antecedent/Consequent.   An *antecedent* is anything that precedes or comes before something else. A *consequent* comes after, or results from, something else. When used in a writing pattern, the antecedent comes before the consequent and usually makes the consequent happen. Another way of looking at the antecedent/consequent plan is as a cause/effect or if/then relationship. As you read the following paragraph, look for the antecedent and consequent.

> One of childhood's saddest figures is the one who hangs around the fringes of every group, walks home alone after school, and sobs in despair, "Nobody wants to play with me." Children can be unpopular for many reasons, sometimes because they are withdrawn or rebellious (Y. S. Smith, 1950; Northway, 1944). They may walk around with a "chip on the shoulder," showing unprovoked aggression and hostility. Or they may act silly and babyish, showing off in immature ways. Or they may be anxious and uncertain, exuding such a pathetic lack of confidence that they repel other children, who don't find them fun to be with. Very fat or unattractive children, children who act in any way that seems strange to others, and slow-learning youngsters are also outcasts.
>
> Papalia, Diane, and Sally W. Olds. *Human Development.* New York: McGraw-Hill, 1978, 233.

Sometimes students have difficulty differentiating between antecedent and consequent. It is helpful to depict the two elements graphically. After you read a paragraph, ask, "What occurs first?" Then ask, "What follows?" Make a diagram, placing the antecedent, whatever occurs first, *above* the consequent.

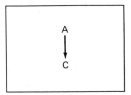

The arrow indicates that the consequent "follows" or "results from" the antecedent. In the above paragraph, the lack of popularity is the consequent. See if you can fill in the antecedents.

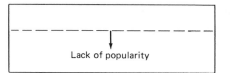

Authors often alert the reader to the type of plan they are using with *signals.* These signals take various forms, including transitional expressions and direct word clues. Transitions that serve as signals for the antecedent/consequent plan include *if, then, so, because, as a result, therefore, since, consequently, so that, in order that, why, accordingly, hence,* and *thus.*

Comparison. The comparison plan presents two or more sides of the issue or gives viewpoints. The views can be similar or different. In a single paragraph an author may present similar views, contrasting views, or both. What two views or sides of the issue are presented in the following example?

> One of the biggest advantages of being single is the opportunity it affords for personal growth. Because single people are under no pressure to accommodate to a spouse and children, they have more time to explore avenues for growth and enrichment. They can try new career options, travel more, have a wider variety of experiences, and expose themselves to the opportunities which lead to personal growth. A married woman's quest for identity and fulfillment can be stifled by the notion that her primary responsibility is not to herself but to her husband and children. A married man can become fearful of losing the job that provides support for his family and fail to risk a change that might prove beneficial.
>
> Green, Ernest J. *Personal Relationships: An Approach to Marriage and Family.* New York: McGraw-Hill, 1978. 407.

Green contrasts single life and married life. In the first half of the paragraph, he gives the advantages of the single life, and in the second half of the paragraph he presents the disadvantages of married life. Notice that the latter half of the paragraph also contains a comparison. The author points out that the married woman and the married man share similar problems.

If you were to depict the paragraph graphically, your general diagram would look like this:

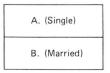

More specifically, you could show in your diagram the comparison of the married woman and the married man in the second part of the paragraph:

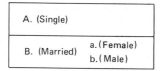

The above diagrams illustrate the *block presentation,* one of the two major ways authors present information when they use the comparison plan to compare and/or contrast elements. Using the block presentation, the author first presents all the information about element A and then all the information about element B. Another type of presentation is the *alternating* presentation in which the author presents one item of information about A followed by one item of information about B, followed by another item about A and another about B, and so forth. A diagram for this type of presentation is:

A.
B.
A.
B.
A.
B.
A.
B.

EXERCISE 13

Rewrite the example paragraph about the advantages and disadvantages of married and single life, using the alternating presentation described above. As you alternate from married to single life, you may want to signal your audience with some of the following transitions:

Either, or, neither, nor, yet, but, even though, though, whereas, whether, however, similarly, on the other hand, likewise, conversely, still, despite, nonetheless, nevertheless.

Description.   When an author uses the description plan, he or she develops the paragraph topic by presenting its attributes, parts, or setting. An author may compose a descriptive paragraph that makes *an impression on the reader's senses* by using details that allow the reader to imagine the thing described. On the other hand, an author may compose a descriptive paragraph that is technical and analytical in that it gives the exact specifications of the thing described rather than a description of it. Compare these two descriptive paragraphs:

A. The fission reaction is the actual source of energy in a nuclear power plant. The core of the reactor contains rods made of the element uranium-235. The fission of a U-235 atom takes place when a neutron strikes the nucleus of the atom and splits the original atom into several smaller atoms. The smaller atoms taken together contain less matter than the original U-235 atom did. At the moment of fission, some of the excess matter is converted directly into energy. This energy is used to heat up water to produce steam. The steam in turn drives turbines that produce the electric power the plant provides. The fission reaction gives off neutrons that are not bonded to atoms. These neutrons can collide with and split other U-235 atoms. The process of one fission reaction leading to another is called a "chain reaction." Chain reactions are kept under control by inserting material into the reactor core that absorbs neutrons and thus slows down the rate at which the reaction spreads through the nuclear fuel.

B. The cold passed reluctantly from the earth, and the retiring fog revealed an army stretched out on the hills, resting. As the landscape changed from brown to green, the army awakened and began to tremble with eagerness at the noise of rumors. It cast its eyes upon the roads, which were growing from long troughs of liquid mud to proper thoroughfares. A river, amber-tinted in the shadow of its banks, curled at the army's feet; and at night, when the stream had become a sorrowful blackness, one could see across it the red, eyelike gleam of hostile camp fires set in the low brows of distant hills.

Crane, Stephen, *The Red Badge of Courage.*

In paragraph A the author gives an exact, technical description of the chain-reaction process. Paragraph B describes a hillside setting: an army is awakening in early morning. The author, Stephen Crane, uses descriptive words and devices, for example, color words such as *brown to green, amber-tinted, sorrowful blackness,* and *red,* and metaphors, such as "eyelike gleam of hostile camp fires set in the low brows of distant hills," to give the reader a vivid impression of the scene. The army is depicted as a person awakening, trembling, and looking out over the land.

Response.   The response plan *first* presents a *statement* and *then* a *response*. The statement-response pattern can take many forms: *question-answer, problem-solution,* and *remark-reply.* What is the form of the following response paragraph?

> Wope (1962) describes the case of a thirty-nine-year-old woman with a severe phobia of riding in an automobile or walking in the vicinity of automobile traffic. Treatment involved the use of reciprocal inhibition and systematic desensitization. The patient was taught to relax, and then relaxation was paired with a series of imagined traffic situations. (For some sessions hypnosis was used to aid the relaxation process.) After fifty-seven sessions the patient was able to walk in the vicinity of traffic without fear, and she was able to ride in cars without any signs of her previous panic.
>
> Silverman, A. *Psychology.* New York: Appleton-Century-Crofts, 1972. 382.

Obviously, the thirty-nine-year-old-woman has a *problem.* The first sentence of the paragraph explains her automobile phobia, and the remaining sentences describe the treatment or *solution* of the problem.

Time Order.   When authors use time-order plans, they order ideas or events *chronologically.*

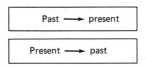

The following paragraph charts the progression of babies' smiles:

> The smile appears early. Babies 1 week old smile spontaneously and fleetingly when their stomachs are full or when they hear soft sounds. At about 1 month, these smiles become more frequent and are directed more toward people. Babies 4 to 5 weeks old smile at having both hands clapped together (Wolff, 1963), or when they can hear a familiar voice (Kreutzer and Charlesworth, 1973). Not until 3 1/2 months will babies smile more to a familiar face than an unfamiliar one.
>
> Papalia, Diane, and Sally W. Olds. *Human Development.* New York: McGraw-Hill, 1978. 104.

EXERCISE 14

Read each of the following paragraphs, identify the author's plan, and explain how the author uses the plan to develop the main ideas.

1. Although modern weather-forecasting techniques include the use of weather satellites and radar, the barometer continues to be an important indicator of weather patterns. Barometers register the atmospheric pressure, the amount the atmosphere pushes down on the earth's surface. In a place where the atmospheric pressure is high, clouds and moisture are pushed away and storm systems flow around the region. Thus a rising barometer is associated with fair weather. When atmospheric pressure drops in a region, clouds can move in readily. Thus a falling barometer is often accompanied with rain and thunderstorms.

2. Persons with little knowledge of accounting may also fail to understand the difference between accounting and bookkeeping. Bookkeeping means the recording of transactions, the record-making phase of accounting. The recording of transactions tends to be mechanical and repetitive; it is only a small part of the field of accounting and probably the simplest part. Accounting includes the design of accounting systems, preparation of financial statements, audits, cost studies, development of forecasts, income tax work, computer applications to accounting processes, and the analysis and interpretation of accounting information as an aid to making business decisions. A person might become a reasonably proficient bookkeeper in a few weeks or months; to become a professional accountant, however, requires several years of study and experience.

   Meigs, Walter, Charles Johnson, and Robert Meigs. *Accounting, the Basis for Business Decisions.* New York: McGraw-Hill, 1977. 3.

3. The chimney swift's flight pattern and flight silhouette are its clear trademarks. The swift's wings beat in alternating strokes giving the bird a choppy, irregular flight pattern rather than a smooth glide. Although much faster, the swift's wing beats remind one of a bat. The silhouette of the bird in flight is particularly distinctive. The long sickle-shaped wings seem too large for the short tailless body.

4. In any monetary system it is necessary to have a monetary standard which states the units of value and the value of the various types of money in use. In early economies there was no need for a monetary standard since there was usually only one or, at the most, two or three types of money. Such money had intrinsic value because it was demanded to meet some need or for use in adornment or decoration; it therefore had value as a commodity, which gave it value as money. Later when governments began to develop coins on which kings placed their seals to guarantee the weight and the quality of the metal, the unit of account came to be the basic coin that was minted by the government. In more modern times, governments developed the monetary system further to help facilitate commerce. The basic money unit of the country was established by law, and the weight and fineness of the precious metal in such a coin was stipulated. Any other money in use had its value ex-

pressed in terms of the standard money. Thus, monetary standards were developed, some based on gold, some on silver, and some on both metals. In recent years the standard in most countries has been paper money issued by the government.

Dauten, Carl, and Merle Welshans. *Principles of Finance.* 4th ed. Cincinnati: South-Western Publishing Co., 1975. 22–23.

What is the gist of the paragraph?

After you have determined the main idea/topic sentence and identified the author's plan, you are ready to combine these two elements to capture *the gist,* or *main idea,* of the paragraph. Let us look again at the paragraphs we analyzed when we were identifying the author's plan. Reread the Papalia and Olds' paragraph on p. 61 that exemplified the antecedent/consequent plan.

The independent clause in the second sentence serves as a good topic sentence for the paragraph: "Children can be unpopular for many reasons." The plan Papalia and Olds use is antecedent/consequent. They first present the consequent, *unpopularity,* and then give reasons to account for it. The gist of the paragraph, then, can be presented like this: *A number of reasons account for unpopularity in children.*

Now return to the example comparison paragraph on p. 62. One might agree that the first sentence of the paragraph is the topic sentence:

One of the biggest advantages of being single is the opportunity it affords for personal growth.

However, only the first half of the paragraph discusses how being single allows one to grow. The latter part of the paragraph explains why marital responsibilities interfere with personal growth. Consequently, the main idea of the sentence is two-pronged: *Whereas the single life affords people opportunities for personal growth, married life carries with it responsibilities that interfere with personal growth.* Combine this main idea with the author's plan, which is to contrast single life and married life, and you have the gist of the paragraph, which can be presented as follows:

Green contrasts single life and married life, pointing out that whereas the single life affords people opportunities for personal growth, married life brings responsibilities that interfere with personal growth.

Notice how we acknowledged the author of the source. *Summaries must always be acknowledged,* just as paraphrases must be.

SUMMARY

In your close reading, as you encounter paragraphs you wish to summarize, follow these four steps:

1. Read the paragraph.
2. Reread the paragraph to determine the placement of the topic sentence—the primary information that tells what the paragraph is about. If the author does not provide a topic sentence, you will have to form one from your underlinings and annotations.
3. After you determine the main idea of the paragraph or topic sentence, identify the author's plan: antecedent/consequent, comparison, description, response, or time order.
4. Combine the main idea/topic sentence with the author's plan and write the gist of the paragraph.

EXERCISE 15

Read carefully each of the paragraphs below and then perform the following operations:

1. Underline the topic sentence, or formulate one of your own.
2. Identify the author's plan and jot it in the margin.
3. Combine the topic sentence and the author's plan and write the main idea, or gist, of the sentence.

1. The experience of writers demonstrates that ideas for novels, short stories, and plays spring from every avenue of life, sometimes so insidiously that an author may be unable to explain how a specific idea came into his mind. The root of a story may be something seen, heard, told, or read. It can be one of the dramas we sometimes see in everyday life: a girl in a railroad station holding a uniformed man tightly to her as though she can never let him go; a dazed motorist staring stupidly down at the body crushed beneath the wheels of his car; the adoring look in a girl's face as she looks down at the ring on her finger; the teen-ager trying to tell his father that he has smashed a fender; a lonely mother on a beach watching her deformed child play in the sand; the look of relief in a woman's eyes as she comes from the confessional. Or it may be as slight a happening as a chance remark heard in a subway, a cry of pain in the night, or a sound of a laugh with no mirth in it.

   Willis, Edgar. *Writing Television and Radio Programs.* New York: Holt, Rinehart and Winston. 1967. 34.

2. What makes a program successful? Certainly a lot depends on such major production elements as the performers, the camera shots, the audio, and

the direction. But there are many other elements, not at all as obvious perhaps but nevertheless important, which contribute to a production. One of these is the use of television graphics—the various titles, photographs, lettering, illustrations, and diagrams that appear in virtually every television program. Graphics generally serve a very utilitarian function: to convey information to the viewer. Yet when graphics are carefully designed and imaginatively used in a production, they are capable of doing much more.

Wurtzel, Alan. *Television Production.* New York: McGraw-Hill, 1979. 251.

3. Once explanations are clearly and explicitly formulated, we wish to find out just how adequate these explanations are. For, no matter how elegant the logical structure of an explanation may be and no matter how complex and numerous the assumptions in the theory that generates the explanation, we want theories that work. The ultimate test of a social science explanation, clearly then, is how well it allows us to predict the way the world is. Prediction involves ascertaining the extent to which observations of behavior agree with what the theory specifies the case should be. The test of the adequacy of a theory then is the answer to the question: How well does the world correspond to the way the theory states the world should look?

Selltiz, Claire, Lawrence S. Wrightsman, and Stuart W. Cook. *Research Methods in Social Relations* 3rd ed. New York: Holt, Rinehart and Winston, 1976. 35.

4. The century between 1815 and 1914 witnessed the virtual transformation of popular life. The rapid proliferation of industrialization and the succcessive reform of the political system of the most powerful and important European states combined to alter radically most facets of social existence. Where before there had been darkness, light was provided; where death had struck unhindered, the power to heal and protect was gained; where men had been politically powerless, sullen, and silent, they obtained a voice in the determination of their nations' destinies.

Cantor, Norman, and Michael Werthman, eds. *The History of Popular Culture.* New York: Macmillan, 1968. 397.

Now that you know how to locate and emphasize the most important ideas in sentences and paragraphs, let us explain how you can do the same in long passages.

What is the author's format?

When you wish to summarize a long passage of two or more paragraphs, for each paragraph follow the steps for locating and emphasizing important ideas: underline the topic sentence, determine the author's plan and make a note of it, and decide on the gist of the sentence and jot it down in the margin. In addition, step back and look at the organizational structure of the total passage.

Look first for *major organizational signals,* such as introductory paragraphs, body paragraphs, and conclusions. Look second for *smaller signals* that are clues to the organization. These smaller signals are often transitional words and phrases—however, moreover, in addition, in conclusion, first, finally.

In the following passage notice how we annotate paragraphs that serve as major signals to organizational structure with roman numerals. When a major division, such as the *body* of the passage, contains more than one paragraph, we label each paragraph with a capital letter. Then we circle words or phrases that act as smaller signals.

Mistakes in Early Speech

I Introduction   Young children's errors of speech are quite similar to their counting errors. (One example) of speech errors that every parent encounters involves the four-year-old who says, "I *goed* to the store" or "He *bringed* the book." Psychologists who have investigated early language point out that mistakes of this type teach us several interesting things.

A. (First) children's language is based on rules. Children never hear "goed" or "bringed" and hence cannot just be mimicking use of these words. (Instead), the words must be the product of a rule to the effect that the past tense is indicated by adding "-ed" to the stem. Of course *II Body* children are not aware of this rule, just as adult speakers are not aware of many language rules. (Nevertheless), rules govern speech.

B. (Second), children's rules are derived in sensible ways from their experiences. Children have frequently heard "-ed" used quite correctly to indicate past tense—for example, "helped" or "waited." So their rule is a sensible one, based on real experience. It is not a figment of their imagination. The main mistake children make is in applying it too widely—to all verbs. They need to learn the exceptions, like "went" and "brought," so that they can avoid overgeneralization. Children's mistakes frequently have a rational basis.

C. (Third), the mistakes children make are the result of a search for meaning. In learning a language, children do not aim merely to imitate what they have heard. (Instead), they look for underlying structure, for what is really going on. They do not simply repeat strings of words; they try instead to construct rules at a deeper level. Sometimes they are wrong, but their mistakes indicate that they are digging below the surface.

III Conclusion   (As we shall see), the same holds true in children's mathematics. Their counting mistakes result from an overgeneralized application of rules; the rules reflect children's experiences; and they are constructed as the result of an attempt to understand. In language as in number, children's intellectual learning is in part a creative, intelligent process. Rote, "mechanical" factors play a secondary role.

Ginsburg, Herbert. *Children's Arithmetic: The Learning Process.* New York: D. Van Nostrand, 1977. 8.

For purposes of illustration we have annotated and marked organizational signals only. As a practice review, reread the passage, and for each paragraph underline the topic sentence, identify the author's plan, and jot down the gist, or main idea.

What is the thesis sentence?

The thesis sentence of a group of paragraphs is similar to the topic sentence of an individual paragraph. In the thesis sentence the author expresses specifically the part or aspect of the general topic that he or she will discuss. The topic of Ginsburg's passage is children's speech errors. It is important to note that often, but not always, the author states the topic in the title of the piece. Now, where does Ginsburg explain what he is going to tell us about children's speech errors? Do not expect the thesis to appear as the first sentence of the passage. Usually you will find the thesis in the introductory paragraph but not necessarily at the very beginning.

After reading Ginsburg's first sentence, we expect him to compare speech errors and counting errors throughout the passage. However, this is not the case. Instead, he reveals some interesting facts about mistakes in speech. Thus the thesis sentence is the last sentence of the introductory paragraph: "Psychologists who have investigated early language point out that mistakes of this type teach us several interesting things."

SUMMARY

When you encounter longer passages or articles you wish to summarize, follow these four steps:

1. Read the passage.
2. Reread the passage to determine the author's format. Annotate the passage as follows:
   a. Place roman numerals next to major organizational signals and divisions like Introduction, Body, and Conclusion
   b. Place capital letters next to individual paragraphs within major divisions
   c. Circle smaller organizational signals

3. Locate and underline the thesis statement
4. For each paragraph underline the topic sentence, identify the author's plan, and jot down the gist, or main idea

EXERCISE 16

Follow the four steps in the summary above as you read the following passage closely:

Broadcast media have a pervasive influence on the average American household, as viewing and listening figures attest.

The built-in advantages of radio advertising include low cost, demographic selectivity, listener mobility, and high frequency. Radio is a particularly good vehicle for reaching the youth market. But the medium has its disadvantages as well, including low reach, shortlived messages, clutter, and limitations on creative approaches.

The cost of a radio spot depends on its duration, the type of audience it reaches, and the time of day it comes on. Availability also has a bearing on rates. Spots are generally sold as discounted weekly packages. For lower rates, the station retains the right to decide when to run an advertising message. The lowest rates of all are for preemptible spots, which allow the station to sell the slots to a higher bidder if one comes along.

Television is expensive because it has a number of built-in advantages. For one, it achieves maximum reach, with some 70 million television-equipped homes in the United States. Maximum frequency is also a possibility with television—for those who can afford message repetitions. TV allows for product demonstration, demographic selectivity, relative cost efficiency, and production freedom.

That is not to say, however, that television advertising has no drawbacks. Advertising clutter is a constant problem. Other problems are the difficulties involved in booking choice spots, and high absolute cost.

The impact of new media on advertising is bound to be significant. Cable TV is now in 8 million homes, and that number is virtually certain to increase drastically. Widespread pay TV is also a sure-fire future development, as are home video centers that are already prevalent. International programming—using satellites, perhaps—may become commonplace. Once again, it will be up to advertising to make the most of new technology, as the industry did when television was in its infancy.

Gilson, Christopher, and Harold Berkman. *Advertising Concepts and Strategies.* New York: Random House, 1980. 350.

CASE IN POINT 7

Read Case in point 6 and reconsider your goals for reading. Now you are ready to return to the Wilson and Arnold article in Appendix B for a close reading.

As you read, use the close-reading strategies to

1. Determine the writer's format and jot it in the margin.
2. Locate and mark the thesis sentence.
3. Locate and underline topic sentences, identify the author's plan, and take notes on the main idea of each paragraph.

Stop here, unless your instructor tells you otherwise. You will have a chance to come back to this assignment later.

POSTREADING/PREWRITING

Reread Your Assignment and Decide What You Will Summarize

When you have completed your close reading, reread your assignment to make certain that summarizing is appropriate for the academic task at hand. If your assignment calls for a straightforward summary or precis of the reading material, obviously you are on the right track. However, if the summary is to be part of a larger assignment in which you will include paraphrases, direct quotations, and other forms of academic writing, at this time you should review the portions of the reading selection that you annotated and underlined and weigh their importance. If every word seems significant as you reread a passage, you may decide to paraphrase or quote directly rather than summarize. If only the gist of the passage is important, however, you may stand by your original plan of summarizing. At the same time, information that you thought was relevant to your assignment topic may now seem unpromising, and you may decide to abandon it altogether.

Reconsider Your Audience

As you reread the passage(s) you have decided to summarize, depending on the type of summary you plan to write, ask yourself these questions:

Will my audience be able to understand the reduced information if it stands alone, or do I need to include more information from the source so that the summary makes sense?

Will my audience be able to understand the reduced information if I include it as a part of a large paper, or do I need to provide more context?

CASE IN POINT 8

Review cases in point 6 and 7, the Wilson and Arnold article in Appendix B, and all of the notes you have taken up to this point. Now you are at the post-reading/prewriting stage. Before you proceed to write your summary, perform the following operations:

1. Reread your assignment and decide what you will summarize.
2. Reconsider your audience.

Stop here, unless your instructor tells you otherwise. You will have a chance to come back to this assignment later.

chapter 6

Writing and Revising the Summary

WRITING

During the planning stage you will perform many operations that lead you to the gist of the information. Sometimes, especially when reducing lengthy sources, the gist is sufficient. Usually you will want a comprehensive summary. This chapter presents two strategies for producing well-written summaries.

Combine the Ideas in the Reduced Information to Produce a Synthesis Sentence

Let us return to our model antecedent/consequent paragraph and review the operations we have performed so far:

Topic Sentence {

~~One of childhood's saddest figures is the one who hangs around the fringes of every group, walks home alone after school, and sobs in despair, "Nobody wants to play with me."~~ Children can be unpopular for many reasons, ~~sometimes~~ (because) they are withdrawn or rebellious (Y. S. Smith, 1950; Northway, 1944). ~~They may walk around with~~ a "chip on the shoulder," ~~showing unprovoked~~ aggression and hostility. ~~Or they may~~ act silly and babyish, ~~showing off in~~ immature ~~ways. Or they may be~~ anxious and uncertain, ~~exuding such a pathetic lack of confidence that they repel other children, who don't find them fun to be with.~~ Very fat or unattractive ~~children, children who~~ act ~~in any way that seems~~ strange ~~to others, and~~ slow-learning ~~youngsters are also outcasts~~.

Description not importan

Consequent

Result of

Antecedents— causes of unpopularity

Papalia, Diane, and Sally W. Olds, *Human Development*. New York: McGraw-Hill, 1978. 233.

75

We have underlined and annotated the paragraph to take account of the close reading we have performed so far. Notice that we have

1. Determined the main idea/topic sentence
2. Identified the author's plan
3. Weighed the importance of the remaining information deciding what to eliminate
4. Condensed the remaining information by scratching out unnecessary words, substituting synonyms, rearranging words, and categorizing ideas

Now as we weighed the importance of the remaining information, we saw that the first sentence describes the unpopular child, and the remaining sentences give the reasons for the lack of popularity.

At this point, after the passage has been marked, scratched out, and annotated, the next step is to synthesize or combine the ideas in a well-written sentence. If we transform all of the reasons for the lack of popularity into adjectives, we are left with a string of thirteen adjectives that we can express in a summary sentence, such as the following:

Children may be unpopular because they are withdrawn, rebellious, aggressive, hostile, silly, babyish, immature, anxious, uncertain, fat, unattractive, strange, or slow-learning.

Use Outlining and Organizational Signals to Write a Précis

Occasionally college instructors will ask you to write a special type of summary called a *précis*. There is one fundamental difference between a regular summary and a précis. *A précis follows the organizational format and the order of ideas of the original source.* In other words, if the source contains two introductory paragraphs, five body paragraphs, and a concluding paragraph, the précis will reflect this organizational distribution. Thus the précis is not only a reduced version of the original; it is also an abridgement or miniaturization of it.

As an illustration of the précis-writing process, imagine that you are a student in a course called Recreation in American Society. In preparation for a unit on exercise in middle age and later life, your professor has assigned a number of short articles and asked different students to summarize them in précis form. Your assigned article is George Sheehan's, "Running Is Forever, and Everyone," from the *New York Times*. We will assume that you have completed the *planning* process: prereading, close reading, and postreading/prewriting;

thus, the article that is reprinted here is thoroughly annotated, marked, and reduced.

Running is Forever, and Everyone

George A. Sheehan, M.D.

I. Introduction
Response:
problem → solution

A   When I took up running at the age of 45 I joined a high school cross-country team. I had to. There were no older runners in my area and extremely few competitive events. So, I kept my gear in my car and would consult the local paper for the time and the place of the meets.

Comparison

B   My teammates quickly accepted me. At the races it was a different story. The opposing teams and their coaches would find it quite odd that someone my age would be running and actually competing. In the races I invariably had to pass a runner twice. The first time he would be unbelieving and immediately put on a spurt. The second time I would put him away.

C   These young runners had not yet had their consciousnesses raised to the marvelous capability of the human body. Nor, indeed, had anyone else. In those days, older runners were eccentrics. And especially in cross-country season when they might appear in longjohns on the roads. No one, including these aging runners, had any idea how little attrition occurs to the human machine with aging.

Comparison

D   The young runners I ran with had a sense of urgency about their performance which I did not have. They would talk to me about two more years or one more year of eligibility. They saw their participation limited to the scholastic career; meanwhile my body was telling me to take the long view. This running, it said, can go on forever.

II. Body
Comparison

A   It was that body wisdom that dispelled my preconceptions about aging—just as women later took to running despite centuries of pronouncements to the contrary. And when they did, I took the role of my high school doubters. Now it was me that a woman had to pass twice. And just as the younger runners finally grasped the truth, so did I. Women of all ages can not only run, they can run well. Some of them can run exceptionally well.

Antecedent/
Consequent

B   Now races are filled with runners over 40 years of age of both sexes. The average times turned in by these older athletes are quite remarkable. They demonstrate just how gradual is the loss of running ability as age progresses. The study on master runners conducted by the Washington School of Medicine in St. Louis, in which I am a subject, has shown this to be in the order of 5 percent a decade. At the age of 63, I have a treadmill endurance which is only 15 percent lower than the 22-year-old miler I am paired with.

III. Conclusion   **A**   What does this all mean? It depends upon your age. If you are a high school runner, you can see that your athletic career need never end. Indeed it must not. In physiology you get what you pay for. The effects of aging are minor as long as you keep your training and weight constant. You can be an athlete at any age, but you have to work at it.

Response: Question → Answer

Antecedent / Consequent   **B**   Those who are older and have deserted exercise and play and sport must get back into it. This is the time to spend your unspent youth. There is no valid reason for doing anything else. No physiological reason to accept the rocking chair and the slippers. The minimal changes due to age would not be apparent in the course of the normal active day.

Comparison   **C**   Fortunately this training need take little time. The fitness requirement is half an hour of movement at a comfortable pace four times a week. The master runners do more than that, of course, and their movement is running. But even for them the outlay is little more than four hours a week devoted to this training.

D   Such activity is needed to satisfy the animal in us. It is what is necessary to make you and me good animals. And that forms the base from which we can operate. Given a sound and healthy and fit body, we can pursue our perfection in various ways. Once we have acquired the energy to make the day easy and the crisis conquerable, age will become the youth we were promised when we were young.

Sheehan, George, "Running Is Forever, and Everyone." *New York Times* 31 Jan. 1982: 25.

A word about organizational breakdowns is important here. As you read academic sources, you will become aware that few professional writers use the classic five-paragraph essay format that you may have learned in high school English class. Do not expect all your sources to have one introductory paragraph followed by a series of body paragraphs and a conclusion.

Your preliminary steps are to use the organizational divisions you have marked on the passage to structure your outline and to write a synthesis sentence of each paragraph next to the appropriate capital letter on your outline.

The next step is to use organizational signals to convert the sentence-summary outline to a précis. Remember to reflect the organizational structure of the original source. In this case you will write three paragraphs, which will correspond to Roman numerals I, II, and III on your outline. In addition to these major organizational signals, you may have to use smaller signals as you combine the summary sentences into cohesive paragraphs. These smaller signals will serve as unifying devices. Examples of smaller signals are transitional words and phrases, repetitions, pronouns, and restatements of ideas. Study carefully the précis that follows.

SUMMARY-SENTENCE OUTLINE CONVERTED TO A PRÉCIS

Sentence Summary Outline

I. INTRODUCTION

    A. When Dr. George Sheehan was 45, he became a member of a cross-country running team at a high school because there were no competitive races for older people anywhere else.

    B. The kids on the team accepted him, but runners on opposing teams found him odd and were amazed that he could pass them on the track.

    C. These young athletes were unaware that the body has terrific potential even as it ages.

    D. Whereas these high school runners were worried about their limited years for eligibility, Sheehan's body was informing him that he could run forever.

Précis

When Dr. George Sheehan was 45, he became a member of a cross-country running team at a high school because there were no competitive races for older people anywhere else. Although the kids on his own team accepted him, runners on opposing teams found him odd and were amazed that he could pass them on the track. These young athletes were unaware that the human body has terrific potential, even in old age. Whereas these highschool runners worried about their limited years for eligibility, Sheehan's body informed him that he could run forever.

II. BODY

    A. Just as Sheehan's preconception about his own body changed, so did his ideas about women runners' ability to run and run well.

    B. The decrease of running ability is only about 5 percent per decade; consequently, male and female runners who are over 40 can and do compete in races.

Just as Sheehan's preconceptions about his own body changed, so did his ideas about women runners' ability to run and compete well. Because the decrease of running ability with age is only about 5 percent per decade, male and female runners over 40 can and do compete in races.

III. CONCLUSION

    A. In effect, an athletic career is endless if the runner regularly works on training and weight control.

    B. Physiologically, if older people exercise and stay active they will experience only minimal changes due to age.

    C. People need to exercise for only half an hour four days per week.

    D. With sound, healthy, fit bodies people can discover their "youth" in old age.

In effect, an athletic career is endless if the runner regularly works on training and weight control. If older people exercise and stay active, they will experience only minimal changes due to aging. They need to exercise only half an hour four days per week. Then, with sound, healthy, fit bodies, in their old age they can discover their "youth."

The précis of the Sheehan essay will satisfy an assignment that calls for a freestanding summary. However, if your plan is to write a component summary that will become part of a larger paper, you will have to do more to weave the reduced information into the longer piece.

EXERCISE 17

After you have completed the prereading and close-reading activities from Chapter 4, write a précis of the following passage by

1. Combining the ideas in the reduced information to produce synthesis sentences
2. Using outlining and organizational signals to compose the précis

Many of the false preconceptions people have about economics are attributable to the fallacy of composition. This is the fallacy of contending that "what is true for the individual or part is true for the group or whole." This is a logical fallacy; it is not correct. The validity of a particular generalization for an individual or part does not necessarily ensure its accuracy for the group or whole.

A noneconomic example may help: You are watching a football game on a sunny autumn afternoon. The home team executes an outstanding play. In the general excitement, you leap to your feet to get a better view. Generalization: "If you, as an individual, stand, then your view of the game is improved." But does this also hold true for the group—for everyone watching the game? Certainly not! If everyone stands to watch the play, everyone—including you—will probably have the same or even a worse view than he had when seated!

Now an illustration from economics: An individual farmer who is fortunate enough to realize a bumper crop is likely to find that his resulting income is larger than usual. This is a correct generalization. Does it apply to farmers as a group? Possibly not, for the simple reason that to the individual farmer, crop prices will not be influenced (reduced) by his bumper crop, because each farmer is producing a negligible fraction of the total farm output. Thus, as all farmers realize bumper crops, the total output of farm products rises, thereby depressing prices. If price declines overbalance the unusually large output, farm incomes fall.

In a sense, these comments on the fallacy of composition boil down to this: There are two essentially different levels of analysis at which the economist may derive laws concerning economic behavior. The level of macroeconomics is concerned either with the economy as a whole or with the basic subdivisions or aggregates—such as government, households, and businesses—which make up the economy. An aggregate is a collection of specific economic units which are treated as if they were one unit. Thus, we might find it convenient to lump together the sixty-nine million households in our economy and treat them as if they were one huge unit. In dealing with aggregates, macroeconomics is concerned with obtaining an overview, or general outline, of the structure of the economy and the relationships among the major aggregates which constitute the economy. No attention is given to the specific units which make up the various aggregates. It is not surprising, then, to find that macroeconomics entails discussions of such magnitudes as total output, the total level of employment, total income, total expenditures, the general level of prices, and so forth, in analyzing various economic problems. The problems of unemployment and inflation, by the way, are the primary topics of macroeconomics. In short, macroeconomics examines the forest, not the trees. It gives us a bird's-eye view of the economy.

On the other hand, microeconomics is concerned with specific economic units and a detailed consideration of the behavior of these individual units. When operating at this level of analysis, the economist figuratively puts an economic unit or very small segment of the economy, under the microscope to observe the details of its operation. Here we talk in terms of an individual industry, firm, or household and concentrate upon such magnitudes as the output or price of a specific product, the number of workers employed by a single firm, the revenue or income of a particular firm or family, and so forth. In microeconomics, we examine the trees, not the forest. Microeconomics is useful in achieving a worm's-eye view of some very specific component of our economic system.

The basic point is this: The fallacy of composition reminds us that generalizations which are valid at one of these levels of analysis may or may not be valid at the other.

McConnell, Campbell R. *Economics: Principles, Problems, and Policies.* New York: McGraw-Hill, 1975. 14–15.

CASE IN POINT 9

Case in point 9 is a continuation of cases 6, 7, and 8. It is in two parts:

Part I. Reread cases 6, 7, and 8 and review all of the annotations, underlinings, and notes you have taken so far.

Part II. Use the two strategies we have presented in this chapter to write a précis of the article "Human Communication" which appears in Appendix B.

Stop here, unless your instructor tells you otherwise. You will have a chance to come back to this assignment later.

REVISING

As we mentioned earlier, you should revise *as* you write as well as *after* you have completed the first draft of your paper. You will find that the changes you make as you write improve the accuracy and the clarity of both short and extended summaries.

Revising Summaries as You Write

As in the case of paraphrasing, when you reduce information, the most significant revisions take place as you write. While you are converting your close-reading annotations and notes to synthesis-sentence summaries and your outlines to précis, you will be revising.

Comparing the Summary to the Original Source. After you have written your summary, be sure to compare it to the source to see if you have preserved the original meaning. The following summarizing pitfalls should serve as your guide:

1. Using too many words from the original
2. Writing telegraphically
3. Including too many quotations
4. Giving too much detail
5. Failing to document

Now let us discuss how you can detect and remedy these pitfalls.

The Pitfall of Including too Many Words from the Original

Original Passage: Mark Twain's *Huckleberry Finn* is often assigned in American schools to adolescent students. In this context, the novel is typically treated as a boy's adventure story, perhaps with some attention paid to morality. However, at an adult level, the book provides a critical examination of American society. Considered in this light, Huck's trip on the Mississippi is a voyage of discovery that uncovers the hypocrisy that Twain felt was at the base of our society.

    Student Summary: Huckleberry Finn, which is often assigned to adolescents as an adventure story, offers a critical look at American society for adults. During his ride on the Mississippi, Huck discovers the hypocrisy at the foundation of his society.

The problem with this summary is that too many words are taken directly from the original. The student has made very few changes. As you summarize, use the rule of thumb we suggested for paraphrasing: Never repeat more than three consecutive words from the original. If you find you are having trouble with this pitfall, you should review the strategies for changing vocabulary and sentence structure that are covered in Chapter 2.

The Pitfall of Writing Telegraphically

Student Summary: Twain's *Huck Finn,* assigned to adolescents and adults, is criticism of hypocrisy at the base of society.

The student who wrote this summary did a good job of omitting unimportant words and details, but then he or she strung together the remaining information without using proper sentence-combining techniques. As a result, the summary reads like a telegram. After you delete unimportant information, be sure to use unifying devices that will enable you to produce a cohesive, smooth-flowing summary.

The Pitfall of Including Too Many Quotations

Read on an adolescent level, *Huckleberry Finn* is adventure, but on an adult level, "the book provides a critical examination," and, "uncovers the hypocrisy that Twain felt was at the base of our society."

The problem with the summary above is that more than half of it is a direct quotation. In a summary it is permissible to quote key words and phrases that capture concisely very important ideas in the original. But you should not quote extensively.

The Pitfall of Giving Too Much Detail

Huckleberry Finn by Mark Twain can be read on both an adolescent level and an adult level. On an adolescent level, the book is read by students in American schools as an adventure. On the adult level, it is a critique of American society. As a critique, Huck's sail down the Mississippi shows the hypocrisy that Twain believed was under American society.

The problem with this summary is that the student has failed to eliminate secondary information, details, and repetitions. Virtually every idea in the original source appears in the summary. Depending on the demands of your assignment and your audience's needs, your summary may include 50 percent, 10 percent or even less, of the information in the original source. In any case, remember that your objective is to reduce the original by compressing its meaning into fewer words.

The Pitfall of Forgetting to Document

Remember that in an academic paper you must give the source of the reading material you summarize. *Failing to document a summary is plagiarism.* Chapter 12 will explain proper methods of documentation. You should make sure that in your notes and in the first draft you have clearly differentiated summarized material from your own ideas.

Although we have discussed the summarizing pitfalls separately, a poor summary will often have several of these problems. Be sure to check the final version of your paper for *all* the potential pitfalls.

Comparing the Summary to the Topic.   As we have pointed out, sometimes as you are writing the first draft of your paper you will change your emphasis or organization. When this occurs, summarized information you planned to include may not fit into the new direction your paper is taking. If you change your writing plan, you must make sure that the summary still helps develop your topic.

Comparing the Summary to Audience Needs.   When you reduce information, one of your chief concerns should be that your audience understands the main idea or primary information the source contains. As you compare your summary to your audience's needs, ask yourself the following questions:

1. By reading the paper up to the point where the summary is included, will your audience acquire enough background information to understand the summary?
2. Will your audience be familiar with all of the vocabulary in the summary?
3. Is there any additional source information that you should include in order to make the summary clearer?

Revising After the First Draft Is Complete

After you have completed the first draft of your paper, you should engage in further revisions and editing before you write another version of it. Your instructor may comment on your first draft or your fellow students may offer their reactions. In any case, before you attempt a second or final draft, see how your summary fits into your overall plan and edit your paper for grammar, usage, and mechanics.

Seeing How Your Summary Fits into Your Overall Plan.   As you read through the completed draft of your paper, see how component summaries fit into the rest of the paper. Be sure that you are using summaries in appropriate places.

The following checklist will help you to evaluate the first draft of your paper.

CHECKLIST FOR REVISION

A. If you have written a freestanding summary précis:
  1. Does your précis follow the major organizational format of the original?
    a. Introduction?
    b. Body?
    c. Conclusion?
  2. Does your précis include background information for your audience?
    a. Author and title of source?
    b. Proper documentation?
  3. Does each of your paragraphs include the necessary elements?
    a. A clearly stated topic sentence?
    b. Supporting sentences?
    c. Transitional and unifying devices?
B. If you have written component summaries that you have included in a longer paper:
  1. Does your paper have clear organizational divisions?
    a. Introduction?
    b. Body?
    c. Conclusion?
  2. Does each paragraph include the necessary elements?
    a. Introduction with thesis sentence?
    b. Body paragraphs with topic sentences?
    c. Sufficient supporting details?
    d. Unifying devices and transitions?
  3. At the places where you have included your own summaries, have you
    a. Provided sufficient context so that your audience will understand the reduced information?
    b. Clearly differentiated between the summarized information and your own ideas?
    c. Provided proper documentation?
C. For both freestanding and component summaries, inquire about pitfalls. Have you
  1. Included too many words from the original?
  2. Written telegraphically?
  3. Included too many quotations?
  4. Given too much detail?
D. Editing—for grammar, mechanics, and usage

CASE IN POINT 10

Reread the précis you wrote for Case 9. Check that your summary does not contain any of the summarizing pitfalls. Then compare your précis to the topic and to your audience's needs as discussed in this chapter. Finally, use the Checklist for Revision to evaluate the revised draft of your précis and then submit the précis to your professor for review and comment.

WRAP-UP EXERCISE FOR REDUCING

The following exercise gives practice in maintaining the balance between completeness and brevity while summarizing.

1. All class members write freestanding summaries of the passage given below.
2. Divide the class into groups of three.
3. Each group member reads the two summaries of his or her partners.
4. Each group works as a unit to make two lists: a list of the separate ideas from the original passage that *all* group members included in their summaries (list 1) and a list of the ideas from the original passage that only one or two of the group members included in their summaries (list 2).
5. Each group discusses the items on list 2 and decides which of these items belong in a summary of the original passage.
6. Each group makes a revised list of the ideas that should be in the summary of the original passage, including all the items from list 1 and the selected items from list 2.
7. Each group writes its revised list on the board. The entire class then discusses and compares the lists. The class arrives at a final list of ideas that should be included in the summary and discusses why specific items were included in, or dropped from, the list.

The power of the sword is more sensibly felt in an extensive monarchy than in a small community. It has been calculated by the ablest politicians, that no state, without being soon exhausted, can maintain above the hundredth part of its members in arms and idleness. But although this relative proportion may be uniform, the influence of the army over the rest of the society will vary according to the degree of its positive strength. The advantages of military science and discipline cannot be exerted, unless a proper number of soldiers are united into one body, and actuated by one soul. With a handful of men, such an union would be ineffectual; with an unwieldy host, it would be impracticable; and the powers of the machine would be alike destroyed by the extreme minuteness, or the excessive weight, of its springs. To illustrate this observation we need only reflect, that there is no superiority of natural strength, artificial weapons, or acquired skill, which could enable one man to keep in constant subjection one hundred of his fellow-creatures: the tyrant of a single town, or a small district, would soon discover that an hundred armed followers were a weak defense against ten thousand peasants or citizens; but an hundred thousand well-disciplined soldiers will command, with despotic sway, ten millions of subjects; and a body of ten or fifteen thousand guards will strike terror into the most numerous populace that ever crowded the streets of an immense capital.

Gibbon, Edward. *The Decline and Fall of the Roman Empire.*

Reading To React

WHAT IS REACTING?

When you react to reading assignments, you respond to them in certain ways. In the chapters on summarizing you learned that one of the most efficient ways to read for the purpose of summarizing is to respond by marking or underlining important parts of the text and by annotating the text with explanatory notes. As you underlined topic sentences, marked structural divisions, and supplied explanatory notes about the writer's plan, you *reacted* to the reading sources in an intelligent, scholarly way, examining relationships among the various parts of the passages.

Another way to react to the material you read is to "move outside" the immediate assignment in order to examine the relationships between the *author's* ideas about a given topic and *your* preexisting knowledge and experiences about the topic. If your sociology professor assigns an article on prejudice, before you read it, ask yourself what you already know about prejudice. A good way to activate previous knowledge is to ask yourself about the topic: Who? What? When? Why? and How? Also ask yourself what bearing your experience has on the topic. Try to make associations based on personal experiences or associations based on other people's experiences, or both. If you have not directly experienced prejudice in your own life, undoubtedly you have experienced prejudice vicariously; that is, you have read about it or seen portrayals of it in films or on television. Jot down all these reactions in your notes.

Then as you read the article, stop from time to time to relate your own ideas to those of the author. Think of the author as a person with whom you are speaking. Carry on a dialogue, interacting with the author as you would with a speaker you were communicating with face to face; once again, write down your reactions. After you have read the article, sit back and reflect on the ideas in it. Try to expand the topic and use your imagination to speculate about it. Spend a few minutes writing down your thoughts.

Definition: Before, during, and after the act of reading, reacting to the academic source means bringing your personal experiences and preexisting knowledge to bear on the topic so that you can put the author's message in a context you understand, carry on a dialogue with the author, and expand and speculate on the author's ideas.

The above definition makes several important points:

1. You can react to a reading source before, during, and after the act of reading. You need not wait to express your reactions until after you have completed the reading.
2. When you react to a topic, you bring to it your previous experiences as well as your previous knowledge about it.
3. Reacting is *good* reading because it enables you to put the author's ideas in an understandable context, carry on a conversation with the author, and elaborate and reflect on the author's ideas.

Consider the following example of a student's reaction to a passage in Lowenfeld and Brittain's textbook, *Creative and Mental Growth:*

Haven't some schools abolished I.Q. tests?

The smart kids usually have large vocabularies.

I don't draw well at all. I wonder if this indicates something about my intelligence!

The whole concept of intelligence as used within our society is essentially that of relating one child's performance to that of all children of the same age. A child who performs tasks typical of an older child tends to be considered more intelligent. Since scribbling is a reflection of the child's total development, we have here an indication of the child's intellectual growth, particularly at a time when the usual group-type intelligence tests are not usable. Therefore, a kindergarten child who is still in the scribbling stage will not be able to perform at the level usually expected of kindergarten children. In first grade the same child could not learn to read. It is obvious that the understanding of scribbling can help us to understand children.

Lowenfeld, Viktor, and W. Lambert Brittain. *Creative and Mental Growth.* 5th ed. New York: Macmillan, 1970. 106.

Student Notes: This is a very interesting idea. Next time I have a chance I'm going to watch my little cousin to see if she still scribbles. Last Christmas she drew a picture of a Christmas tree on the card she sent us. I guess she's pretty advanced for a three-year-old.

Observe how the student annotated the passage with her reactions. Also notice the informal nature of her notes. Reactions are usually written in an expressive writing style called free writing. When you free write, you can let your thoughts flow, be imaginative, and experiment with words. Usually you will be the only person who sees your free-writing notes. However, in some courses your professors may ask you to keep your reactions in journals that they will collect and review from time to time.

In addition to reacting informally in journals, you may react formally in assignments that call for your impressions of books, articles, lectures, and films or in personal-experience essays. You may also include reactions when you write a critique, an illustration of an idea, or your judgment about a particular concept or theory. Remember that the focus of academic reactions is on the sources, not on you or your opinion. You must treat the original authors fairly and represent their ideas accurately. You react in order to learn more about the issues raised in the sources, not just to get your licks in. Reactions in academic papers should clarify issues rather than cloud the truth or bias and confuse the reader.

At this point it is important to emphasize that reactions are not always appropriate in academic assignments. Some professors may structure assignments specifically to avoid student reactions. Other professors may impose constraints on what is appropriate in a reaction. Be sure to check with your professor if you are unsure about the type of reaction that is permissible.

Reacting vs. Paraphrasing and Summarizing

1. Reacting goes beyond the literal content of the text. It requires you to bring to the text meaning that is not stated explicitly. Paraphrasing and summarizing are bound to the literal content.

2. Reacting may include your *subjective* interpretations. The *I* emerges, where your paraphrases and summaries are completely *objective*.

3. Reacting does not require you to follow the order of the source. You might first react to the author's final point and then comment on a point midway in the passage. Paraphrases and summaries usually follow the author's order of presentation.

4. Reacting focuses partially on *you,* the reader; paraphrasing and summarizing focus exclusively on the author of the text.

5. Reacting allows you to include paraphrases or summaries of the parts of the reading passage to which you are referring. Paraphrases and summaries do not contain reactions.

Reacting is:

A way to put the topic in a familiar context before the careful reading

A way to have a dialogue with the author during the reading

A way to expand and speculate on the author's ideas after the reading

Reacting is not:

Just giving your own opinion

A way to twist the author's ideas

An excuse to use unsubstantiated opinions

A free license to attack the author

A technique that is appropriate for *all* academic assignments

HOW REACTING FITS INTO THE ACADEMIC WRITING PROCESS

Planning
  Prereading
    1. Clarify the assignment and topic.
    2. Consider the audience's needs.
    3. Preview the academic source and write your thoughts on the topic and a personal definition.
    4. Set goals for reading.
  Close reading
    1. Connect new ideas with previous knowledge and experience.
       (a) Annotate the passage.
       (b) Take separate notes.
  Postreading/Prewriting
    1. Reread the assignment and decide what you will react to.
    2. Reconsider your audience.
Writing
    1. Write freely in order to expand the topic and speculate about it.
    2. Select and order your reactions.
    3. Order your essay.
    4. Summarize the source and write reaction paragraphs.
    5. Write introductory and concluding paragraphs.
Revising
  As you write
    1. Compare paper to the original source and search for pitfalls.
    2. Compare reaction to topic and assignment.
    3. Compare reaction to audience needs.
  After you write
    1. Edit for grammar, usage, mechanics.

chapter 7

Planning the Reaction

At the planning stage make your preexisting knowledge and experiences available by reacting to the reading source *as* you are overviewing it, *while* you are performing a careful, close reading of it, and *after* you have read it. If you activate your background knowledge *before* you read, you will better comprehend the assignment because you will be fitting it into a context or framework you already understand. Then *as* you read the passage, be aware of the fundamental relationships between your own ideas and those of the author. Annotate the passage with your reactions. Based on your knowledge and experience of the topic, converse with the author: agree or disagree, or approve or disapprove of the ideas. Write a note about a reading association or give an example of the topic from your personal experience. *After* you read the passage, close the book and spend fifteen or twenty minutes expanding and speculating about the topic, writing your thoughts, sensations, memories, and associations. Make these notes as detailed as possible. Later you may be able to select and order some of these reactions and use them in a paper.

PREREADING

Clarify the Assignment and Topic

As we pointed out in the introduction to this section, instructors may have varying opinions about whether or not you may use reactions when you respond to academic assignments. Carefully study the assignment to see if any reaction is permissible. If some reaction is appropriate, ask yourself if the conventions of the field of study impose any limits on the types of information you may include. For example, your sociology professor may permit you to use examples from your personal experience whereas your psychology professor may not.

Consider Audience Needs

The reading source that triggers your reaction is familiar to you, but your audience may not know as much about the source as you do. Unless you present some background information about the source, your audience will not appreciate fully the reaction. Look at how one student reacted to her English assignment.

> *Assignment:* The main characters of all three novels we read this term were violent men who were sentenced to death. Do you agree totally with the sentence these men received? Is there any character you would have found innocent to a certain degree?
>
> *Student Reaction:* I do not think Bigger was totally guilty. Mary, herself, was partly responsible because of the way she acted with Bigger in the restaurant and in the car. Besides it was Mary's fault that Bigger was in her room. Bigger panicked because of the situation he was in. But it was Mary who got him into the predicament in the first place. Because of this, I would not have sentenced Bigger to the electric chair. Mary was just as guilty as he was.

This paragraph is a good example of writer-based prose. The student, who knows the plot of Richard Wright's novel *Native Son* perfectly, writes for herself. She forgets to consider the needs of her reader and leaves the reader with many questions: Who is Bigger? What is his crime? Who is Mary? What were Mary's actions in the restaurant and in the car? What kind of predicament was Bigger in? As you react to a reading source, anticipate the needs of your reader. A good way to give your reader necessary background information is to summarize briefly the parts of the source to which you are reacting.

Preview the Academic Source

To preview the reading material, use the procedure you followed in earlier chapters, with two additional steps. As previously, do an overview of the passage, reading the title, author, and first sentence of each paragraph and making note of the writer's format (introduction, body, and conclusion). Then perform two other operations that will enable you to put the reading topic in a context you already understand. These two operations will activate your pre-existing knowledge and previous experiences. First, in an expressive, free-writing style write down your thoughts and understanding of the topic. Second, write your own personal definition of the topic based on your previous knowledge and experiences with it. As you work through the following case, you will get a good idea about how to use these two operations.

> Assume you are a student in educational psychology. Your professor has assigned the following excerpt from the beginning of a long essay. She expects you to summarize briefly the excerpt's main ideas and react to them.

A Young Person's Guide to the Grading System

by Jerry Farber

There's no question that the grading system is effective in training people to do what they're told. The question is: what does it do for learning?

Grades focus our attention. But on what? On the test. Academic success, as everyone knows, is something that we measure not in knowledge but in grade points. What we get on the final is all-important; what we retain after the final is irrelevant. Grades don't make us want to enrich our minds; they make us want to please our teachers (or at least put them on). Grades are a game. When the term is over, you shuffle the deck and begin a new round. Who reads his textbooks after the grades are in? What's the point? It doesn't go on your score.

Oddly enough, many of us understand all of this and yet remain convinced that we need to be graded in order to learn. When we get to college, twelve years of slave work have very likely convinced us that learning is dull, plodding and unpalatable. We may think we need to be graded: we assume that without the grades we'd never go through all that misery voluntarily. But, in fact, we've been had. We've been prodded with phony motivations so long that we've become insensitive to the true ones. We're like those sleeping pill addicts who have reached the point where they need strong artificial inducement to do what comes naturally. We're grade junkies—convinced that we'd never learn without the A's and F's to keep us going. Grades have prevented us from growing up. No matter how old a person is—when he attends school, he's still a child, tempted with lollipops and threatened with spankings.

Learning happens when you *want* to know. Ask yourself: did you need grades to learn how to drive? To learn how to talk? To learn how to play chess—or play the guitar—or dance—or find your way around a new city? Yet these are things we do very well—much better than we handle that French or Spanish that we were graded on for years in high school. Some of us, though, are certain that, while we might learn to drive or play chess without grades, we still need them to force us to learn the things we don't really want to learn—math, for instance. But is that really true? If for any reason you really want or need some math—say, algebra—you can learn it without being graded. And if you don't want it and don't need it, you'll probably never get it straight, grades or not. Just because you pass a subject doesn't mean you've learned it. How much time did you spend on algebra and geometry in high school? Two years? How much did all those years of force-fed grammar do for you? You learn to talk (without being graded) from the people around you, not from gerunds and modifiers. And as for writing—if you ever do learn to write well, you can bet your sweet ass it won't be predicate nominatives that teach you. Perhaps those subjects that we would never study without being graded are the very subjects that we lose hold of as soon as the last test is over.

Still, some of us maintain that we need grades to give us self-discipline. But do you want to see real self-discipline? Look at some kid working on his car all weekend long. His parents even have to drag him in for dinner. And yet, if that kid had been compelled to work on cars all his life and had been continually graded on it, then he'd swear up and down that he needed those grades to give him self-discipline.

Farber, Jerry. "A Young Person's Guide to the Grading System." In *The Student as Nigger*. New York: Simon and Schuster, 1970. 67–68.

First, overview the passage. You note that the title is "A Young Person's Guide to the Grading System," that the author is Jerry Farber, and that the piece is excerpted from a book. A quick reading of the first sentence of each paragraph reveals that the topic of the passage is grades.

Second, begin to activate your preexisting knowledge of the topic—grades. Recall your previous experiences with grades. Write informally and express your thoughts freely. Explain how you feel about the topic. Be creative and experiment with words. Ask yourself questions, such as:

What do I think about grades?

How do grades affect me?

Am I interested in grades?

What feelings do grades evoke in me?

Have I had positive experiences with grades?

Have I had negative experiences with grades?

This can be a journal exercise. A *journal* is a record of your expressions. It is similar to a diary except that a diary is written for the writer alone whereas journal entries may be shared with an audience. When you write your reactions in a journal, you have to be concrete and specific so that your reader—either the professor or your classmates, or both—is able to appreciate your response.

A typical prereading journal entry on the subject of grades might read as follows:

> In my opinion grades are a bad method of evaluating. People can judge how others function by seeing how they perform over time. I would be able to understand someone a lot better by talking to that person for months or days, rather than hours as on a regular examination. Grades really don't show your true identity. Grades are a way for teachers to tell how well students achieved in school, not in their social background. Grades should be done away with. I think another way of evaluation should be created. I know of a lot of people who don't succeed on tests but understand the material that was previously covered.
>
> Shep Becker

Third, now that you have written down your thought on grades, try to compose your own personal definition of this topic. The following sentence-completion exercise will serve as a guide.

Grades are _____.

Grades are a type of _____ that _____
_____.

Grades are_____ but not _____
_____.

Grades are like _____.

After you have recalled your previous knowledge and experiences with the topic and composed a definition of it, you will have established an advanced scheme or framework that will help you to understand better the ideas you examine as you read closely the Farber passage. Now let us turn to the final step in the prereading stage of the planning process.

Set goals for reading

Before you proceed to the close reading, review your assignment and establish your goals for reading. Remember that when you read for the purpose of reacting, you continue to bring your own ideas to bear on the author's ideas *as* you read and *after* you have finished the passage.

CASE IN POINT 11

Assume you are a student in Introduction to Sociology. Over the course of the semester, your professor has been assigning brief commentaries on social behavior and asking students to react to them. You have just received this week's assignment:

In "A Red Light for Scofflaws" Frank Trippett makes a number of observations of social behavior, supported by concrete examples, that lead him to generalize that the U.S. is becoming a nation of people who disregard the law. What is your reaction to Trippett's claim?

You will find Trippett's essay in Appendix B.

Plan your prereading response to this assignment. Follow the procedure described in the beginning of this chapter.

1. Clarify the assignment and topic.
2. Consider your audience's needs.
3. Preview Trippett's essay. Next, freely write out your thoughts and understanding of the topic. Then write your own definition of the topic.
4. Set goals for your close reading.

Stop here, unless your instructor tells you otherwise. You will have a chance to come back to this assignment later.

CLOSE READING

As you read the source, connect the new ideas you are encountering with preexisting ideas from your store of knowledge and experiences. Carry on a dialogue with the author, writing your reactions as marginal annotations or separate notes. You may agree or disagree with the author, recall a previous association, ask or answer a question, express satisfaction or dissatisfaction, or approve or disapprove. Normally as we read we react in hundreds of ways, but we are not fully conscious of these reactions. When you bring them to a conscious level and jot them down, you will get a better understanding of how you think about the topic, and you will also acquire increased knowledge about yourself.

If you have been a passive reader for ten or eleven years, learning to carry on a dialogue with the author may take a little practice. At first, you should try to jot down every reaction that comes into your head. Study the following student reactions to the first two paragraphs of the Farber passage.

There's no question that the grading system is effective in training people to do what they're told.* The question is: what does it do for learning?* Grades focus our attention. But on what? On the test.* Academic success, as everyone knows, is something that we measure not in knowledge but in grade

That's for sure. If you don't do as you're told you'll flunk!

It makes you learn what they tell you to learn.

That's why I spent 4 hours cramming for my history exam last night. But grades are also important for paper assignments. In this course, we don't have tests but we get graded on the papers.

points.* What we get on the final is all-important; what we retain after the final is irrelevant.* Grades don't make us want to enrich our minds; they make us want to please our teachers (or at least put them on). Grades are a game. When the term is over, you shuffle the deck and begin a new round. Who reads his textbooks after grades are in? What's the point? It doesn't go on your score.

I agree. I got an 86 on the geometry final, but I don't remember any of it.

That's true. Once you psyche out the teacher and give her what she wants, you've got it made.

Yeah and you're playing against the teacher!

Does it ever stop?
I sell my books. Nobody keeps school books.

Notice that as the student reads, essentially, she expresses her agreement. She agrees with Farber on a number of points. She also recalls concrete personal experiences that illustrate Farber's ideas, asks a question, and supplies a counterexample (writing papers as opposed to taking tests).

As we mentioned earlier, there are hundreds of ways to express reactions. However, because many of us are passive readers who rarely react on a conscious level, we need to be reminded of ways to have an active dialogue with the author. Most students react to academic sources in three ways. First, they react with unquestioning acceptance: "If the ideas are published and assigned by my professor, they must be true. That's all there is to say about it." This is the typical reaction of the passive reader. Second, students react with confusion: "How am I to remember this? It makes no sense." Third, students may express too much confidence in their previous knowledge: "This is obviously simple-minded." Unfortunately, these three ways of reacting—with unquestioning acceptance, with confusion, or with confidence—are quite passive. The reader's reaction is limited to an observation and a comment. There is very little interplay between the reader and the author of the text.

Throughout this book we have suggested strategies and techniques that will help you to think of reading as an active process that involves two partners—you, the reader, and the author of the text. We have stressed that reading is not a one-way communication process. The text you read was written by a real person. Try to keep this person in mind as you read. "Talk" directly to the author in your mind and in your notes. Let the author know what you think of the text. Think of reading as an *inter*-personal rather than a personal experience.

In order to keep the interaction between you and the author of the text dynamic, ask yourself questions as you read. Following are a number of useful questions. At first you will have to make a conscious effort to ask these questions as frequently as possible. But with practice you will find yourself stopping intermittently to have a dialogue with the author in a natural, effortless way.

Twelve Questions to Ask Yourself as You Read

1. Can I add any information to what the author is saying?
2. Do I agree with the author's views here? Do I disagree? Why?
3. Do I approve of the author's ideas? Do I disapprove? Why?
4. Am I satisfied with what the author has to say on the topic? Am I dissatisfied? Why?
5. How do I feel or what do I believe about this topic?
6. Do I have a question for the author? Have I answered any questions the author has raised?
7. Based on what the author has said, can I make a prediction?
8. Can I think of an example that illustrates the author's point? Can I think of a counterexample?
9. Have I had any personal experiences with this topic?
10. Can I recall previous associations I've had with this topic or with these ideas?
11. Can I make a generalization based on elements in common between the author's ideas and my own ideas?
12. Can I think of an analogy to illustrate what the author is saying?

There are times when you will abbreviate your answers to the above questions and write your reactions in the form of marginal annotations. On other occasions you may want to write out your reactions as separate notes, particularly as entries in a course journal. We will discuss such journals later.

EXERCISE 18

Study the twelve reacting questions presented above. Then return to the selection from Jerry Farber's article, "A Young Person's Guide to the Grading System." As you read the article, carry on a dialogue with Farber, stopping after each paragraph and asking the twelve questions. Write your answers in the margins.

CASE IN POINT 12

This case is a continuation of Case 11. Review Case 11 and reread your pre-reading-reaction notes. At this point, you are ready to begin your close reading. As you read "A Red Light for Scofflaws," you will be doing a lot of annotating. We have provided you with large margins for this purpose. You might want to make a copy of the article and annotate it, instead of writing in your book. In any case, as you read the article, have an active discussion with Trippett. We have inserted asterisks as reminders for you to stop and ask questions. Feel free, however, to stop and ask questions before you come to an asterisk, if you wish. Use the Twelve Questions to Ask Yourself as You Read as a guide.

Stop here, unless your instructor tells you otherwise. You will have a chance to come back to this assignment later.

POSTREADING/PREWRITING

Reread Your Assignment and Determine the Portions of the Reading Sources to Which You Will React

After you have completed your close reading of the source, you should reread your assignment to determine whether you will write a *freestanding* reaction or a reaction that will be a *component* of a larger paper. The reaction will be freestanding if it satisfies the assignment sufficiently. For example, an assignment that includes a poem and asks you to react to it is freestanding. However, if the material to which you will react is not included as part of the assignment, you should summarize it before you react to it.

For some assignments, a brief summary of the source followed by a reaction will suffice. For others, you may have to include a critical review of the material. We will discuss the characteristics of the review later in this book. If you are unsure about how much or how little reaction to include in your essay, be sure to consult your instructor.

Reconsider Your Audience

Remember that although you are very familiar with the source to which you are reacting, your audience may not know it well. When you use just a portion of a source, you will have to provide your audience with the context into which the portion fits. You may have to summarize the information that comes before the portion as well as the information that comes after it.

CASE IN POINT 13

This case is a continuation of cases 11 and 12. Review these two cases, Frank Trippett's "A Red Light for Scofflaws," your prepreading-reaction notes, and your close-reading annotation. Then return once again to the assignment:

> In "A Red Light for Scofflaws," Frank Trippett makes a number of observations of social behavior, supported by concrete examples, that lead him to generalize that the U.S. is becoming a nation of people who disregard the law. What is your reaction to Trippett's claim?

After you have reread the assignment, determine whether your reaction will be freestanding or accompanied by other forms of academic writing. Then reconsider your audience. Decide how much background information you will provide.

Stop here, unless your instructor tells you otherwise. You will have a chance to come back to this assignment later.

chapter 8

Writing and Revising the Reaction

WRITING

When you reach the point where you are reacting in continuous writing, you will have already reacted in free writing at the prereading stage and in annotation at the close-reading stage. During the writing stage you will engage in five operations:

1. Write freely in order to expand and speculate on the author's ideas.
2. Select and order your reactions.
3. Decide on your organizatonal plan and the essay format.
4. Summarize the source and write your reaction paragraphs.
5. Write your introductory and concluding paragraphs.

In order to illustrate these operations, let us return to the Farber selection and review your activities during the prereading stage. After you previewed the Farber passage, you freely wrote down your thoughts about grades and composed your own definition of this topic. Then as you closely read the passage, you had a dialogue with Farber by asking reaction questions and annotating the text. Up to this point, you have *reacted* and *interacted*. Now it is time to *reflect*.

Write Freely in Order to Expand and Speculate on the Author's Ideas

Take out your journal or another notebook and spend fifteen to twenty minutes reflecting on the new ideas you have read. Try to expand or elaborate on Farber's ideas and begin to speculate about them. Record all of your reflections.

You can expand an author's ideas by asking what bearing your experiences have on what you have read. Remember, you are not limited to autobiographical events. In addition to your personal experience, consider friends' experiences and vicarious experiences you have had through reading or viewing television or films. Try to

1. Recall an incident or dramatized scenario from your own life
2. Recall someone else's experiences, vicarious experiences, or hypothetical incidents
3. Provide additional details, examples, or elaborations

Here are some excerpts from journal entries of students who used these techniques.

Recall a Personal Incident or Dramatized Scenario

I would prefer that teachers stop grading students. I can learn better if the grading system changes. When I was at high school, whenever we had a test I got panicky. After reading the questions, I would forget everything I studied because I worried that I would fail instead of getting good grades. This semester I am taking a course in which we do not have tests or any kind of grades, but we will have a final grade. I am working as I work for any other course and so are the rest of the students. I want to prove that students who are attending college or schools will work hard even though they are not being graded, on one condition— that they are there to learn and not hanging around having fun. On the other hand, when one feels that someone is watching him and will evaluate his work, he will do his best to please the person who is watching him. For example, when my mother asked me to do some housework I would do my best because I knew she would come after me and say that I was not doing my job as I should have done. Now, since my mother is not with me, I do not take care of my closet because nobody is going to evaluate my job. But to tell the truth, I feel guilty in doing so.

Shoghig Missirian

Recall Someone Else's Experiences

Another time students don't need grades as motivation is when they are studying for a profession; they will be motivated without being graded. For example, my brother pulled "A's" in law school, whether he was graded or not. When he made errors on exams, he would always correct his mistakes and learn from them, even though his grades weren't changed.

Howard Kaminsky

Provide Additional Details, Examples, or Elaborations

I agree with Farber when he states that people learn better when they want to learn, but there are so many more things that grades are directly involved with. Job positioning is a prime example of this. How is an interviewer supposed to base his judgment on employee prospects? Employers need to know how competent their workers are, and grades serve as a good basis for an evaluation. I know that if I get good college grades, I will have a better chance at getting a job than if I never attended college.

Jim Volz

You can *speculate* on an author's ideas by letting your imagination run freely. There are three techniques that will help you to prime the pump and stretch your imagination:

1. Ask questions about the direct consequences of the author's ideas.
2. Draw personal implications from the author's ideas.
3. Assume a role and apply the author's ideas to the new situation.

Reading the journal entries of students who used these techniques will help you to see how they are used.

Ask Questions About the Direct Consequences of the Author's Ideas

I feel that if the grading system was abolished today, numerous problems would surface, like lack of incentive for hard work. Because grades represent rewards for hard work, it is conceivable that their elimination would have a negative impact on the incentive to work hard. Another consequence would be the reluctance of students to go to classes. As all of us know, academic accomplishment is something we measure in grade points not in wisdom. Therefore, a person would not feel compelled to attend classes if he or she was not going to receive a grade. For myself, it would seem like a waste of time if I were not going to receive a grade.

Casey Tillman

Draw Personal Implications from the Author's Ideas

There are alternatives to grades, such as progress reports or ratings. I think that some form of evaluation of a student's performance is essential. I would not feel safe if I knew that the doctor operating on me was not evaluated on his knowledge of science and medicine. The documentation of a student's progress serves a greater importance than motivation in a learning situation and evaluations apply outside the classroom.

Robin Arnheim

Assume a Role and Apply the Author's Ideas to the New Situation

If I were a teacher at Ithaca College, I would want my students to enjoy my course. I wouldn't want them to feel that they had to come to class. In addition, I would want them to remember most of what I taught them and learn for the sake of learning and not for the grade.

Wendi Barbesh

Student reactions like the ones above are often written as journal entries. Some college instructors require their students to keep a journal in which they record their reactions to the course and/or to the reading assignments. Often instructors collect student journals and comment on them; however, they rarely grade them or correct students' writing. The purpose of journal writing is to express your thoughts freely and to experiment with different types of writing without worrying about spelling, grammar, or mechanics.

If your instructor does not assign a journal, you may decide to keep one yourself. The journal not only affords an opportunity to develop more fully your reactions to the topics you read, it also develops your awareness of how you think about these topics. A reading journal can serve as a documentary of your academic growth. Your prereading reactions and your postreading journal reflections are a record of your evolving awareness about an assignment topic. At the end of each week, you should reread your journal entries and reflect on your intellectual progress.

EXERCISE 19

This exercise contains five excerpts from students' journal reactions to the selection from Jerry Farber's essay, "A Young Person's Guide to the Grading System." Read carefully each entry to determine which of the following techniques the student used to expand and speculate on Farber's ideas:

1. Recall an incident or dramatized scenario from your own life.
2. Recall someone else's experiences, vicarious experiences, or hypothetical incidents.
3. Provide additional details, examples, or elaborations.
4. Ask questions about the direct consequences of the author's ideas.
5. Draw personal implications from the author's ideas.
6. Assume a role and apply the author's ideas to the new situation.

Identify the technique and explain how the student used it. There may be more than one technique per excerpt.

Example: Student Journal Entry

I agree with Farber. I can recall studying for a calculus test the night before the exam. I had to get a good *grade* to keep my average up. When I really think about it, I was pressuring myself into a form of study which made me very bored and frustrated. I gained very little knowledge.

Michael Athanas

The student recalls a personal incident when he crammed for a calculus test but really learned little from it.

Just receiving grades from teachers that don't really know that much about you or why you are at school seems slightly worthless. That's why I feel school grades should be less crucial. But, if I was to be operated on by a surgeon who didn't receive any grades throughout school, I doubt I would proceed with the operation. Surgeons who make their way through medical school must be pretty good, but without a grading system we wouldn't have any criteria for knowing who is a better doctor.

Lori Leipzig

I think the major question is if all grades were abolished tomorrow, would anyone continue to work? This pertains not only to students in schools, but also to today's working person. If employees were not monitored or evaluated on how well they do their jobs, would the quality of work be the same? This decision could have a major effect on our economy! It could also have a very big effect on professions where quality is extremely important. I know I'd feel much safer having a lawyer that had good grades all through college, than one that wasn't graded at all.

Tim Torrey

As far as I can remember, I have always hated history, so I never did anything for the class. (Psychology I liked so I did the work and learned as much as I wanted to.) I also enjoyed playing the piano, and I knew I wasn't being graded on it so I tried my best and learned a lot.

Cynthia Satenspiel

People seem to lose their values when all they care about are their grades. I hate to see someone having to drop a class because he's getting a D in it. They feel they need to drop the class because their grade point average might go way down. However, they forget each class is costing them $500 and the opportunity to increase their knowledge.

Marvin Maltz

I feel as Farber does. Farber says that grades make us want to please our teachers and focus our attention on tests. I often find myself wanting to please a teacher with a good grade, especially once I get to know her over a certain period of time. In high school I became really close to a history teacher over a three-year period. When I finally had her for class, I saw myself becoming more aware of the tests. I also saw myself studying more, so that I could please her with a good grade.

Another point which Farber brings up is that in learning to talk or write it isn't modifiers or predicate nominatives that help us learn, but rather the people we listen to. To some extent I believe this is true. Surely we learn from others, but in actuality is everything we hear correct? It seems as though Farber disregards the fact that we need the understanding of modifiers and predicate nominatives to help us begin to talk or write.

David Dasch

EXERCISE 20

Review the excerpt from Jerry Farber's article, "A Young Person's Guide to the Grading System." Remember that you have already written your prereading reactions to grades and interacted with Farber as you read closely. For fifteen to twenty minutes write freely to expand and speculate on Farber's ideas. Use as many of the reacting techniques as possible.

CASE IN POINT 14

This case is a continuation of cases 11, 12, and 13. It is in three parts. First, review cases 11, 12, and 13, Frank Trippett's "A Red Light for Scofflaws," your prereading notes, and your close-reading annotations. Second, for fifteen or twenty minutes use the six techniques for expanding on and speculating about the author's ideas to free write your reactions to Trippett's essay.

Third, compare your prereading reactions and the free writing you have just completed. Take five more minutes to write about the differences between your earlier and later notes.

Stop here, unless your instructor tells you otherwise. You will have a chance to come back to this assignment later.

Select and Order Your Reactions

The next step is to review all of your reactions, your prereading reactions, close-reading annotations, and postreading journal entry in order to select the reactions you will include in your essay. Combine similar reactions, eliminate isolated reactions, and reorder remaining reactions. To illustrate, let us look at the reactions of freshman Eileen Pizarro to "A Young Person's Guide to the Grading System."

Prereading Reactions

I think we have to have grades to motivate us to study and do well in school, especially in courses we find boring or have little interest in. We also need grades to compare people and measure who is doing a better job. All through life, we are graded. I've had a lot of negative experiences with report cards, especially in elementary school and junior high. When I came to this country, I spoke only Spanish and it took me a long time to adjust to American schools. Grades used to affect me negatively, but now I realize that if it weren't for grades, I wouldn't work very hard. Grades keep me on my toes.

I would define grades as a type of measurement that is used to motivate people and compare their capacities.

List of Close-Reading Annotations

I disagree. If I didn't have grades I wouldn't know where I'm at.

What's wrong with pleasing the teacher?

Well, I *need* to be graded. Look what happened in Spanish!

It's not just people in school who are tempted with lollipops.

True I learned to swim without being graded.

Yeah, but if we did away with grades, how would we measure?

But everything is graded, even food.

Grades are not just in school. I was evaluated by my boss last summer.

This doing away with grades is a great idea but it wouldn't work. What will replace grades?

Journal Expansion and Speculation on the Topic

If we did away with grades around here, no one would go to classes! Or else they would only go to the classes they liked. All the kids would party all day. It would be total chaos.

I need grades to motivate me. If I wasn't being graded, I wouldn't have done well in Spanish. Because I'm Spanish, I thought I didn't have to study at all. But the grades that I got showed me where I needed the most help—grammar.

Mostly everything in life is graded. Food and services are graded. There are different grades of meat and grade A and grade B hotels. Employees are graded, too. When Elia and I worked for Manpower last summer, we got a job in the same firm. The boss gave us a two-week trial period to see what kinds of jobs we could do best. I got a good grade for filing, and Elia got a good grade for typing, so I got a clerical job and she got a secretarial job.

Even doctors and lawyers are graded. I'd rather be operated on by a doctor who had an A than someone who barely passed the course.

After reviewing her reactions, Eileen decided to focus on her disagreement with Farber and to stress the negative consequences of Farber's ideas. After eliminating irrelevant reactions, she reordered her reactions as follows:

If we abolished the grading system, there would be negative consequences:

people wouldn't go to classes or would go only to classes they liked—total chaos, e.g., Spanish course.

unrealistic because we need to grade food, services, jobs, professors, etc., e.g., summer job with Elia, doctors.

Eileen can use this breakdown as a preliminary outline for the reaction section of her essay.

EXERCISE 21

Review all of your own reactions to the excerpt from Farber's "A Young Person's Guide to the Grading System." Combine similar reactions, eliminate isolated reactions, and reorder the remaining reactions. Now, like our student, Eileen, you are ready for step 3.

Decide on Your Organizational Plan and the Essay Format

At this point, let us review the reaction assignment:

You are a student in a course in educational psychology. Your professor expects you to summarize briefly the main points of "A Young Person's Guide to the Grading System" and react to the essay.

Of the five writer's plans we discussed in Chapter 5—antecedent-consequent, comparison, response, description, and time—it is clear that you will choose response for this essay. First, you will present your statement—the summary of the source—and then you will give your response—your reaction to the Farber essay.

The most effective format for a freestanding-reaction paper uses four major organizational signals: introduction, summary, reaction, and conclusion.

Usually you will keep your summary of the source brief because the focus of the paper is *your* reaction to the author's ideas, not the author's ideas themselves. To continue our illustration, using the suggested format and her reordered reaction breakdown, our student, Eileen, constructed the following outline for her paper.

Paragraph 1—Introduction
Paragraph 2—Summary of Farber passage
Paragraph 3—Reaction
   Negative consequences in many areas (food, services, etc.)
Paragraph 4—Reaction
   Negative consequence for students
Paragraph 5—Reaction
   Negative consequence for other people
Paragraph 6—Conclusion

Now Eileen is ready for step four.

Summarize the Source and Write Down Your Reaction Paragraphs

You will use the summarizing strategies you learned in chapters 4, 5, and 6 to reduce the reading source to one lengthy paragraph. First, write your own summary of the Farber passage and then consider Eileen's version:

According to Farber, the grading system is good for teaching us to do things as we're told, but we are not really learning. Farber says that success in school means pleasing the teacher and doing well on the tests. The game is to get a good score and to measure points, and not to enrich our minds. We finally reach the point where we become "grade junkies" and we start convincing ourselves that A's and F's are needed to learn, when, in fact, grades have stopped us from growing up. Farber also says that we only learn things that we have interest in, enjoy, or want to learn. Some people learn to drive, play chess or even do math problems if they want to, but if they were to get grades on these things, they would not want to do well. What it all comes down to is that some people say they need grades to give them self-discipline, but Farber says if these people had a strong desire to learn, they would learn without grades.

Eileen Pizarro

When you complete the summary, move on to the reaction paragraphs. Flesh out your preliminary outline and use it as a guide. Write three reaction paragraphs. For each paragraph, use one of the five writer's plans, compose a clear-cut topic sentence, and use organizational signals as unifying devices. If you need to review any of these elements, reread the section on summarizing. We have annotated Eileen's reaction paragraphs in order to show you how she used the various techniques.

Topic Sentence	Mostly everything in life is graded. If we were to do away with the grading system, the situation wouldn't be realistic. First of all, we need the grading system to measure the quality of our food and services. If we were to abolish the grading system from our society, we wouldn't have a choice between grade A and grade B peaches or different qualities of meat. People would not be aware of the differences. The consequence would be the same if we abolished the grading system in our schools. If we didn't have it, we wouldn't know the difference in quality of school work.	Prediction of consequences

Antecedent/consequent — marked on the left of the first paragraph.

Transition-signal and **Implication** — marked on the right.

Topic Sentence	If we were to abolish the grading system, students wouldn't bother going to classes they didn't like. Grades give a reward that classes don't give. Students would only attend the classes they like most, not classes that are required for their major. This would cause total chaos. If I didn't have grades to show me where I'm at, I don't think I would go to my classes. I need grades to keep me on my toes doing my work. For instance, I'm taking Spanish for the first time. I wouldn't have done so well if it weren't for my being graded on my work and exams. I came	Prediction

Antecedent/consequent — marked on the left of the second paragraph.

Signal and **Personal experience** — marked on the right.

into class thinking that just because I'm Spanish, I didn't have to study at all. But the grades that I got showed me where I needed the most help, which is in my grammar. Now I can concentrate more on improving my grammar than wasting time speaking Spanish.

Topic
Sentence

Antecedent/
consequent

Grades also motivate people other than students to do better and they are used to compare and measure how well people perform on their jobs. Most people would prefer having surgery performed by a doctor who received an *A* in his anatomy course than by one who got a *D*. They need to compare the capacity to see which doctor can do a better job. This is one of the many reasons why people need the grading system. Another good example is an experience I had with a girlfriend in the city. We got a job in the same firm, and because we were from the same high school and had the same major, our employer didn't know what kinds of jobs each one of us could do. So, he decided to give my friend and me a trial period of two weeks. During this time, he gave us miscellaneous jobs to do like filing, typing, and answering phone calls. He graded us on our work and found our weaknesses and strengths. Because he was grading us, we knew we had to work harder. The tension helped make us realize what we liked to do. Our employer recognized my interest in filing, so he gave me a clerical job, and he gave my friend a secretarial job.

Implication

Signal

Personal
experience

Eileen Pizarro

These three reaction paragraphs and the summary will comprise the body of Eileen's paper. Now she is ready to write her introduction and conclusion.

Write Your Introductory and Concluding Paragraphs

The purpose of your beginning paragraph is to introduce the general topic and state your thesis. The best way to do this is to give your readers some background information about the topic, and prepare them for what you will say about it. You might also tell them your writer's plan and try to capture their interest. Let us consider each of these pieces of information and examine how Eileen used them to construct an introductory paragraph.

General topic: "A Young Person's Guide to the Grading System" and my reaction to it.

Background information: Jerry Farber wrote the passage. It is excerpted from his book.

What I will say: I disagree with Farber's ideas. If we do away with grades, there will be many negative consequences.

My plan: Statement/response. I will summarize Farber's article and then react to it.

How I will interest reader: I think I'll begin with a startling quotation from Farber's passage.

Putting It All Together

"We're grade junkies," claims Jerry Farber "—convinced that we'd never learn without the A's and F's to keep us going." In "A Young Person's Guide to the Grading System," Farber criticizes the grading system and suggests that students would learn better without it. I disagree with Farber because if we did away with grades, there would be negative consequences.

Eileen selected a quotation for the opening sentence. If your reading source contains a striking quotation, you may want to use this technique. Eileen could have begun the paper with a statement of her thesis or with background information. There are a number of ways to open a paper. If you have difficulty deciding how to begin, use one of the techniques in the following list.

Paper Openers

1. Quotation—use a direct quotation from the reading source or a famous quotation.
2. Question—ask your reader a rhetorical question, for example, "Are you a grade junky?"
3. Anecdote or brief story—I got an A on the typing final even though I could only type eleven words per minute. I was slow but accurate.
4. Fact—Children learn to feed and dress themselves and to walk and talk without grades.
5. Generalization—Students learn more when they take courses pass-fail than for letter grades.
6. Contradiction—Grades are a pain that we can't do without!
7. Thesis statement—I disagree with Jerry Farber's position against grades in "A Young Person's Guide to the Grading System" because abolishing grades would have negative consequences.
8. Background—In "A Young Person's Guide to the Grading System," Jerry Farber criticizes the grading system and suggests that students would learn better without it.

Use one of the eight paper openers to begin your reaction to the Farber passage. Then write the rest of your introductory paragraph.

Finally, we are ready to move on to the last paragraph of the essay. The concluding paragraph should do more than recapitulate the high points of the paragraphs that come before it. A summary of the main points you have made is justified, but you should also use techniques, such as (1) stressing the significance of your thesis; (2) predicting the consequences of the author's ideas; (3) calling your readers to action; and (4) ending with a question, anecdote, or final quotation.

Read Eileen's conclusion. In addition to summarizing, which of the techniques did she use?

> In the last analysis, we need to grade people, like students and doctors, as well as things, like services and food. If we abolished grades, we would not be able to differentiate between good and poor quality. If you paid a top price for grade A sirloin, would you be satisfied with chuck?

Notice that Eileen began her conclusion with a phrase that signaled the reader. In addition to *in the last analysis,* there are other signals for conclusions, such as *finally, in sum, in conclusion, lastly, in closing,* and *thus.* Eileen then rephrased her thesis and ended the paper with a question.

At this point, reread the introduction, summary, and reaction paragraphs you wrote for Farber's essay. Use the techniques presented above to write an interesting concluding paragraph.

CASE IN POINT 15

This case is a continuation of cases 11, 12, 13, and 14 based on the assignment to read and react to Frank Trippett's "A Red Light for Scofflaws." To recapitulate: You have written prereading-reaction notes, close-reading annotations, and a postreading journal entry.

Select and order these three sets of reactions. Now you are ready to complete the remaining steps in the writing process:

> Decide on the organizational plan and the format you will use for your essay.
>
> Summarize the Trippett passage and write your reaction paragraphs.
>
> Write your introduction and conclusion.

Stop here, unless your instructor tells you otherwise. You will have a chance to come back to this assignment later.

REVISING

You will probably revise reactions more *as* you write than after you have completed a first draft. While you are selecting and ordering your reading notes, and as you are composing your first draft, you will be making a number of changes in order to convert your personal, free-writing prose to a more formal, audience-based prose. Moreover, after you complete the first draft you will continue to revise your paper, searching for pitfalls and correcting grammatical mistakes. The task of revising a reaction paper is complex because you must check for reaction pitfalls, summarizing pitfalls, and even paraphrasing and quoting pitfalls if you have restated or repeated any of the source material. In addition, you must make changes that will improve your total paper.

Revising Reactions as You Write

Comparing the Paper to the Original Source. As you write the brief summary that accompanies your reaction, check that you have avoided problems such as using too many words from the original, writing telegraphically, including too many quotations, and giving excessive details. If you need suggestions for solving these problems, review the summary pitfalls in Chapter 6.

As you write the reaction paragraphs, be aware of three other pitfalls:

1. Presenting unfair bias in personal reaction
2. Giving uninformed opinions
3. Being unaware of the limits of experiences

Now let us discuss how you can detect and remedy these problems. Consider examples of pitfalls in students' reactions to Farber's essay.

Presenting Unfair Bias in Personal Reaction

I don't think Farber's ideas hold water. He sounds like the type that just doesn't want to study. People who complain the loudest about grades are usually the laziest.

The problem with this reaction is that the student is biased. The student is disinclined to believe Farber because of her own personal prejudices. As you react to an author's ideas, try to be impartial. Do not let your personal views prejudice you in any way.

Giving Uninformed Opinions

I just don't believe any learning can take place without grades.

Here the student expresses what she believes is true but offers no information to support the opinion. It is all right to use opinions in your reaction paper.

However, your opinion should be a conclusion you draw from evidence of some sort. It is unreasonable to expect your audience to agree with an uninformed opinion.

Being Unaware of the Limits of Experiences

Students in my high school, which is a typical all-American school, were not grade junkies.

The problem with this reaction is that it contains an overgeneralization. The assumption is that the students from one high school represent all of the students Farber discusses. When you use personal experiences in reaction papers, recognize their limitations.

Comparing the Reaction to the Topic. As we have pointed out in earlier chapters, sometimes as you are writing the first draft of your paper you change your emphasis or organization. When this occurs, information you planned to include may not fit into the new direction of the paper. If you change plans or decide to shift emphasis, be sure your reaction still helps develop your topic.

Comparing the Reaction to Audience Needs. As you write your first draft, be mindful that your readers need sufficient background information about the source if they are to appreciate the content of your reactions. In addition, they need organizational clues that will enable them to follow your line of thought. As you compare your paper to your audience's needs, ask yourself:

1. By reading the paper up to the point where the reaction is included, will your audience acquire enough background information to appreciate the reaction?
2. Is there any additional source information that you should include so that your readers will better understand your reaction?
3. Have you provided your readers with major organizational signals, introduction, body, and conclusion?
4. Have you supplied your readers with a thesis sentence that indicates your main idea?
5. Have you provided your readers with minor organizational signals, such as transitional words and phrases?

Revising Reaction after the First Draft Is Complete

After you have finished the first draft of your paper, edit it for faults in grammar, usage, and mechanics and use the Checklist for Revision to recheck the organization and content.

CHECKLIST FOR REVISION

A. Does the paper have an appropriate title?
B. What is the thesis of the paper?
C. In the introductory paragraph do you inform your audience of the title and author of the passage to which you are reacting?
D. Is the summary complete? Do you need more information?
E. Do you provide transitions between the summary and the reaction section?
F. Which of the following techniques do you use in the reaction section? Do you
    1. provide a personal incident or dramatized scenario?
    2. provide someone else's experiences, vicarious experiences, or hypothetical incidents?
    3. provide additional details, examples, or elaborations?
    4. ask questions about the direct consequences of the author's ideas?
    5. draw personal implications from the author's ideas?
    6. assume a role and apply the author's ideas to the new situation?
G. In the reaction section section, do you
    1. present unfair bias in personal reactions?
    2. give uninformed opinions?
    3. lack awareness of the limits of experience?
H. Editing—Are there any problems with grammar, usage, or mechanics?

CASE IN POINT 16

This case is a continuation of cases 11, 12, 13, 14, and 15 based on the assignment to read and react to Trippet's "A Red Light for Scofflaws." For Case 15 you composed the first draft of your essay. Before you submit your paper to your instructor, revise it, using the above Checklist for Revision.

CASE IN POINT 17

Assume you are a student in an introduction to psychology course. For the next class meeting you have been assigned the passage from William Lambert and Wallace Lambert's text, *Social Psychology* that appears in Appendix B. Your professor has pointed out that in the passage, Lambert and Lambert present psychologist Stanley Schachter's findings on birth order.

Before you read the passage, activate your preexisting knowledge and previous experiences on the topic of birth order. In a journal, write your personal definition of birth order and freely record your answers to the following questions: What do I think about birth order? How does my position in my family's birth order affect me? What feelings does my position evoke in me? What have I noticed about people with different positions in birth order?

Next, read the passage carefully, carrying on a dialogue with the author and jotting down your reactions to Schachter's ideas.

Then without looking at your earlier journal entry, write another definition of birth order and an informal response to Lambert and Lambert's passage.

Finally, in writing compare your prereading and postreading entries. How did you grow academically? What did you learn about position in birth order? What are your reactions to this new knowledge?

CASE IN POINT 18

Take the informal reactions you collected for Case in point 17. Select and order them, and use them in a personal-experience essay based on Stanley Schachter's theory of birth order. In light of your own experiences, do you agree or disagree with Schachter's ideas? Be sure to use all of the reacting strategies you learned.

CASE IN POINT 19

The English instructor has asked your freshman English class to read the following poem by Katharyn Machan Aal and write their impressions of it in their course journals. Use the strategies you learned in chapters 7 and 8 to write a free-flowing, but detailed, 250-word journal reaction.

one night the dogs
come running yelping
the stink of the kennel
on them   the men
silently walking
the guns
glinting in the night
the light from the moon
a big round mouth
open

far down the creek
she hears before the sound
stops her   begins
to run tasting
salt in her throat
runs knowing she must
escape
their eyes
the flecks of spit
flying from their tongues

she climbs
high the big pine
tallest in the forest
swaying
against the mouth of moon
the dogs below
howling
the men
shouting jeering
she reaches the top

the instant
of death and life laughing
she jumps

her stomach ballooning
legs and head spread wide
jumps
past the moon
that would swallow her
rushing down and

down
she hits
the firm ground
bouncing tumbling

the pack still yelps
at the empty sky
furious impotent blind*

WRAP-UP EXERCISE FOR REACTING

This exercise will help you appreciate the diversity of reactions that academic ideas can produce.

1. Read the first of the sentences listed below.
2. Write freely in reaction to the sentence you read. Do not stop writing for ten minutes.
3. Look over your free writing and select the one sentence that best expresses your reaction to the sentence you read.
4. Reduce the sentence you chose in step 3 to five words or less.
5. All students write their reduced reactions on the board.
6. The class discusses the nature of the differences between the student reactions.
7. Repeat steps 1 thru 6 for sentences 2 and 3.

Sentence 1: Like their ape ancestors, human beings are inherently violent, and thus war is inevitable.

Sentence 2: Studies show that homes without television produce children who are better students.

Sentence 3: Political libertarians claim that the American government does not respect the rights of the individual.

*Aal, Katharyn Machan, *The Raccoon Book.* Ithaca, N.Y.: McBooks Press, 1982.

Reading to Review

WHAT IS REVIEWING?

In chapters 1 through 6 we assumed that as you paraphrase or summarize a source, you come to understand its meaning. This way of thinking indicates that your search for meaning has a definite end where you understand the original source completely. In chapters 7 and 8, we explained how you can enrich understanding for both yourself and your audience by reacting to ideas. However, there is still more that you can do to expand understanding of written sources and incorporate the information more usefully into your own writing. Specifically, you can objectively *analyze* the ideas you read about. Analyzing is the central technique in the process of *reviewing*. Reviewing helps broaden your understanding of what you read and helps you gain more from the source than just the literal content.

Although the purpose of both reviewing and reacting is to expand your understanding of the original source, they do so in distinctly different ways. When you react, you draw from part of your personal view of the world and bring it to bear on the academic material. When you review, you use certain commonly accepted strategies that do not depend on your personal outlook to look more closely at the meaning of the source. You do not rely on your personal experiences and views as evidence. Reacting is a personal response. Reviewing is an objective response.

The distinction between reacting and reviewing is extremely important to college students because instructors often ask students to avoid reactions in written assignments. We mentioned earlier that a personal reaction is not always appropriate. At the request of a particular instructor or in response to a particular subject, you may find that you must review rather than react.

Definition. Through reviewing you broaden both your own and your audience's understanding of an academic source by objectively analyzing the content of the source. Academic reviews are not based on personal reactions but rather on techniques that can be applied by anyone familiar with the field of study.

ANALYZING IDEAS FOR REVIEWING

Analyzing ideas can involve a wide range of activities. These activities could be grouped in four main categories:

1. Strategies that help you detect the parts of the message that are not stated outright
2. Strategies that help you decide the value of the ideas
3. Strategies that help you apply the ideas
4. Strategies that help you see the relationships between sources

The thrust of all four types of analysis strategies is to go beyond the author's literal message and do something new with the author's ideas. In this sense, reviewing is creative just as reacting is. However, reviewing must be *objective.* You should not rely on personal reactions and perspectives but rather base your analysis on reasoning that anyone could follow whether or not he or she understands your personal feelings and perspectives. Analyzing is done according to standards that would be acceptable to most people. Common sense is perhaps the most basic of these standards. The scientific method is an example of a standard that is used in a number of academic fields to analyze arguments. Later we will give you a list of analysis strategies that are commonly used in many different fields of study.

Although our list of strategies will help you deal successfully with a great variety of assignments that require analysis, you should keep in mind that each subject area may also have its own standards for analyzing ideas. When you become educated in a particular field of study, you learn the methods of analyzing ideas that are typically used in that field. For example, in a literature class you might learn that poems can be analyzed according to meter—the number and sequence of accents per line. Make sure that you keep track of the standards for analysis that are presented in each class and use them when you read and write in that field.

Reviewing vs. Quoting, Paraphrasing, Summarizing, and Reacting

Assignments that ask you to review will often require quoting, paraphrasing, and summarizing as well. A review will not make sense unless you first clearly express the content of the material that you are reviewing. This will probably involve summarizing the ideas in the original source and may also involve either quoting or paraphrasing specific sections of the text. You must let your audience know the overall content of the material you are reviewing for your review to be fair.

Reacting is subjective. It involves bringing in your personal view of the world. Reviewing is objective. It involves analyzing and connecting ideas in ways that do not involve using personal reactions.

SUMMARY:

What reviewing is:

A means of going beyond the literal content of a source
A tool for connecting ideas from academic sources
A means of objectively analyzing ideas
A way of providing support for opinions
A means of evaluating your own opinions

What reviewing is not:

Expressing subjective views and personal opinions
Offering only negative criticism of a source while ignoring the positive
Summarizing only

HOW REVIEWING FITS INTO THE ACADEMIC WRITING PROCESS

Planning
  Prereading
    1. Clarify assignment and topic.
    2. Consider your audience's needs.
    3. Consider the author's intended audience.
    4. Consider the author's objectives.
    5. Set goals for reading.
        What analysis questions will you use to guide your close reading?
  Close Reading
    1. Search for answers to analysis questions:
        What are the answers to field-specific analysis questions?
        What assumptions does the author make?
        What particular aspects of the topic does the author emphasize?

What do the ideas, evidence, or explanations in the source suggest or prove?
How do the ideas in the source interact with those in other sources?
How can the author's ideas be used or applied?

2. Make notes on the content.

Postreading/Prewriting

1. Reconsider your answers to analysis questions.
2. Determine the limitations of the source.

Writing

1. Compare your analysis-question answers to the assignment topic.
2. Look for organizational patterns.
3. Arrive at a thesis that ties your thoughts together.
4. Organize your paragraphs around the results of your analysis.

Revising

As You Write

Search for reviewing "pitfalls."

After You Write

1. Compare your thesis to the assignment.
2. Compare your conclusion to the assignment and to your thesis.
3. Check the relationships between paragraphs.
4. Clarify the dividing lines between summary, reaction, and analysis and check for the relative proportions of each.
5. Check paraphrases and summaries for accuracy.

chapter 9

Planning
The Review

Successful reviewing requires careful planning. Assignments that ask you to review (to critique, to analyze, and so on) are typically harder to approach than assignments that ask you to summarize or react. Students who plunge into writing reviews without sufficient initial planning frequently become lost or merely turn assignments into extended summaries or reactions. Without the proper preparation, it is almost impossible to write a good review.

PREREADING

Clarify the Assignment and Topic

When you face a reviewing assignment, you must clarify the exact topic area, as we have mentioned in earlier chapters, but you must also pay close attention to the way in which the assignment asks you to write your review. Reviewing potentially involves such a wide range of activities that you need to make sure that you know exactly what your assignment calls for. Some review assignments may be extremely specific, but others may leave you with questions. When you are trying to clarify a review assignment, you should ask your professor the following questions:

How much of my paper (if any) should be a summary of the source(s)?

How much (if any) of my paper should be a personal reaction?

How much (if any) of my paper should be an analysis of the source(s)?

The answers to these questions will let you know to what extent you are expected to review, if at all. If you find that you are expected to review, you should ask your professor one more question:

What aspects of the source should I analyze or review?

The answer you receive to this question may range from "It's up to you" to a very detailed description of the review process that the assignment calls for. Remember that a particular field of study may require special reviewing strategies. In such a case, your professor will usually explain the assignment in detail. Later in this chapter we provide a list of reviewing strategies that are appropriate for a wide range of reviewing tasks. For open-ended assignments, you can refer to this list to get ideas of what aspects of a source you could review.

Consider Your Audience's Needs

As we mentioned earlier, an important part of reviewing is to go beyond the literal content of the source. As you review, you first come to an understanding of the literal content of the source and then use a variety of strategies to extend its meaning. In most cases your written review must take your audience through the same steps from literal content to extended meaning. Your finished paper should allow your audience to answer each of the following questions:

What is the literal content of the source?

How does this essay extend the meaning of the source?

What is the extended meaning of the source?

Consider the Author's Intended Audience

Figuring out the audience that a piece of writing is meant for can be extremely important when you are trying to interpret a piece of writing. Understanding the perspective can make the material more meaningful to you and make it easier for you to decide how to use the information. For example, imagine that you are writing a research paper on the risks to society resulting from gene-splicing technology. You know that the issue is highly controversial, and that there are strong arguments to both support and oppose further development of gene-splicing technology. The technology can help scientists create new microorganisms that could, for example, possibly attack and kill human cancer cells, thus curing the disease. However, it is also possible that the new technology would create new disease microorganisms that, if allowed to escape from the lab, could kill thousands of people. You want to consider both sides of the controversy in your paper. In the course of doing your research, you find that a certain well-known biologist is a leader of the group that supports developing gene-splicing technology. You find three sources in which he argues in favor of the new technology. The chart summarizes the contents of these three sources.

Source 1	*Source 2*	*Source 3*
Stresses the reliability of science and reviews improvements science has made in everyday life.	Stresses the value of gene splicing as a biology research tool.	Gives an explanation of safeguards used to prevent infection from gene-splicing experiments.

Notice that the contents of these sources vary a great deal. Why would the biologist present three entirely separate arguments? Did he change his mind about which argument provides the best support for developing the new technology? Which argument does the biologist feel is the strongest? Which argument should you concentrate on in your paper? Thinking about the audience for which each of these sources is intended would help you answer these questions.

For example, source 1 might be a newspaper feature story; source 2, an article in a biological-science journal; and source 3, a report to a congressional committee studying the safety of gene splicing. The newspaper article is most likely intended for the general public. The biologist may feel that the average person will tend to oppose gene-splicing technology due to a general distrust of science. Thus, the article stresses the reliability of the scientific method and how it has helped improve our lives. The article for the scientific journal is meant for an audience of other biologists, people who may actually use the new technology. This article explains the advantages of gene splicing as a means of advancing knowledge in the field of biology. The author knows that other biologists will be interested in a technique that can help them to make major advances in their field of study. The article for the congressional committee centers on safeguards against the serious health problems that could result from the research. The biologist knows that the committee will be concerned with the potential dangers of the new technology and how these dangers can be avoided.

In this example, the author's basic opinion did not change from article to article. Rather, the author chose the details that would make most sense to each specific audience. Remember your assignment is to write a paper on the risks to society resulting from gene-splicing technology. Since your hypothetical paper topic deals with the issue of safety, the congressional committee report would probably be the most useful to you since its intended audience is a group of informed people who want to know the specific hazards of gene splicing and the possible ways to avoid these hazards. This source will probably present the strongest case for the opinion that gene-splicing technology can be developed safely. The other two sources contain reasonable and possibly valid arguments, but they are geared for audiences for whom the details concerning safety are not the central issue in evaluating the subject.

The number of audiences that an author might write for is virtually limitless. The following list suggests a few possible audiences:

General public
College-educated readers
Experts in a particular field
Scientists
People who read widely
People who keep up with current events
People with particular job experiences

EXERCISE 22

Below are brief descriptions of various pieces of writing. In each case, describe the author's *most likely* audience. Use the list of possible audiences as a guide.

1. A textbook on the neurophysiology of the visual system.
2. A newspaper article on a new art exhibit at a local museum.
3. A textbook on academic writing and reading.
4. A research study on cutting production costs for high-carbon steel.
5. A textbook on the psychology of aging.
6. A feasibility study on a national health insurance plan.
7. A sermon.
8. An article on the use of pantomime in early productions of Shakespeare's *King Lear*.
9. A review of a play produced by your college's drama department.
10. A textbook on the full range of approaches to literature.

Consider the Author's Objectives

When authors write, they usually have both their main ideas and their specific objectives in mind. The main ideas are the thoughts about their topics that they want to develop. Thus far in this book, we have discussed paraphrasing, summarizing, and reacting to authors' main ideas. *Authors' objectives are the general effect they want their writing to have on their audiences—what they want to accomplish by writing*. The author's objectives are frequently not part of the literal content. For a variety of reasons, from working for an indirect writing style to deliberately attempting to hide certain intentions, writers may not state their objectives directly. Thus, *as a reader, you should search for the author's overall objectives.* If you look for the author's objectives as you read, you are less likely to get bogged down if the details are complex or otherwise confusing. Also, locating and writing about the author's objectives can form a valuable part of a written review.

It may seem to you that the author's objective is very similar to the author's main idea. Certainly, the goal and the main idea are closely related. However, the same main idea can be expressed by different authors to achieve different goals. Consider the following example:

Main idea: Studies have shown that making students work through grammar exercises does not improve their writing.

Objective 1:   Help teachers choose the best teaching techniques.

Objective 2:   Persuade students to reject traditional approaches to education.

Objective 3:   Inform scholars who study writing theory of new research findings.

Objective 4:   Criticize the writing curriculum in a particular college.

The sample main idea could be the focus of a paper with any of the four suggested objectives. As you preview a source, you should look not only for the main ideas but also for the author's objectives. Clues that point to the author's objectives can be found in the same places as the clues to the main ideas, largely in the beginnings and endings of sources. Notice in the example that each objective suggests a particular audience. Figuring out the audience for a piece of writing will give a good hint as to its overall objective.

EXERCISE 23

Below are brief descriptions of pieces of writing. Determine each author's *most important* objective. Remember that a piece of writing may have several objectives, but you are looking for the most important one.

1. A lab report on an experiment conducted in a chemistry class
2. An article in a business magazine that analyzes opportunities for investment created by a new corporate merger
3. An English teacher's statement in her course syllabus concerning policies on plagiarism
4. A technical report issued by a committee of politically active scientists on the risks of stockpiling biological weapons
5. A leaflet handed to you on campus announcing a political rally in support of unionizing campus workers
6. An article describing an experimental treatment for leukemia

7. A poem describing the details of a criminal's death in the electric chair, written by an author who opposes the death penalty
8. A diary written by a father covering the first year of his new child's life
9. A chapter in an archeology textbook giving the steps in an archeological dig

Set Goals For Reading

Analysis of a source is largely a matter of asking the right questions about it as you read. We will see in the next chapter that these questions and their answers can provide both the content and the structure for a review paper. Thus, you set your goals for reading by determining which analysis questions are appropriate for your assignment. We have just considered two analysis questions, involving the author's intended audience and general goals, that you can answer based upon your preview. We will now consider questions that can be answered only by closely reading the source.

Before you begin to read an academic source, you should decide what analysis questions will work best for your assignment. Your goal in reading will be to answer these questions. The following list contains the most general analysis questions:

1. What analysis techniques specific to your field of study have you learned? Which of these does the assignment require?
2. What is the author's intended audience? (determined by previewing)
3. What are the author's objectives? (determined by previewing)
4. What assumptions does the author make?
5. What particular aspects of the topic does the author emphasize?
6. What do the ideas, evidence, or explanations in the source demonstrate or support?
7. How do the ideas in the source interact with those in other sources?
8. How can the author's ideas be used or applied?

Not all of these questions will work for any given assignment. In fact, for most assignments you will probably center on a few or perhaps even just one of these questions, to guide your close reading of the source. When you have clarified the topic and previewed the source, you should then decide which of the questions will serve you best. Your assignment will often indicate that you should use particular questions as your reading goals. For example, consider the following sample assignment:

One of the most influential documents in the history of socialism is *The Communist Manifesto* by Karl Marx and Frederick Engels. During the nineteenth century when this document was published, many people felt that it exposed the social injustice of the capitalist economic system. However, some scholars now argue that modern capitalism is considerably different from the system that Marx and Engels criticized. Are the criticisms of capitalism found in *The Communist Manifesto* still valid when applied to capitalism today?

In order to write this paper, you must *summarize* Marx and Engels's criticism of capitalism and try to *apply* the same criticisms to modern capitalism. Thus as you read, you will need to concentrate on the following modification of one of the basic analysis questions:

Basic analysis question: How can the author's ideas be used or *applied?*
Modification: How can Marx and Engels's ideas be applied to today's society?

It is very helpful if you start out with a clear understanding of your reviewing goals before you read. In this way, you avoid getting sidetracked and thus writing a paper that does not really speak to the assignment you were given. Notice that the sample assignment is based on evaluating how well the ideas in *The Communist Manifesto* work today, not how well they worked in the nineteenth century. Thus it would be irrelevant to your topic to examine how Marx and Engels's writing affected their nineteenth-century audience. You must focus on the analysis questions that are appropriate for your particular topic.

In addition to providing the substance for a review paper, analysis questions encourage you to think carefully and intelligently about what you read. In fact, the thought process that these questions stimulate can be more valuable to you than the actual answers to the questions. Indeed, when analyzing some sources, it may be impossible to come up with an answer to a particular review question that is definitely "correct." However, asking analysis questions will extend your understanding even if you are unsure of the ultimate answer. If nothing else, this questioning process helps clarify the literal meaning and cements it more firmly in your memory.

CLOSE READING

Search for Answers to Analysis Questions about the Source

Throughout this book we have stressed the importance of using specific questions to guide your close reading. You should now realize that this is particularly important when your goal is to review the source. Since a source can be reviewed from so many different perspectives, it is crucial that you understand what you want from a source so you can search for the relevant information as you read closely. We will discuss what you should look for when you attempt to answer analysis questions during your close reading.

What analysis questions specific to your field of study have you learned? Which of these does the assignment require?

To guide your close reading, *always* use the specific analysis strategies that you have learned in the course or that the assignment indicates. Often, the entire purpose of an assignment is to detect how well you use the analysis strategies that are standard in a particular field of study. Try to make a list of these special strategies *before* you read.

What is the author's intended audience?

As you read closely, try to check on the judgment you made at the preview stage as to the author's intended audience. If your close reading indicates a different audience than your preview did, make the necessary alterations in your preview notes.

What are the author's objectives?

Use your close reading to check on your initial impression of the author's objectives. Make any necessary changes in your notes.

What assumptions does the author make?

Almost every piece of writing is based on certain *assumptions* of the author. Assumptions are ideas or facts that authors take for granted as they write. Usually authors make no attempt to describe their assumptions in any detail. However, at times authors will clearly identify their basic assumptions as they write. The following well-known sentence from the Declaration of Independence is a good illustration.

> We hold these truths to be self-evident, that all men are created equal, that they are endowed by their Creator with certain unalienable Rights, that among these are Life, Liberty and the pursuit of Happiness.

This sentence contains one of the basic assumptions on which the Declaration of Independence is based: All people have certain basic rights. When Thomas Jefferson wrote this document, he discussed this assumption explicitly. More often, authors' assumptions are not stated outright, and thus the reader has to figure out what assumptions underlie the ideas in sources.

Most authors' assumptions can be classified into two groups: (1) assumptions about what is true and (2) assumptions about what the intended audience knows. In the previous example, Jefferson made an assumption about what was true, namely, that people were born with "certain unalienable rights."

In the following passage the author makes an assumption about what the intended audience will know. See if you can identify this assumption.

> After the Michaelson-Morley experiment results were accepted as fact, scientists such as Albert Einstein began to search for an alternative to the theory that light was transmitted through an invisible, undetectable substance that was at one time thought to exist throughout the universe.

This passage is based on several assumptions. The most important assumption is that the audience will be familiar with the Michaelson-Morley experiment. Most people who have studied basic physics would probably have some notion of what this experiment demonstrated. However, even if you are unfamiliar with the experiment, you can figure out what it must involve from the other information in the passage. You can reason that the Michaelson-Morley experiment must have shown that light does not travel through an invisible substance. Thus, by thinking about the author's assumptions, you could have learned something from this passage that was not part of its literal content.

Quite often you cannot understand academic writing until you understand the assumptions on which it is based. This creates problems for students who are just beginning to read the academic prose in a field of study. In order to understand the material, the students must first identify the assumptions and figure out how they contribute to the author's meaning.

Examining the author's assumptions not only extends your understanding but also can form the basis for a review of the source. Indeed many academic reviews say nothing about the literal content and concentrate totally on the author's assumptions. This is particularly true if the author's assumptions do not seem reasonable. We will discuss assessing the reasonableness of assumptions later in this chapter.

EXERCISE 24

Each of the following passages is based on at least one fact that the author does not state explicitly. Find this unstated fact for each passage using the information the author does provide.

1. In the early 1980s, a substantial number of cardiologists began to revise their previously strict opposition to having their patients eat food containing high levels of cholesterol.
2. Modern drama producers take more risks when they stage Shakespearean drama than did the producers of Shakespeare's time. One major factor that accounts for this difference is the elaborate sets that modern audiences expect. Current productions of Shakespeare's plays must do very well at the box office to cover costs.

3. Although feudal kings were rarely known for their good will, England's King John was particularly notorious for his unfair administration. His callous lack of regard for the rights of the English nobles led them to force him to sign the Magna Carta. For centuries to come, this document helped to hold the English monarchs in check when they attempted to claim absolute power over their subjects.

4. Of the two major types of processes that create islands, the slowest is definitely the formation of islands from the remains of small living creatures such as coral and algae.

5. Bound as we are by Western ideas about religion, it is often difficult for us to understand Eastern religions. Our culture supports the notion of a single God with humanlike qualities that created everything in the world. Also, Western religions tend to have strict doctrines that explain exactly how this God should be worshipped.

CASE IN POINT 20

Assume that you are a student in the course Introduction to Communications. As a reserve reading, you are assigned the article "Communication Without Words" by Albert Mehrabian. The article appears in Appendix B. Your professor gives you the following paper assignment:

> All human communication experts agree that we use both verbal and nonverbal methods to convey messages to each other. However, there is considerable controversy as to the relative importance of verbal and nonverbal communication modes. Write a two-page review of Albert Mehrabian's article "Human Communication" that clarifies the relative importance of these two communication modes.

Decide what analysis questions would be appropriate to guide your reading for this assignment. Then read the article and write out the answers to the analysis questions as you find them.

Stop here, unless your instructor tells you otherwise. You will have a chance to come back to this assignment later.

What particular aspects of the topic does the author emphasize?

One way of looking at writing is as a series of choices an author makes about what to include and what to leave out. Rarely do authors put down all they know about their topics. Instead, they carefully select the parts of their total knowledge that are best suited to their goals and audiences. We saw this clearly in the example of the biologist who supported developing gene-splicing technology. He changed his emphasis each time he addressed a different audience. What authors emphasize depends on their goals and intended audiences. Emphasis can also reflect the author's assumptions. If you can figure out how authors limit their content, both what they choose to mention and what they leave out, you can often come to conclusions about their goals and audiences as well as determine their assumptions.

Below is a passage written about pregnancy. As you read it, think of what you know about the subject and consider what the author emphasizes or leaves out.

> Every pregnancy begins when an egg in the female's body is fertilized by a sperm cell from a male. In order to fertilize an egg, sperm must travel through the vagina, through the uterus to a point high up in the fallopian tube. Under normal circumstances, only around one out of a million sperm cells is able to make this journey successfully. If the path to the fallopian tube is effectively blocked, no sperm will be able to reach the egg.

Considering the author's emphasis, can you suggest a possible goal and audience for this passage? First notice all that is ignored about pregnancy. For example, the author ignores the sociological and psychological significance of child bearing, and instead stresses the process of becoming pregnant and how this process can be interrupted. Thus, we might guess that this passage is part of a longer piece with the goal of explaining how certain birth-control methods work. The author describes the process in detail and assumes very little knowledge of reproduction, so we can assume that the intended audience is the young teenage reader.

EXERCISE 25

Read each of the following passages *carefully*. Decide what aspects of the topic the author has emphasized. Also mention some areas that the author has ignored.

1. Hydrocarbons such as oil and coal are America's primary sources of energy. As we move into the twenty-first century, these precious resources will be in short supply on the world market. Thus, we will need to intensify our exploration for coal and oil deposits if we are to maintain our current rate of economic growth.

2. Computers are particularly well suited to educational tasks. A computer has infinite patience with even the slowest student and never tires of giving individual attention. It can present the learner with a combination of words, pictures, and sounds that is captivating to even the youngest child. A single computer can contain a huge variety of instructional modules that surpass the knowledge of even the best-educated teacher. Finally, computers treat all children equally and fairly.

3. Even the largest and most successful industries suffer occasional slumps in sales. Thus, in order to maintain their margin of profit, industries need to have a fluid work force that they can expand during growth periods and contract when the market for goods is slow. If the size of the work force can be easily and rapidly altered in response to market fluctuations, profits will be maximized.

4. In many cases, forest and brush fires create favorable growing conditions for plant life. For example, blueberries that prefer soil with high acidity thrive in burned-over areas. In fact, commercial blueberry growers often intentionally burn their land to increase the berry yield.

5. During the Industrial Revolution, increased mechanization created many jobs that did not require brute strength and thus could be performed equally well by members of both sexes. Consequently, large numbers of women were able to work at factories and mills. However, women were typically segregated from men in the work place and invariably received lower pay than men. In addition, these new working women often retained the traditional responsibilities of women in the home, such as child care, cooking, and housework.

What do the ideas, evidence, or explanations in the source suggest or prove?

Very often authors write to show that their main ideas are true or reasonable; they write with the objective of proving something. As a result, sources usually include both main ideas and information that is intended to *support* the main ideas. When you read for literal comprehension, your primary goal is to locate the main ideas. But when you want to extend your understanding of these main ideas, you try to see how they are supported by the author. Thus, *you analyze the connection between the main ideas and the information that supports them.*

Trying to figure out how the main ideas are supported will help you zero in on the content of a source. You can sometimes miss parts of the content if you fail to understand main ideas/support connections. To get a sense of this problem, read the following passage and try to pick out the main idea:

One way of assessing the significance of a particular crime is to determine its economic and social impact on the community. For example, heroin addiction is responsible for literally millions of dollars of robbery and shoplifting annually in each large city in the United States. The crimes of heroin addicts raise the cost of consumer goods and of police protection. In addition, heroin addicts are responsible for a large percentage of violent street crimes. Thus, heroin-related crime increases fear and restricts personal freedom in a community. The economic and social damage done by heroin indicates that it is a serious criminal problem.

The main idea is in the first sentence of the passage. This sentence states that we can judge the importance of crimes by the economic and social problems they cause. The rest of the passage supports this idea by giving a specific example. However, if the readers do not see this main idea/support pattern, they may very well miss the point of the passage. One of our students attempted to summarize the passage as follows:

> The main idea is about heroin addiction and how it tends to cause a lot of other problems in our society. It gives examples of how heroin addiction links with economic problems through stealing and how it also makes people afraid to walk the streets of large cities. Heroin hurts us both economically and socially.

As you can see, this student thought the passage was about heroin, not about a method for determining the importance of crimes. The student most likely centered in on heroin because most of the sentences in the passage concern heroin. However, when we look for the main idea/support pattern in the passage, we realize that heroin is only used as an example to illustrate the main idea. Thus, trying to understand how main ideas are supported can make the source more meaningful to you.

Analyzing the main idea/support connections as you read will sometimes *suggest* to you main ideas other than those the authors mention. In this way, you can use information in the source to come to your own conclusions. This process helps you develop the ability to think independently about the academic sources and can form the basis for some of the most creative review papers. However, you cannot fit just any conclusion of your own to the ideas from the source. Your own conclusions must logically follow from the evidence, just as the author's conclusions must.

How do the ideas in the source interact with those in other sources?

Too often students think that only research papers need to be based on more than one source. And even when students write research papers, they often merely list the main ideas of the sources without trying to connect them. *You should always think of how the material you are reading connects with other academic sources.* Academic books and articles don't exist in isolation. Every academic field of study is a network of interrelated ideas. Scholars rarely come up with entirely new ideas but rather build on, or respond to, the ideas of other scholars. As a result, there are numerous *interactions* between any given academic source and other publications in the same field. An important part of reviewing is uncovering and explaining these connections.

Suppose for the moment, that you are taking a psychology course and are studying models of human intelligence. You have learned that many psychologists describe the brain as a complex computer while others maintain that brains and computers operate in entirely different ways. Your professor asks you to write on this controversial issue. She has put on reserve for your class an article by a well-known psychologist in which you read the following passage:

> The deep difference between the thinking of men and machines has been intuitively recognized by those who fear that machines may somehow come to regulate our society. If machines really thought as men do, there would be no more reason to fear them than to fear men. But computer intelligence is indeed "inhuman": it does not grow, has no emotional basis, and is shallowly motivated. These defects do not matter in technical applications, where the criteria of successful problem solving are relatively simple. They become extremely important if the computer is used to make social decisions, for there our criteria of adequacy are as subtle and as multiply motivated as human thinking itself.
>
> Neisser, Ulric. The Imitation of Man by Machine. *Science* 18 Jan. 1963: 197.

As you read this passage, you think of something you read in a textbook for a computer-science course. You turn to your computer text and read the following:

> In the subset SP/4 you learned how to handle character strings; you could join strings together, select parts of strings, and determine their lengths. As well, you learned how to compare strings, either for the purpose of recognizing particular strings or for putting various strings in order. In this chapter we will show how these capabilities can be used to create the illusion that the computer does things that we normally associate with people, and we might say that it is "intelligent." We say it has an artificial intelligence, since it is of course *not* human, and thinking is what humans do. The field of artificial intelligence in computer science concerns itself with getting the computer to perform acts that we think of as the province of humans. Of course, when we see how it is done, we realize it is just a mechanical process. It has to be mechanical or a machine could not do it. But if you do not know how the "trick" is performed, it does seem as if the machine can "think."
>
> Hume, J. N. P., and R. C. Holt, *Structured Programming*. Reston, Va.: Reston Publishing Co., 1975. 129.

What is the relationship between the two passages? The passages are discussing the same issue from different perspectives. Neisser explains that computers are fundamentally different from the human mind; he looks at artificial intelligence from a psychologist's point of view. Hume and Holt discuss how computers can be programmed so they seem to behave in an intelligent manner; they look at artificial intelligence from a computer programmer's point of view.

Taken together, the two passages explain more about the basic nature of artificial intelligence than either passage does separately.

When you are working to expand your understanding of a source, you might want to connect it to other sources for any of the following reasons:

To provide additional background information
To provide additional detail
To find general trends
To compare
To contrast
To support
To contradict

How can the author's ideas be used or applied?

Ideas are often interesting in themselves, but your education serves you best when you can think of ways to apply the ideas you learn. In any learning situation, you should try to understand how the information you study can be *used*. Some of the best reviews center on the uses of academic ideas. When you show your audience how to use ideas, you will make the ideas both clearer and more valuable.

Read the following example in which a student both summarizes and analyzes information from academic sources.

Many studies show that first-born children generally receive more one-to-one attention from parents and are more strictly supervised than later-born children. Studies also show that first-born children are more dependent on adults and seek interaction with adults more often than their brothers and sisters. These findings have direct implications for elementary school teachers. Teachers will likely find that first-born children are more receptive to adult supervision than children with older siblings.

The first two sentences in this passage summarize the findings of a number of research studies. The last two sentences tell how these studies can be used to help understand the behavior of children in school. Thus, the student writer has tried to come to a conclusion about the research studies that will make them more meaningful and useful.

Take Notes on Your Answers to the Analysis Questions

Don't trust your memory. Make sure that you write down the answers to the analysis questions as you discover them during your close reading of the source. We have discussed in earlier chapters how difficult it is to remember the literal content of academic sources; it is usually even more difficult to remember complex analyses. Record your answers completely as soon as you have read enough to respond to one of the analysis questions. We will see in the next chapter that your paper will grow directly out of these notes.

POSTREADING/PREWRITING

After you have finished your close reading of the source you intend to review, you should take a few minutes to reflect on what you have read and what your analysis has shown you so far. Good analysis requires careful thought. One of the best times to organize your thoughts about the source is immediately after you have finished your careful reading, while the ideas and details from the source are still fresh in your mind. Pausing to think at this stage may also save you time since it can eliminate the need for rereading the source at the writing stage.

Reconsider Your Answers to the Analysis Questions

After you have finished your close reading, go back through all the answers you recorded to the analysis questions. At this point, you have more perspective on the source than you did while you were involved in the close reading and thus may find you need to either add to or delete from your original answers. Don't hesitate to reread parts of the source if you are having trouble answering a question. Immediately after you have finished reading, you will be able to find the relevant sections of the text much more quickly than you will later. *Don't stop working until all the questions are adequately answered.* The process will only get more difficult and time consuming if you decide to wait.

Determine the Limitations of the Source

Up to this point in the chapter, we have discussed analyzing sources as a way to *extend meaning.* However, we can also analyze to *determine the limitations of the source.* By limitations, we mean the constraints on how useful the information in a source is to us and on how confident we are in the truth of the information. Both of these concerns can be an important part of the reviewing process. Although the limitations of a source may sometimes occur to you as you read, you often need to finish your close reading before you have enough perspective to assess its limitations.

For an example of how a source may have limitations, let's look again at the various arguments supporting gene-splicing technology that we examined earlier (see p. 127).

The article written for the newspaper (source 1) may be accurate, reasonable, effective, and useful. A scientist might write such an article in a community where a plan to build an important gene-splicing facility was endangered by the voters' suspicions about science in general. In such a case, it would be important for the scientist to help remove the voters' unfair prejudice. Although the newspaper article might be perfectly legitimate given its objective and audience, it would still have certain limitations. For example, the article does not specifically discuss the safety factors involved in gene-splicing procedures and thus would not be a good source for a research paper that examines the potential risks of gene splicing.

When you analyze academic material, you will rarely find a source that is either totally useless or completely unreliable. Rather, the source may have a certain range of usefulness, or there may be certain factors that influence to what extent the information in the source is true. As you read the rest of our comments on limitations, remember that finding a source has limitations does *not* mean that it is a bad source or that it should not be used. In one way, all sources have limits to both their usefulness and validity. By understanding these limits, you can write more intelligently and effectively about the source.

The following questions will help you determine the limitations of a source. We have organized them around the topics covered by our original analysis questions.

Audience

1. Would the author's ideas be appropriate for only a special audience?
2. Does the intended audience have any special needs that the author is trying to meet?

Objectives

1. Does the author's objective suggest that he or she has any goals other than presenting the truth?
2. Are the author's goals intentionally hidden? If so, why?

Assumptions

1. Does the author assume things are true that may in fact be false?
2. Does the author assume that something that is true in a few cases will necessarily be true all of the time?

Emphasis

1. Does the author's emphasis indicate a definite bias?
2. Does the author leave out any important ideas or facts that seem crucial to the issue?

Conclusions

1. Does the evidence presented clearly lead to the author's conclusion?
2. Is there an alternative conclusion that fits with the evidence as well as the author's conclusion does?

Interaction With Other Sources

1. Do other sources contradict the source you are working with?
2. Is your source consistent with general thought in the field?

Usefulness

1. Can you think of any problems in applying the conclusions in the source to real-world situations?

CASE IN POINT 21

Imagine that you are taking a history course in which you are studying the fall of the Roman empire. The instructor has covered several different explanations that scholars think might account for the fall of Rome. As an exam question, the instructor has asked you to read the following excerpt and respond to it analytically.

> The fall of the Roman empire has been attributed to such diverse causes as the influence of Christianity and the use of poisonous lead in Roman water pipes. However, the fate of any civilization ultimately rests in the hands of its military establishment. Clearly, if the Roman legions had continued to be as successful as they were at the height of the empire, then the glory and power of Rome would never have faded. The main reason for the decline of the Roman military was its failure to evolve from an army that was based on a traditional infantry to a more mobile and effective fighting force that depended primarily upon cavalry.
>
> The Roman legions continued to rely upon the traditional combat methods that had brought them their initial success and thus did not change with the times. Genghis Khan later demonstrated the tremendous effectiveness of horse mounted troops when his cavalry terrified and decimated European armies. If the Roman legions had developed similar cavalry strategies, they would have been completely invincible in Europe. Such military strength would have preserved the Roman empire indefinitely.

As you read through this source, you are struck by its limitations and decide to concentrate on these in your short essay. Luckily, it is an open-book exam, and you happen to have your copy of *Academic Writing* with you. You open to Chapter 9 and ask the series of questions about the limitations of the source. Do this now and write out the answers.

You now pick out what seem to you the three most important limitations of the source. You decide to write a complete paragraph on each of these limitations. Do this now.

You decide to use the three paragraphs you have just written as the body of your essay. Add an introduction and a conclusion to complete the essay.

chapter 10

Writing the Review

At the planning stage of writing a review, you think about the source analytically and make notes on your thoughts. This careful thought must be the basis for any review. However, even the most careful analytic thought does not produce a paper in itself. In fact, as we have already pointed out, many students experience the frustration of knowing they have "good ideas" on an academic subject while being unable to communicate these ideas to someone else. During the writing stage, you must develop the structure that will tie together your analytic thoughts.

WRITING THE FIRST DRAFT

The following steps will help you develop your analysis into the first draft of a review:

Compare Your Analysis-Question Answers to the Assignment Topic

Answering the analysis questions is basically a way of gathering information for your review. Usually not all the information you collect will fit into your paper. You need to sift through your prereading and close-reading notes to get a sense of what information is relevant to the topic and what information will not contribute to your paper.

Remember that professors' ideas of how to write reviews vary widely. Each of your professors may have different expectations of how you should analyze sources. Thus, you must search through your analysis notes for the information that best matches your specific topic. As an example of how you might edit your analysis notes, imagine that your psychology professor has assigned the following paper topic:

> Over the past century, millions of people have been diagnosed as "schizophrenic" by psychologists and doctors. Although the diagnosis is common, there is considerable controversy over what causes the behavior pattern characteristic of schizophrenics. Each of our three reserve readings gives a different view of what causes schizophrenia. Choose one of these sources and write a two page *discussion* of its explanation of the causes of schizophrenia.

Is a discussion a summary, a reaction, or a review? You question the professor, as we suggested earlier, to further define the assignment. In response to your questions, your professor tells you to concentrate on *analyzing* in your paper as opposed to summarizing or reacting. The professor further says that it is up to you to pick the analysis strategies that you will use.

You carefully read all the sources, using the analysis questions as a guide. In your notes, you write a brief summary of each source as described below:

Source: Laing, R. D. *The Politics of Experience*. New York: Ballantine Books, 1967. 100–130.

Content: Laing believes that schizophrenia is a natural mechanism that people use to cope with an unlivable social environment. He feels that schizophrenia is not an illness but rather a legitimate response to extreme conditions.

Source: Gottlieb, Bill. "Healing Sick Minds With Food." *Prevention*. 31.10 (1979). 99–103.

Content: Gottlieb believes schizophrenia is actually a number of separate diseases each of which results from a biochemical deficiency and can be cured with proper nutrition.

Source: Krech, David, et al. *Elements of Psychology*. 4th ed. New York: Alfred A. Knopf, 1982. 617–618.

Content: The authors explain that research supports the conclusion that genetic and environmental factors interact to produce schizophrenia. According to this view, one must not only have a genetic predisposition but also face conflict in his or her life for the disease to develop.

You read through each of the sources carefully and find R. D. Laing's ideas particularly interesting. Thus, you decide to discuss the Laing source for your paper. You then look over your answers to the general analysis questions on the Laing source. For each question, you decide whether or not the answer is relevant to your topic.

What is Laing's intended audience?

Laing writes for the general educated public. Readers can follow his argument without any special background in psychology. The issues he addresses pertain to the general public.

Evaluation: This answer is not relevant to the assigned topic. Identifying Laing's readers as the general educated public says nothing about his view of schizophrenia.

What is Laing's objective?

Laing wants to persuade us to reject the commonly accepted view of schizophrenia as an inherited disease and accept his theory that schizophrenia is a legitimate way to respond to an impossible social environment.

Evaluation: This answer is relevant to the assigned topic. It highlights the fact that Laing sees his ideas as a significant departure from traditional theories.

What assumptions does Laing make?

Laing assumes that the environmental conflicts that lead to schizophrenia result from problems with our society as a whole. He assumes that our social organization is to blame for creating the situations that lead to schizophrenia.

Evaluation: This answer is not directly relevant to the topic. Although Laing does make certain assumptions that are essentially political, his discussion of the causes of schizophrenia does not depend on these assumptions. Schizophrenia could still be a response to difficult social conditions even if these conditions are not a direct result of our political/social system.

What particular aspects of the topic does Laing emphasize?

Laing emphasizes the real-life situations that lead to schizophrenia. He discusses the personal experiences of the patients, a factor that he believes traditional psychology has ignored.

Evaluation: This answer is definitely relevant to the topic. Laing's emphasis on the real-life experience of the schizophrenic is what he feels distinguishes his approach from that of many other psychologists.

What do the ideas, evidence, or explanations in Laing's source demonstrate or support?

Laing supports his view that schizophrenia is caused by the social environment by referring to research he conducted along with A. Esterson. All the schizophrenics Laing and Esterson studied were seemingly forced into their mental conditions by dilemmas in their lives. Laing also cites the work of Gregory Bateson, who originated the idea that schizophrenia is the result of a person's being caught in a mental "double-bind" where any course of action will lead to unacceptable consequences.

Evaluation: This answer is relevant to the topic. The strength of Laing's argument can be measured by the validity of the support he provides for it.

How do the ideas in Laing's source interact with those in other sources?

Laing's theory sharply conflicts with Gottlieb's. If correcting chemical imbalances can cure schizophrenia as Gottlieb claims, then it would be difficult to accept Laing's view of schizophrenia as a result of social conflicts.

Krech et al. conclude that research indicates schizophrenia results when a person with a genetic predisposition for the disorder faces serious conflict in his or her social environment. Laing's theory is to some extent compatible with this view. Laing does not argue that everyone who is put into a double-bind situation will develop schizophrenia. Thus, it is possible that the double-bind Laing describes will lead to schizophrenia only when the genetic factor mentioned in Krech et al. is present.

Evaluation: This answer is definitely relevant to the topic. Laing's theory becomes clearer when compared and contrasted with other sources. The comparison to Krech et al. shows how Laing's views stack up with the standard theory about schizophrenia.

How can Laing's ideas be used or applied?

Laing's theory of the causes of schizophrenia has definite implications for the treatment of the disorder. If schizophrenia is not a disease but rather a reasonable response to intolerable conditions, then the medical approach to therapy, using drugs and hospital confinement, makes little sense. In fact, Laing believes that treating a schizophrenic as someone who is sick will only deepen the condition. Laing's ideas suggest that the therapist try to understand what the schizophrenic is experiencing, approach it as a legitimate response to the world, and help the patient work through the experience.

Evaluation: This answer is relevant to the topic. It is important to understand the consequences of Laing's theory for actual practice if we are to assess its value.

Look for Organizational Patterns

After you have reviewed your answers to the analysis questions and decided which answers are relevant, you begin to look for any organizational patterns that can readily fit with the material. You cannot merely take the questions in order and discuss your answers to each of them. You must establish a pattern for your paper so that it seems like a coherent whole, not like a scattered list of answers to questions.

Two useful questions to ask are, How do the parts of your analysis interrelate? and How should you order your analytic thoughts? In answering the first, see if any of the answers to analysis questions can be linked together. Write out the answers that seem relevant to your topic on one sheet of paper and think about how the ideas interconnect.

Objectives

Laing wants to persuade us to reject the commonly accepted view of schizophrenia as an inherited disease and accept his theory that schizophrenia is a legitimate way to respond to an impossible social environment.

Emphasis

Laing emphasizes the real-life situations that lead to schizophrenia. He discusses the personal experiences of the patients, a factor that he believes traditional psychology has ignored.

Support

Laing supports his view that schizophrenia is caused by the social environment by referring to research he conducted along with A. Esterson. The schizophrenics Laing and Esterson studied were seemingly forced into their mental conditions by dilemmas in their lives. Laing also cites the work of Gregory Bateson, who originated the idea that schizophrenia is the result of a person's being caught in a mental "double-bind" where any course of action will lead to unacceptable consequences.

Interaction With Other Sources

Laing's theory sharply conflicts with Gottlieb's. If correcting chemical imbalances can cure schizophrenia as Gottlieb claims, then it would be difficult to accept Laing's view of schizophrenia as a result of social conflicts.

Krech et al. conclude that research indicates schizophrenia results when a person with a genetic predisposition for the disorder faces serious conflict in his or her social environment. Laing's theory is to some extent compatible with this view. Laing does not argue that everyone who is put into a double-bind situation will develop schizophrenia. Thus, it is possible that the double-bind Laing describes will lead to schizophrenia only when the genetic factor mentioned in Krech et al. is present.

Uses

Laing's theory of the causes of schizophrenia has definite implications for the treatment of schizophrenia. If schizophrenia is not a disease but rather a reasonable response to intolerable conditions, then the medical approach to therapy, using drugs and hospital confinement, makes little sense. In fact, Laing believes that treating a schizophrenic as someone who is sick will only deepen the condition. Laing's ideas suggest that the therapist try to understand what the schizophrenic is experiencing, approach it as a legitimate response to the world, and help the patient work through the experience.

The types of connections that exist between the answers to analysis questions will, of course, vary greatly depending on the source and type of analysis used. When you work on your schizophrenia assignment, you notice that the three obvious connections betweeen the different parts of the analysis involve *justification, conflict,* and *compatibility.* These connections, which are explained below, will help cement together the various parts of your analysis as you write.

Justification: Laing's evidence clearly provides support for his emphasis.

Conflict: Gottlieb's explanation of a biochemical basis for schizophrenia conflicts with both Laing's evidence and his emphasis on the social origins of schizophrenia.

Compatibility: Laing's emphasis on the social origins of schizophrenia can be at least partially reconciled with the commonly accepted theory of the causes of schizophrenia outlined by Krech et al.

We now come to the second of the two questions suggested on page 148, How should you order your analytic thoughts? Although your instructor has said that you are not to devote a lot of your paper to summarizing, you do need to start with a very brief statement of Laing's theory. The information on Laing's emphasis logically comes next since it helps further clarify his theory by explaining his general orientation to the topic. After Laing's theory is clearly explained, it makes sense to consider what evidence he offers to show that his theory is correct; thus, you bring in how Laing supports his theory. Next, you work to put the source in perspective by adding your analysis of Laing's overall objectives. Along with this you include the information from Krech et al. and the discussion of how Laing's ideas can fit within the standard theory of the causes of schizophrenia. You then turn to Gottlieb's theory that contradicts Laing's. Finally, you discuss the implications of Laing's source for actually helping schizophrenics and tie this in with his overall objective. You reorganize your notes according to this pattern and begin to rough out the structure for the paper. After you include the brief summary and reorganize your notes, your rough structure looks like this:

> Laing believes that schizophrenia is a natural mechanism that people use to cope with an unlivable social environment. He feels that schizophrenia is not an illness but rather a legitimate response to extreme conditions.
>
> Laing emphasizes the real-life situations that lead to schizophrenia. He discusses the personal experiences of the patients, a factor that he believes traditional psychology has ignored.
>
> *Laing justifies his emphasis.*
>
> Laing supports his view that schizophrenia is caused by the social environment by referring to research he conducted along with A. Esterson. All schizophrenics Laing and Esterson studied were seemingly forced into their mental conditions by dilemmas in their lives. Laing also cites the work of Gregory Bateson, who originated the idea that schizophrenia is the result of a person's being caught in a mental "double-bind" where any course of action will lead to unacceptable consequences.
>
> Laing wants to persuade us to reject the commonly accepted view of schizophrenia as an inherited disease and accept his theory that schizophrenia is a legitimate way to respond to an impossible social environment.
>
> *Laing's view is compatible with current theory in the field.*
>
> Krech et al. conclude that research indicates schizophrenia results when a person with a genetic predisposition for the disorder faces serious conflict in his or her social environment. Laing's theory is to some extent compatible with this view. Laing does not argue that everyone who is put into a double-bind situation will develop schizophrenia. Thus, it is possible that the double-bind Laing describes will lead to schizophrenia only when the genetic factor mentioned in Krech et al. is present.
>
> *Laing's theory does conflict with at least one current theory in the field.*
>
> Laing's theory sharply conflicts with Gottlieb's. If correcting chemical imbalances can cure schizophrenia, as Gottlieb claims, then it would be difficult to accept Laing's view of schizophrenia as a result of social conflicts.
>
> Laing's theory of the causes of schizophrenia has definite implications for its treatment. If schizophrenia is not a disease but rather a reasonable response to intolerable conditions, then the medical approach to therapy, using drugs and hospital confinement, makes little sense. In fact, Laing believes that treating a schizophrenic as someone who is sick will only deepen the condition. Laing's ideas suggest that the therapist should try

to understand what the schizophrenic is experiencing, approach it as a legitimate response to the world, and help the patient work through the experience.

CASE IN POINT 22

This case is a continuation of Case 20. Look back at your answers to the analysis questions on the Mehrabian article. Then compare your answers to the assignment. Decide which answers will fit into your paper. We will repeat the assignment:

> All human communication experts agree that we use both verbal and nonverbal methods to convey messages to each other. However, there is considerable controversy as to the relative importance of verbal and nonverbal communication modes. Write a two-page review of Albert Mehrabian's article "Human Communication" that clarifies the relative importance of these two communication modes.

After you have decided which analysis questions are relevant to the assignment, look for an organizational pattern that will tie all the information together. Reorganize your notes using this pattern to form a rough structure for your paper.

Stop here, unless your instructor tells you otherwise. You will have a chance to come back to this assignment later.

Find a Thesis That Ties Your Thoughts Together

Finding a thesis statement that expresses the main idea for an entire paper requires careful thought, especially when you are writing a review. After you have identified the connections between the various parts of your review and arranged the ideas in a logical order, you need to tie the entire paper together. Your thesis must let your audience know in general what you found when you analyzed the source. You need to pick out the common threads, the unifying ideas that run throughout your analytic thought. The following three steps can help you write a thesis statement based on your analysis notes.

List The Main Conclusions Of Your Analysis.   For the schizophrenia paper, you might summarize your analysis like this:

1. Laing emphasizes the real-life situations that lead to schizophrenia.
2. Laing's emphasis is supported by a body of research.
3. The explanation of the causes of schizophrenia that is supported by current research is compatible with Laing's view.

4. Gottlieb's theory contradicts Laing's.
5. Laing's theory implies a treatment for schizophrenia that is at odds with common practice.

As you look over these conclusions, you realize that conclusions 1, 3, and 5 are the most important since they imply more general conclusions about Laing's ideas than conclusions 2 or 4 do. Thus, you decide to make these more important conclusions the focus of your thesis.

Tie Together the Main Points of Your Analysis in One or Two Sentences.   The thesis of a paper is a *compact* statement of its main idea. Thus, when possible the thesis of a short essay should be a single sentence. However, when you are writing reviews, you often come up with a number of different analytic thoughts that cannot easily fit together in one sentence. Your guiding principle in writing a thesis should be to compress your ideas as much as possible without leaving out any crucial information.

As you work on the thesis for your schizophrenia paper, you come up with the following two sentences:

Laing's emphasis on the social environments that produce schizophrenics, although revolutionary at the time he wrote, is now accepted more readily by psychologists and is compatible with standard theory in the field. However, Laing's ideas do imply a treatment for schizophrenia that is at odds with common practice.

Write an Introduction Based on the Thesis.   In a short essay, the thesis often comes at the end of the first paragraph, as part of the *introduction*. The sentences before the thesis introduce the general topic while the thesis gives the main ideas that will be developed in the paper. Whenever an essay is written about an academic source, the source should be clearly identified in the introduction. When properly written, the introduction lets the reader know exactly what the essay will be about. One way of beginning an introduction is with a paraphrase of all or part of the original assignment. This can help assure that the paper will speak to the assigned topic. For your schizophrenia paper, you paraphrase the first two sentences of the assignment as follows:

Although schizophrenia is a relatively common mental disorder, experts disagree on what causes it.

You decide that the next part of your introduction will be the brief summary of Laing's theory. Since you are asked to concentrate on analyzing and not summarizing, the short summary can be used to introduce the results of your analysis. Combining the paraphrase of the assignment, the brief summary, and the thesis, you come up with the following introduction:

Although schizophrenia is a relatively common mental disorder, experts disagree on what causes it. In his book <u>The</u> <u>Politics</u> <u>of</u> <u>Experience</u>, R. D. Laing (1968) argues that schizophrenia is not an illness but rather a natural mechanism that people use to cope with unlivable social circumstances. Laing's emphasis on the social environments that produce schizophrenics, although revolutionary at the time he wrote, is now accepted more readily by psychologists and is compatible with standard theory in the field. However, Laing's ideas do imply a treatment for schizophrenia that is at odds with common practice.

CASE IN POINT 23

This case is a continuation of cases 20 and 22. Look over the rough essay structure that you created in Case 22. Find a thesis that ties together the thoughts in your rough structure. Then write an introductory paragraph for the essay based on your thesis.

Stop here, unless your instructor tells you otherwise. You will have a chance to come back to this assignment later.

Organize Paragraphs Around the Results of Your Analysis

When you look for organizational patterns in your notes, you are actually figuring out the structure for your paper. This process gives you the different ideas that can be developed in separate paragraphs, the order in which these paragraphs will appear in your paper, and the transitions that will link these paragraphs together. By fleshing out this basic structure, you develop a series of interconnected paragraphs that form the body of the first draft of your essay.

Look back at the set of reorganized notes for the Laing paper. These notes are chunks of information that are linked together by the italicized ideas. You now read through these notes and decide where two or more chunks should be combined into a single paragraph and where new paragraphs should begin. You then write out the first draft of your paper, fleshing out the skeleton as you go. Following is the first draft of the paper. Since the paper topic concerns psychology, APA documentation style is used. We will explain the APA style in Chapter 12.

Although schizophrenia is a relatively common mental disorder, experts disagree on what causes it. In his book <u>The</u> <u>Politics</u> <u>of</u> <u>Experience</u>, R. D. Laing (1968) argues that schizophrenia is not an illness but rather a natural mechanism that people use to cope with unlivable social circumstances. Laing's emphasis on the social environments that produce schizophrenics, although revolutionary at the time he wrote, is now accepted more readily by psychologists and is compatible with standard theory in the field. However, Laing's ideas do imply a treatment for schizophrenia that is at odds with common practice.

Laing emphasizes the real-life situations that lead to schizophrenia. He discusses the personal experience of the patient, a factor that he believes traditional psychology has ignored. By examining schizophrenics' social backgrounds, particularly their interactions with their families, Laing attempts to show how they are literally forced to withdraw from their environments into their own inner worlds.

In addition to explaining the logic behind his understanding of schizophrenia, *Laing provides evidence for his theory* by referring to research he conducted along with A. Esterson. All the schizophrenics Laing and Esterson studied were seemingly forced into their mental conditions by dilemmas in their lives. Laing also cites the work of Gregory Bateson who originated the idea that schizophrenia is the result of a person being caught in a "double-bind" where any course of action will lead to unacceptable consequences.

Writing in the late 1960s, Laing intended to persuade his audience to reject the commonly accepted view of schizophrenia as an inherited mental disease. *However,* in recent years Laing's theory has received attention from even the more traditional psychologists. In a recently revised introductory psychology textbook, Krech, Crutchfield, Livson, Wilson, and Parducci (1982) cite Laing's work as an example of the growing body of literature devoted to the families of schizophrenics. Looking at the full spectrum of research on schizophrenia, Krech et al. state that strong evidence indicates that schizophrenia results when a person with a genetic predisposition for the disorder faces serious conflict in the social environment. Although the conclusions of Krech et al. are not identical with those of Laing, the two views are to some extent compatible. Laing does not argue that everyone who is put into a double-bind situation will develop schizophrenia. Thus, it is possible that the double-bind Laing describes will lead to schizophrenia only when the genetic factor mentioned by Krech et al. is present.

However, at least one current theory of the causes of schizophrenia is completely incompatible with Laing. Gottlieb (1979) suggests that schizophrenia is a cluster of diseases each of which is caused by a specific nutritional deficiency. If correcting chemical imbalances can cure schizophrenia, as Gottlieb claims, then it would be difficult to accept Laing's view of schizophrenia as a result of social conflicts.

Laing's emphasis on the social origins of schizophrenia does have revolutionary implications for the treatment of the disorder. If schizophrenia is not a disease but rather a reasonable response to intolerable conditions, then the medical approach to therapy, using drugs and hospital confinement, makes little sense. In fact, Laing believes that treating a schizophrenic as someone who is sick will only deepen the condition. Laing's ideas suggest that the therapist should try to understand what the schizophrenic is experiencing, approach it as a legitimate response to the world, and help the patient work through the experience. Indeed, adopting Laing's approach to therapy would change the entire nature of psychiatric treatment.

Laing's theory of what causes schizophrenia has seemingly had an impact on the development of thought in the field. The shift in emphasis that Laing called for in the late 1960s has to some extent taken place. The social environment of the schizophrenic is now given more serious attention. However, new approaches, such as the treatment of schizophrenia as a nutritional deficiency, raise serious questions as to the adequacy of Laing's approach. Laing's shift in emphasis does have profound implications for the treatment of schizophrenics that are in sharp contrast with current practices.

References

Gottlieb, B. (1979). Healing sick minds with food. <u>Prevention</u>, *31*(10), 99–103.

Krech, D., Crutchfield, R., Livson, N., Wilson, W., & Parducci, A. (1982). <u>Elements of psychology</u> (4th ed.). New York: Alfred A. Knopf.

Laing, R. D. (1967). <u>The politics of experience</u>. New York: Ballantine Books.

In addition to creating paragraphs from the material in your notes, you also added a concluding paragraph that summarized your main ideas and brought your paper to a close. In a review where the logical connections between the parts of the paper may be complex, it is especially important to end with a summary of your main points.

You will notice we have not suggested one or several organizational patterns that can be used for any given review. Rather, we have given you a process you can work through to discover the pattern that will work best for the particular assignment you are faced with. Professors' writing assignments vary so much that no standard pattern can be applied to any given assignment. You can discover the best pattern by using the strategies we have described to fit the pieces of your analysis together logically.

CASE IN POINT 24

This case is a continuation of cases 20, 22 and 23. Look over the rough essay structure you wrote for Case 22 and the introductory paragraph you wrote for Case 23. Develop the rough structure into a series of interconnected paragraphs and complete the first draft of your essay.

CASE IN POINT 25

Assume that you are given the assignment at the beginning of this chapter concerning the causes of schizophrenia. Instead of writing on the Laing source as we did in the chapter, you decide to write on the Gottlieb source, which suggests schizophrenia results from nutritional deficiencies. Go to your college or public library, locate and read the Gottlieb source, and write a review of it similar to the one we provided on the Laing source. The complete reference for the Gottlieb source is given below:

> Gottlieb, Bill. "Healing Sick Minds With Food." *Prevention* 31.10 (1979):99–103.

CASE IN POINT 26

As you read through the sample assignment on schizophrenia in this chapter, you may have recalled a section of the article used in cases 20, 22, 23, and 24. Mehrabian's article, "Communication Without Words," in Appendix B, mentions schizophrenia as an example of one application of theories on nonverbal communication. Reread the Mehrabian article. Once again, assume that you have been given the assignment on page 145 concerning the origins of schizophrenia. Write an essay in which you review Mehrabian's article concentrating on how his ideas interact with suggestions of Laing, Gottlieb, or Krech as to the causes of schizophrenia.

chapter 11

Revising the Review

Reviews pose the most significant revision problems we have discussed thus far. As a writer/reviser of a review, you have several different roles to keep in mind. When you revise a review, you not only evaluate your treatment of ideas from sources. You also judge the value of your independent thought as well. Remember that a review can contain reaction and summary along with analysis. You may need to keep separate your analysis, your reaction, and your summary, each of which you produce while acting in a different role as a writer. With the increased complexity of your role as a writer comes an increased complexity in the thoughts expressed in your paper and thus more difficulty in keeping the paper organized and coherent. In short, reviews demand much of you as a writer and as an editor of your own writing.

REVISING AS YOU WRITE

Revising is built into the process we described in the two previous chapters for developing a review from the answers to analysis questions. As you use this process, you are revising and reorganizing your notes both before and as you write and thus are modifying your ideas about the content and structure of your paper. However, as you write a draft of the paper, you should be aware of the following reviewing pitfalls.

1. Failing to analyze
2. Criticizing instead of reviewing
3. Plunging into analysis without an adequate summary
4. Ignoring specific analysis strategies that the assignment calls for
5. Leaving out sections of multipart questions
6. Confusing ideas from different sources
7. Losing the focus
8. Losing coherence
9. Developing an illogical or far-fetched analysis
10. Repeating the professor's analysis
11. Confusing analysis with summary or reaction

Failing to Analyze

Often students merely summarize sources when the assignment specifically calls for analysis. When you are asked to analyze, the professor wants to see how well you can go beyond the literal content of the source. If you only summarize, you are not writing an adequate review. Also, analysis assignments help you develop your ability to think about the information you are studying. You will miss out on this if you stick to summaries of the literal contents of sources.

Criticizing Instead of Reviewing

The main purpose of reviewing is to extend your understanding of an academic source. In some cases, the process of reviewing may involve assessing the *limitations* of a source. Some people get the impression that the best reviews are those centering on weaknesses, those that criticize. However, the value of your review does not depend on how many weaknesses you can find in the source. For the most part, your professors will ask you to review reputable sources that are taken seriously by experts in the field of study. Although you may find limitations in these sources, you probably will miss a lot if you center only on these limitations. Also, you have an obligation to be fair to sources that you review. If you decide at the outset that you will concentrate on the limitations of a source, you are not being fair to the author or to the ideas expressed in the source.

Plunging into Analysis without an Adequate Summary

Since the point of reviewing is to extend the meaning of a source beyond its literal content, it makes little sense to use the review process until the literal content is clear. Summarizing comes first, analysis second, both as you read and as you write. Your readers can only appreciate your analysis of a source after they understand what the source is about.

The amount of summarizing you need to do when you write a review depends upon your intended audience. You may receive assignments that require relatively little summarizing. For example, the sample assignment on schizophrenia that we looked at in Chapter 10 asked you to concentrate on analysis. Accordingly, the sample paper on this assignment contains only a few sentences of summary that briefly give the author's main idea. By asking you to limit your summary, the professor, in effect, makes you write for an audience that is already familiar with the ideas in the source. However, other reviews may require extensive summarizing. When you write a research (library) paper, quite often you will use sources that your professor has not read. In this case, summarizing becomes very important.

Ignoring Specific Analysis Strategies That the Assignment Calls For

Remember that in each field of study there are analysis questions that are typically used by the experts. You may be expected to use, as you write, particular analysis strategies you have learned in the course. Sometimes the assignment may specify the strategies you are to use. Even when you are using the analysis questions from Chapter 10, you may find that you need to modify them to fit the particular subject area you are working with. Always check with your professor if you are unsure about what analysis strategies are appropriate.

Leaving Out Sections of Multipart Questions

Quite often, professors organize review assignments around several specific questions that require analysis. In these cases, you must cover each part of the assignment adequately in your review. Consider the following sample assignment for a literature course:

> Certain common elements run throughout the tragic drama written in Western culture. Some of these common elements are listed below.
>
> 1. The inevitability of tragedy
> 2. Flaws in character that create the potential for tragedy
> 3. Decisions based on partial information that lead to tragedy
>
> Pick one of the three tragedies we have read this semester (*Oedipus Rex, Hamlet, Death of a Salesman*). Write an essay in which you show how these three elements function in the play you have chosen.

Notice that this assignment asks you to analyze the source in three different ways. You must make sure that your essay develops each of these analyses fully. It is best to organize the paper so it is obvious that you are looking at the play in three distinct ways. You could do this by referring to all three methods of analysis in both the introduction and the conclusion and clearly indicating in the body of the paper when you stop discussing one method of analysis and begin discussing another.

Confusing Ideas from Different Sources

When you write reviews, you sometimes rely on more than one source. In these cases, you must make sure that your audience will be able to tell at all points in your paper what the source is for the ideas you are discussing. Confusing the source of the ideas can make your paper difficult to follow and is considered irresponsible use of references. In order to avoid this problem, make sure you do the following: (1) Identify clearly both the author and the title the first time you refer to a source; (2) mention either the author or the title each time you shift your discussion from one source to another; (3) make sure you provide complete bibliographic information for all sources you use, in either footnotes or a reference list.

Losing the Focus

Asking the analysis questions we covered earlier along with any your professor suggests will very likely give you a great number of ideas that will help extend the meaning of a source. Remember that not all the analysis questions are appropriate for any given assignment. However, once you have come up with a good answer to a specific analysis question, you may feel that you want to include it in your review even if it is not entirely appropriate.

Once you have invested time, effort, and thought in coming up with a good response to an analysis question, it may be hard for you to leave this analysis out of your paper. You must include only information that is directly relevant to your topic even though it may be tempting to put in your other insights. Including information that is not directly related to the topic may destroy the focus of your paper and leave your reader wondering what you are writing about.

Losing Coherence

One of the main purposes of reorganizing your analysis notes, as we suggested previously, is to keep your paper a coherent whole rather than a list of separate points. The *transitions*—the links between paragraphs in the paper—come in part from the connection that you make between the various answers to analysis questions. Make sure that you preserve these transitions as you write drafts of your paper.

Using Illogical or Far-Fetched Analysis Techniques

Good analysis is based on logical, well-supported thought. Illogical or unsupported thinking leads to a poor review no matter how well the ideas are expressed in the paper. Consider the following analysis of the Laing source on schizophrenia that we referred to in Chapter 10:

Laing says that schizophrenia results from pressures in the environment. If this is true, then why don't soldiers all become schizophrenic in the middle of combat? Why isn't schizophrenia more common among poor, starving people than among the rich? Lots of people face a lot of pressure in their lives without going crazy.

This analysis is based on a misunderstanding of Laing's argument and is also illogical. The physical hardships this student describes are not the same as the double-bind situations that Laing says lead to schizophrenia.

The student who wrote the analysis given above might defend his or her work by claiming, "Well, that's the way I see it." Unfortunately, this defense is never adequate. There is a difference between careful, sound analysis and unreasoned comments. Remember that your most basic purpose in writing is to communicate something to an audience. Thus, the logic of your argument must make sense to your readers as well as to you.

Repeating the Professor's Analysis

When you are asked to write a review, the professor wants to see how well you can develop your own thoughts on academic sources, not how well you can paraphrase or summarize the interpretations of sources you have heard in class. When you write a review, don't ask yourself, "What does the professor want me to say?" Rather, analyze the source on your own and then think of how you can communicate your thoughts to the professor. If you merely parrot back the ideas from class lectures, you are unlikely to do well on the paper and will miss out on an important learning experience.

Although you should always analyze on your own, when you are reviewing sources, this does not mean that your conclusions must be different from those of the professor. If you strain too hard for originality, you may end up with an illogical analysis, as we described above. It is important that you go through the process of analysis independently, not that you arrive at a conclusion no one has ever thought of before.

Confusing Analysis with Summary or Reaction

Some assignments may require that you analyze along with summarizing and/or reacting. For example, the sample assignment on Gandhi that we have used in the introduction to this book asks you to use all three of these approaches. In such cases, you must make sure that your audience will be able to tell when you are merely summarizing the source, when you are reacting, and when you are analyzing. The most common confusion is between summarizing and analyzing. When you confuse these two, your reader cannot tell which ideas were actually stated in the source and which ideas are your own extension of the source. This distinction is very important.

CASE IN POINT 27

Use the list of reviewing pitfalls to check your use of analysis strategies in the first draft you wrote for Case 24. Make any neceessary revisions.

REVISING AFTER THE FIRST DRAFT IS COMPLETE

Compare Your Thesis to the Assignment

Since your thesis is a record of the main idea you are trying to develop, it should *directly* answer the question in the assignment. Your reader will look for a statement of your main idea in the introduction to your paper and will expect it to match the assignment. If you find at the revising stage that your thesis is not appropriate for your assignment, you must check to see if the thesis is consistent with the rest of your paper. It is possible that the thesis does not reflect the idea that you actually develop in the body of the essay. In this case, you merely need to alter the thesis to fit your discussion better and then compare it to the assignment. If, however, the thesis does accurately reflect the ideas in the rest of your paper, you need to do some serious and perhaps extensive revising. Read through your paper slowly and cross out or alter any information that is not directly relevant to the assignment. As you did when you wrote the first draft, try to list the main ideas from the material that remains. Then write a new thesis that ties this remaining information together. Now compare this new thesis to the assignment. You may have to go back to academic sources for new information if much of your original information has to be discarded.

Compare Your Conclusion to the Assignment and to Your Thesis

Sometimes students drift unconsciously away from the assignment as they write. The analysis process often yields ideas that are not directly relevant to the topic. Exploring these extraneous ideas can take you away from your original assignment. However, the drift to irrelevant material can be so gradual that you do not notice it as you write. Organizing your information as we described in Chapter 10 will help you stay on the topic. However, a good check is to compare your conclusion with both your thesis and your assignment. Your thesis and your conclusion *must* be consistent. Although you may change your mind about an issue many times as you analyze sources, your final draft must have a consistent view from beginning to end. Also, like your thesis, your conclusion must be directly relevant to the assignment.

If you find that your conclusion does not fit with either the thesis or the assignment, trace back through your paper to locate the point where you depart from your objective. You may have to rewrite the entire paper from this point on. Write down the main idea of each paragraph whose relevance is questionable and compare the main idea directly to the thesis and assignment. Take out any paragraphs that are not directly relevant.

Check the Relationships between Paragraphs

In Chapter 10 we stressed that you must organize the ideas in your paper to form a coherent whole. Check for this at the revising stage by reading through the entire paper, checking to see that: (1) the evidence, discussion, examples, and so on, in each paragraph tie in with your thesis; and, (2) the transitions between paragraphs are smooth and logical.

Your thesis serves as the master plan for the entire paper, and thus all paragraphs must tie in with the thesis. In addition, the relationships between body paragraphs are important. Check to see that the transitions that guide the reader from paragraph to paragraph are smooth and make sense. If the transitions do not seem right, ask the following questions:

1. Is there a better way to order the paragraphs?
2. Do I need to insert any transitional sentences or short transitional paragraphs to show my reader how the thoughts in adjacent paragraphs are related?

Clarify the Dividing Lines between Summary, Reaction, and Analysis, and Check for the Relative Proportions of Each

An important part of the planning stage is deciding whether the assignment calls for summary, reaction, or analysis. Some assignments call for more than one of these approaches. When you work with assignments that ask you to summarize, react, and analyze, you must make sure that your reader can distinguish among these activities. For example, your summary and analysis must be distinct; your reader must not confuse the literal content of the source with your attempts to extend the meaning. Also, you must make sure that you devote an appropriate proportion of your paper to each approach you take. When your assignment asks primarily for analysis, you might include a short introductory summary, but you cannot let this summary dominate the paper. In this instance, the bulk of your writing must be analysis.

Check Paraphrases and Summaries for Accuracy

Follow carefully the procedures for editing paraphrases and summaries. Be particularly careful that you include accurate documentation in every place you have used information from a reading source. Make sure that the beginning and end of each paraphrase and summary are clearly indicated.

CHECKLIST FOR REVISION

A. Does your paper have clear organizational divisions?
1. Introduction?
2. Body?
3. Conclusion?
B. Does your paper have a thesis that clearly states the main finding(s) of your analysis?
C. Does the organization of your review reflect the results of your analysis?
D. Does your review include background information for your audience?
1. Proper documentation of all sources used?
2. Summaries of the literal content of all sources you analyze?
E. Does each of your paragraphs have the necessary elements?
1. Topic sentences?
2. Supporting information?
3. Transitions?
F. Is your analysis objective?
G. Does your analysis speak directly to the assignment?
H. Have you avoided the review pitfalls of
1. Failing to analyze?
2. Criticizing instead of reviewing?
3. Plunging into analysis without an adequate summary?
4. Ignoring specific analysis strategies that the assignment calls for?
5. Leaving out sections of multipart questions?
6. Confusing ideas from different sources?
7. Losing the focus?
8. Losing coherence?
9. Developing an illogical or far-fetched analysis?
10. Repeating the professor's analysis?
11. Confusing analysis with summary or reaction?
I. Editing—Are there any problems with grammar, usage, or mechanics?

CASE IN POINT 28

Use the Checklist for Revision to finish editing the rough draft of your review of the Mehrabian article that you wrote for Case 24. Produce a final draft of your review.

CASE IN POINT 29

Imagine that you are a student in the course Introduction to Communications. Your professor gives you the following assignment:

> We have recently read four articles that discuss the basic nature of human communication. The articles are "Communication Without Words" by Albert Mehrabian, "Human Communication" by John Wilson and Carroll Arnold, "Everyone Communicates" by Anabel Dean, and "How Communication Works" by Wilbur Schramm. Write a five-page paper that defines human communication based on your analysis of these four articles.

Complete both the rough and final drafts of this essay. All four articles are in Appendix B.

WRAP-UP EXERCISE FOR REVIEWING

Although analysis is a route to objective truth, assignments that require analysis do not always have a single "right" answer. The methods of analysis that different individuals use to approach a particular assignment often vary widely. Different methods of analysis often lead to different conclusions. Sometimes two markedly different methods of analysis will be equally valid. Other times one method will have clear advantages over another. The following exercise will help you understand how and why individual methods of analysis differ.

1. Make sure that all students bring to class the final draft of a review essay that has been assigned to the entire class.
2. Divide the class into groups of three.
3. Read the essays of the other two students in your group.
4. Working with the other two students in your group, list the techniques of analysis used in each of the three essays.
5. Note any differences among the three lists of analysis techniques. Decide which methods seem best from all three lists. Make a combined list of only the best techniques.
6. Have each group report to the class on its list of the best analysis techniques. Each list should be copied on the board.
7. Compare the lists on the board. Discuss any differences as a class and come up with a final list of the best techniques.

Reading To Repeat

WHAT IS REPEATING?

The process of repeating and reproducing exactly someone else's words is called *direct quoting*. Academic writers repeat authors' ideas when they incorporate *direct quotations* into their work. Many types of nonacademic materials also contain direct quotations. In newspapers reporters quote witnesses or persons being interviewed, and in fictional writing writers quote characters engaged in conversations. In all of the materials you read in which one person is speaking with another, you will notice that the author uses some device to differentiate the words of the individual speakers.

Cartoonists use one of the simplest techniques of handling direct quotations. Over the characters' heads they suspend "balloons" that contain the speakers' words. At the bottom of the balloon a little tail points directly to the character that is speaking. Since the text is fully illustrated, the cartoonist can show graphically who is speaking in each frame. When dramatists and scriptwriters portray conversations or dialogue, they differentiate between speakers by beginning each speaker's statement with his or her name on a new line of text.

In addition to drawing balloons and beginning speakers' statements on new lines of text, another signal that writers use to inform their readers that someone is speaking is quotation marks. We excerpted the following passage from Mark Twain's essay "Fenimore Cooper's Literary Offenses." Notice how

Twain acknowledges Brander Matthews and signals a direct quotation from Matthews.

> We must be a little wary when Brander Matthews tells us that Cooper's books "reveal an extraordinary fullness of invention." As a rule, I am quite willing to accept Brander Matthews's literary judgments and applaud his lucid and graceful phrasing of them; but that particular statement needs to be taken with a few tons of salt.

Direct quoting is a writing technique you will use in college when you want to repeat another person's statement word for word. You should always alert your reader that you are repeating someone else's words by placing the quoted words between quotation marks (". . .").

Some typical academic situations call for direct quoting:

> When you give the direct testimony of another person
>
> When you copy the exact phrase or sentence of a lecturer
>
> When you include an apt phrase or sentence from another author in your own essay or research paper

Can you think of other times when you will write quotations?

> *Definition:* When you repeat an author's ideas, you reproduce the words *exactly* and place quotation marks before and after them. You must *always* accompany a direct quotation with some identification of the source.

This definition makes several important points about direct quotations:

1. The quotation must be an exact reproduction of the original. Be sure to proofread quotations and check them against the original material.
2. A set of quotation marks (") should precede the first word and follow the last word of quoted material.
3. The direct quotation must always include a reference to the original source. We will discuss the details of correct referencing in this chapter.

Direct Quoting vs. Paraphrasing

When you paraphrase other writers, you "translate" their words by substituting synonyms and changing sentence patterns. Nothing is left out. When you quote other writers, you copy and reproduce their words exactly the way they wrote them. In order to distinguish your words from words that belong to someone else, set off the other writer's words in quotation marks.

It is important to point out that you may combine paraphrasing and direct quoting in your writing. You may decide to paraphrase part of the source but quote key ideas or phrases you have difficulty restating in your own words.

Direct Quoting vs. Summarizing

When you summarize, you reduce the source by eliminating secondary information and emphasizing the main idea. A summary may contain a direct quotation.

SUMMARY

What repeating is:

A writing technique that enables you to repeat someone else's words and differentiate them from your own writing
An exact reproduction of the original source

What repeating is not:

An unidentified or unacknowledged direct quotation

In order to quote directly from an academic source locate the words, sentences, or passages that best serve your purpose and reproduce them word for word in your paper.

HOW REPEATING FITS INTO THE ACADEMIC WRITING PROCESS

Planning
  Prereading
    1. Clarify the assignment and the topic.
    2. Consider audience needs.
    3. Use a systematic approach for previewing the reading source.
    4. Set goals for reading.
  Close reading
    Decide what you will quote and annotate the text.
  Postreading/Prewriting
    1. Reconsider assignment and audience.
    2. Decide which documentation style you will use and record appropriate data.
Writing
    1. Weave quotations into your essay.
    2. Make adjustments for special cases.
    3. Develop a list of references or works cited.

Revising
  As You Write
    1. Compare quotation to original.
    2. Compare quotation to topic and assignment.
    3. Compare quotation to audience needs.
  After You Write
    1. Compare quotation to overall plan.
    2. Edit for grammar, usage, mechanics.

chapter 12

Planning, Writing, and Revising Quotations

PLANNING

Prereading

Clarify the Assignment and the Topic

When you receive an assignment that requires you to use academic reading sources, study it carefully and do not proceed to read the sources or to write until you answer two crucial questions:

1. How will I use the reading sources in my writing; will I paraphrase, summarize, or quote them?
2. Which types of material shall I repeat word for word rather than rephrase or reduce?

The choice of paraphrasing, summarizing, or quoting is up to you unless your professor has cautioned you against quoting. Occasionally, professors will ask you to use your own words as a safeguard against excessive quoting or plagiarism. As we mentioned earlier in this book, many students use too many direct quotations when they write. Instead of summarizing parts of the text and paraphrasing important information, they string together endless direct quotations. Use quotations sparingly, one to two per typed page.

171

Consider Your Audience's Needs

Remember that when you quote from a reading source, you cannot assume that your audience will understand the quotation unless you provide some background or context for it. Think about your audience even before you begin to read because the intended audience will affect the amount and type of background or contextual information you will include with the quotation. Ask yourself the questions like the ones you posed before paraphrasing and summarizing:

1. How much general background information or how much of the context will your audience need in order to understand the quotation?
2. Will your audience be familiar with any field-specific vocabulary in the quotation?

Preview the Academic Source

To preview the reading source use the same system you used for summarizing. Ask the following questions:

1. What is the title of the source?
2. Who is (are) the author(s)?
3. What are the subdivisions of the source?
4. What do the study aids tell you about the content of the source?
5. Can you make connections between the topic and the ideas in the source?
6. What are the major organizational signals?
7. What are the smaller organizational signals?

Set Goals for Reading

Lastly, before you begin your close reading, decide what you want to accomplish. Review the section on prereading in Chapter 1 and ask goal-directed questions:

1. What do you expect to learn from the source?
2. What clues will help you to find the information you want?
3. Will you read all or only part of the source?

CASE IN POINT 30

Let's establish a setting for the cases. You are a student in Introduction to Communications. For your first paper for the course, your professor has assigned a five-hundred-word essay on a topic of your choice. You have decided to write on animal and human communication. One of the articles the professor has placed on reserve, Anabel Dean's "How Animals Communicate," is especially relevant for your topic. You will find Dean's article in Appendix B. Before you read closely, be sure you have performed the following prereading activities:

1. Clarify assignment and topic.
2. Consider the audience's needs.
3. Review the source.
4. Set goals for reading.

Stop here, unless your instructor tells you otherwise. You will have a chance to come back to this assignment later.

Close reading

Decide What You Will Quote and Annotate the Text

Repeat word for word only material that is exceptionally well expressed. If an author has phrased a sentence in a striking or unusual way, you may decide to quote it rather than restate it in your own words. You may also want to quote special forms of writing, such as definitions, key concepts, clever sayings, testimonials, and poems. There are other types of writing that you will choose to paraphrase or summarize, such as narration, the author's account of a story or anecdote, explanations, or facts. Facts and data may be important pieces of information to include in a paper; however, unless they are striking, you should paraphrase the sentence or context in which they appear. For an example, consider the following passage:

> ODOR. What's true for taste is also true for your sense of smell. Most people can easily agree about what odors they like the least (burnt rubber or vomit, for example), and to a lesser degree the ones they especially like (fresh strawberries, honeysuckle), but there's no real consistency about whether most smells are good or bad. For example, in one study people ranked their preference to 132 different odors. Bay leaf (a spice commonly used in cooking) ranged from 9th to 98th; peppermint from 1st to 76th; and raw onion from 5th to 110th. Age and sex do seem to play some part in people's odor preferences. Children and men generally like sweeter fruit odors, while women prefer them less sweet; men ranked musky-smelling perfumes higher than women did; and children tolerate odors such as feces more than adults do.
>
> Adler, Ron, and Neil Towne. *Looking Out/Looking In: Interpersonal Communication.* San Francisco: Rinehart Press/Holt, Rinehart & Winston, 1975, 124.

The odor passage contains some interesting statistics; however, the authors present them straightforwardly so there is no unusual wording to preserve. The information in this paragraph is appropriate for summarizing or paraphrasing. Compare the odor passage to the following:

> With malice toward none; with charity for all; with firmness in the right, as God gives us to see the right, let us strive on to finish the work we are in; to bind up the nation's wounds; to care for him who shall have borne the battle, and for his widow, and his orphan—to do all which may achieve and cherish a just, and a lasting peace, among ourselves, and with all nations.
>
> Abraham Lincoln, "Second Inaugural Address"

It would be possible to summarize Lincoln's words but if you paraphrase them it would be difficult to preserve the parallel structure ("to finish . . . to bind . . . to care . . . to do") and capture Lincoln's style. A well-crafted paragraph like this one should be quoted.

Once you have selected the lines of text that you will quote directly, annotate the text or jot down a reminder in your notes so that you can easily locate the material during your postreading.

EXERCISE 26

Read carefully each of the following passages. If a passage contains material that is quotable, underline the quotable parts and explain why you would quote them. Some passages may have no quotable material or may need to be entirely quoted.

Example

The dreams of childhood—its airy fables; its graceful, beautiful, humane, impossible adornments of the world beyond: <u>so good to be believed in once, so good to be remembered when outgrown</u>.

Charles Dickens, *Hard Times*

Answer: This is clever, memorable wording that would be difficult to paraphrase successfully.

1. To provide health care in its modern concept, the talents of a rapidly expanding number of health care personnel and disciplines are being utilized. Previously the three recognized health professions were medicine, dentistry, and nursing. Today there are over 200 health careers,

only a small segment of which were in operation prior to World War II. Although the physician and nurse are usually constant members of the health team, each of the other members is vital to the mission. There is specialization on all levels. Various care-giving agencies are being linked together to provide an imposing group of resources, technologies, and skills (Fig. 1-1).

Brunner, Lillian Sholtis, and Doris Smith Suddarth. *Textbook of Medical-Surgical Nursing.* 3rd ed. Philadelphia: J. B. Lippincott, 1975. 4.

2. Some books are to be tasted, others to be swallowed, and some few to be chewed and digested.

Francis Bacon, "Of Studies"

3. Remember that a construct is something unobservable and not directly measurable, such as motivation, ideas, and even time.

Owen, Steven V., Robin D. Froman, and Henry Moscow. *Educational Psychology: An Introduction.* 2nd ed. Boston: Little, Brown, 1981. 76.

4. Even the most sophisticated, modern, high-resolution electron microscope gives only indirect evidence of an atom's existence. Why then do we have so much faith in it? The answer is that the body of knowledge we can account for is so vast and so elegantly simplified by thinking in terms of atoms that we accept the atom as a physical actuality.

Sienko, Michell J., and Robert A. Plane. *Chemistry: Principles and Applications.* New York: McGraw-Hill, 1979. 2.

5. When a particle of light strikes a molecule of chlorophyll, an electron is jolted out of the molecule and raised to a higher energy state. Within a fraction of a second, it returns to its previous energy state. All life on this planet is dependent upon the energy momentarily gained by the electron.

Raven, Peter H., Ray F. Evert, and Helena Curtis. *Biology of Plants.* 2nd ed. New York: Worth Publishers, 1976. 1.

CASE IN POINT 31

Let us continue working on the assignment for Case 30. As you read Anabel Dean's "How Animals Communicate," select two or three sentences that are suitable for use as direct quotations. Annotate the article so that you will be able to locate quotable material readily as you postread and prewrite.

Stop here, unless your instructor tells you otherwise. You will have a chance to come back to this assignment later.

Postreading/prewriting

Reread Your Assignment and Decide
What You Will Repeat

When you have completed your close reading, reread your assignment to make certain that quotations are acceptable. Also, check with your professor about the documentation style he or she wishes you to use. *To document is to furnish your reader with additional information about the source of the quotation.* Let us say that you have included the following sentence in your paper:

> According to Randel, a conga is "a long, single-headed, Latin-American drum, often with a shell that bulges in the middle" (115).

You have given your reader the author's name, used quotation marks to signal Randel's words, and furnished the number of the page on which the quoted material appears. But the interested reader will want additional information: the title of the book, the date of publication, and the location and name of the publishing house. You will supply this information in a list at the end of your paper. The format you will use to arrange the additional information in the list will depend on the *documentation style* your professor requires. There are many different documentation styles. We will focus on the two most widely followed styles: the style of the Modern Language Association, called MLA style, and the style of the American Psychological Association, called APA style. Be sure to ask your professor which style is preferred.

After you determine the documentation style, reread the quotable material in the source and weigh its importance. If the quotations still look promising, copy them onto index cards or into your notes. Also copy the information you will need to include in the list at the end of your paper. Be sure to record (1) *author's full name;* (2) *title* of the article, chapter, or book; (3) *facts of publication*. The facts of publication for books are city of publication, publisher's name, and publication date. You will find the city of publication and publisher's name on the title page of the book. The publication date appears on the reverse side of the title page. The facts of publication for articles are full name of the journal or magazine, date of publication, volume number, and numbers of the first and last pages of the article. For an example of documentary information for a book, return to the above quotation about the conga. Here is the information that should appear on the index card.

Author	Don Michael Randel
Title	Harvard Concise Dictionary of Music
Publisher's name	The Belknap Press of Harvard University Press
City of publication	Cambridge, Massachusetts
Publication date	1978

For an example of documentary information for articles, consider the following:

Author	STROBE TALBOTT	
Article title	"In Central America, No Quick Fix"	
Magazine title	Time, August 8, 1983	Date of publication
Volume number	Vol. 122, pp. 79–80	Inclusive pages

If you are ever in doubt about how much documentary information to record, it is better to copy down more information than you may need rather than to lack information later.

Reconsider Your Audience

As you reread the material you have decided to quote, ask yourself if your audience will be able to understand the quotation when it is incorporated into your paper, or if you need to provide more background information or context. You may want to paraphrase or summarize the material that came before or after the quotation. If that is the case, write the additional information on the reverse side of the index card or in your notes.

CASE IN POINT 32

To continue working on the assignment for cases 30 and 31 return to Anabel Dean's article. Reread the material you selected for direct quoting. On an index card or in your notes, record the necessary documentary information. Reconsider your audience's needs. Paraphrase or summarize additional background information.

Stop here, unless your instructor tells you otherwise. You will have a chance to come back to this assignment later.

WRITING

In this section we discuss three basic techniques that will help you to use quotations intelligently and correctly. During the planning stage you selected quotable material and recorded necessary information for documentation. During the writing stage you will weave the quotations into your essay, allow for special types of quotations, and develop the list of references or works cited.

Weave Quotations into Your Essay

There are a number of ways you can weave quotations into your writing. You can inform your reader of the author of the quotation either by documenting the author in parentheses or by acknowledging the author right in the text. When you acknowledge the author in the text, you can cite the name before the quotation, within the quotation, or after it. For example, let us say you are quoting the definition of paraphrasing presented earlier in this book. Here are your options:

(a) "When you paraphrase a piece of academic writing, you write a passage that has *exactly* the same meaning as the original piece of writing but is different enough in both the choice of words and the arrangement of ideas to be considered your own work" (Kennedy and Smith 9).

(b) *Kennedy and Smith write,* "When you paraphrase a piece of academic writing, you write a passage that has *exactly* the same meaning as the original piece of writing but is different enough in both the choice of words and the arrangement of ideas to be considered your own work" (9).

(c) "When you paraphrase a piece of academic writing," *according to Kennedy and Smith,* "you write a passage that has *exactly* the same meaning as the original piece of writing but is different enough in both the choice of words and the arrangement of ideas to be considered your own work" (9).

(d) "When you paraphrase a piece of academic writing, you write a passage that has *exactly* the same meaning as the original piece of writing but is different enough in both the choice of words and the arrangement of ideas to be considered your own work," *observe Kennedy and Smith* (9).

Option a allows you to insert the quotation without acknowledging the author(s) in the body of the text. Instead, you inform your audience of the author's identity in parenthetical documentation. Options b, c, and d include author(s) acknowledgments within the text. You may acknowledge the author(s) before the quotation (option b), within the quotation (option c), or after the quotation (option d). Note that all four options require that you cite the page number in parentheses.

If you are using MLA style, the above method of documentation will suffice. APA style is slightly different in that the publication date follows the author's name, and the abbreviation for *page* is included. For example, for option a, you would write (Kennedy & Smith, 1986, p. 9) and for options b, c, and d, you would write the date in parentheses: Kennedy and Smith (1986) and include "p." before the page number: (p. 9).

When you use the MLA format, if you refer to more than one source written by the same author(s), you need to add an abbreviated source title to the parenthetical documentation. Consider the following example that contains references to the books *The Divided Self* and *The Politics of Experience* by R. D. Laing:

> Laing's careful analysis of the origins of schizophrenia (<u>Divided</u>) led him to develop a theory that attempted to explain the problems of our society as a whole (<u>Politics</u>).

In the example the parenthetical documentation shows that Laing's analysis of schizophrenia appears in *The Divided Self* while his theory concerning society as a whole can be found in *The Politics of Experience*.

In the APA format, the publication date would distinguish between Laing's two books:

> Laing's careful analysis of the origins of schizophrenia (1960) eventually led him to develop a theory that attempted to explain the problems of our society as a whole (1967).

If you want to reference several sources published by the same author in the same year, put lowercase letters after the year to make the distinction:

> Jones (1963a, 1963b) provides further information on this point.

It is important to remember that when you use option a, you must provide transitions between your own ideas and the ideas you quote. Inexperienced writers sprinkle their papers with direct quotations that appear to have little connection with the rest of the text. You can avoid this problem by *leading into* the quotation. A common lead-in is used in the following:

> *Academic Writing* offers some interesting advice: "When you write a passage that has exactly the same . . . (Kennedy and Smith 9).

Other ways to lead into quotations are to paraphrase or summarize the information that precedes the quoted material in the reading source. If you have difficulty coming up with lead-ins, use options b, c, or d. As you cite the author, try to vary the verb or verb phrase that you use. Note that in the previous examples, we used: "Kennedy and Smith *write*," "*according to* Kennedy and Smith," and "*observe* Kennedy and Smith." Here is a list of useful acknowledgments:

In the words of ⎫
                 ⎬   Kennedy and Smith
According to   ⎭

Kennedy and Smith . . .

admit	demonstrate	propose
add	discover	question
ask	evaluate	remark
ascertain	explore	reply
analyze	examine	refer to
assess	expound on	review
argue	emphasize	report
agree (disagree)	envision	rationalize
address	furnish	state
answer	find	suggest
believe	investigate	show
categorize	inquire	say
compare (contrast)	identify	survey
critique	list	synthesize
consider	measure	stress
concur	make the case	stipulate
conclude	note	summarize
cite	observe	trace
describe	prove	view
delineate	postulate	warn
determine	point out	write
define	present	

EXERCISE 27

Following is the first draft of a paragraph from a student paper followed by four quotations that could be used in the paragraph. Rewrite the paragraph and weave in all four quotations. You may change sentences from the original passage as long as you preserve the overall meaning. All quotations are fictitious as are their sources.

Although we all use the term *science,* few people stop to consider its precise meaning. When asked what science means, most of us immediately think of such things as the space program, modern medicine, and computers. However, these are merely the products of science. Science is more than just a list of technological accomplishments. All scientists realize that science is in part a body of knowledge about how the world works. These facts and statistics can be used in a variety of ways to achieve a number of different purposes. But most scientists maintain that science is a method of investigation as much as a list of facts. Some feel that science is a systematic procedure that, when carefully followed, will always lead to the truth. Others are less confident in the total reliability of science but still feel it gives a more objective view than personal experience. In any case, most scientists see the basic methods they use as applicable to virtually any field of study, not just biology, chemistry, physics, and advanced technology. Indeed, scientific method has implications for us that go far beyond the technological marvels with which we are all familiar.

"Science rarely leads to absolute certainty but rather to a best guess." (physicist Adam Orbut in "Science For Its Own Sake")

"Any discipline that methodically and objectively studies an aspect of humans or their environment can be called a science." (psychologist May Ratnick in *Behavioral Studies*)

"Science is the most powerful method known for arriving at the correct solution to any given problem." (statistician Norman Bell in *Numbers and You*)

"Science's primary role is to systematically categorize and record what is known about the world." (biologist Jean Splisar in *An Introduction to Biology*)

A Note About Mechanics.   Your professor will expect you to use proper punctuation and capitalization when you quote. Keep in mind the following rules:

Capitalization

1. Begin the direct quotation with a capital letter if the direct quotation is a complete sentence:

>   Kennedy and Smith point out, "Just as your summary can contain brief paraphrases, it can also include brief quotations from the original work" (47).

2. Begin the quotation with a lowercase letter if the quotation itself is not a complete sentence:

> According to Kennedy and Smith, "the phrase or brief sentence that expresses more specifically the part or aspect of the large subject area of the sentence kernel that the author discusses" is called the "gist" of the sentence (53).

3. Begin the quotation with a lowercase letter and omit the comma if the quotation is preceded by the word *that*. For an example, look again at the quotation in rule 1. You will see that the quotation begins with a capital letter. We have capitalized it in our example because *Just* begins a complete sentence. However, if we were to introduce the quotation with *that*, we would change the first letter to lower case:

> Kennedy and Smith point out that "just as your summary can contain brief paraphrases, it can also include brief quotations from the original work" (47).

4. Do not capitalize the opening word of a continued quotation unless it begins a complete sentence or is a proper noun:

> "Just as your summary can contain brief paraphrases," write Kennedy and Smith, "it can also include brief quotations from the original work" (47).

Punctuation

1. Set off the quoted material with double quotation marks "...".
2. Set off quoted material within a quotation with single quotation marks '...'. (We explain this rule on page 184.)
3. Separate the verb of acknowledgment from a short quotation with a comma and from a long quotation with a colon.
4. Close a quotation by placing the period or comma after the parenthetical documentation of the page number:

> Kennedy and Smith state that the primary goal of summarizing is "to make the original shorter without changing its meaning" (45).

5. When you acknowledge a source, you must set off the title with underlining or quotation marks. Underlining signals your audience that you are quoting from a long source: a book, full-length play, journal, magazine, or long poem. Quotation marks signal a shorter work: a chapter or section within a book, an article in a journal or magazine, a poem, or a short story:

> In <u>The Stranger</u>, Albert Camus describes . . . .
> James Joyce's "The Dead" concerns . . . .
> In "Reading to React," section III, Kennedy and Smith discuss . . . .
> <u>Romeo and Juliet</u>, a play by Shakespeare and a film by Zeffirelli, shows how . . . .

Punctuating titles also helps avoid confusion. In the following sentence, the punctuation enables the reader to differentiate between the novel and the whale: Is Moby Dick the central character in <u>Moby Dick</u>?

EXERCISE 28

Turn back to your revision of the paragraph in Exercise 27. Reconsider your use of punctuation and capitalization in the four places in which you wove quotations into the original passage. Rewrite your paragraph using correct punctuation and capitalization of the four quotations.

Allow for Special Types of Quotations

As you weave quotable material into your writing, there will be times when you may want to alter the quotation in some way. You may decide to omit part of the quotation or to work it in with your own words. You may also quote lengthy material or material that contains a quotation within a quotation. Let us look first at the practice of omitting words within a quotation.

Ellipses. Ellipsis points are three dots that are inserted where quoted material is left out. For example, let us say you are interested in the following quotation from Thomas Carlyle's *On Boswell's Life of Johnson*:

> There is a tolerable traveling on the beaten road, run how it may; only on the new road not yet levelled and paved, and on the old road all broken into ruts and quagmires, is the traveling bad or impracticable.

However, you would like to capture the idea that the old road is superior to the new road in as few words as possible. In order to signal your audience that you have omitted words, you use three spaced periods (. . .) called *ellipses*:

> There is a tolerable traveling on the beaten road, . . . only on the new road . . . is the traveling bad or impracticable.

If you use ellipses at the end of a sentence, be sure to add a fourth period.

Interpolation. Interpolation is inserted material. If you find it necessary to insert your own ideas into a quotation, you must signal your audience by placing your words within brackets. Let us say you are quoting Washington

Irving's *The Sketch-Book:* "The happy age when a man can be idle with impunity." You want to interject a detail. You would place your interpolation within brackets: "That happy age [around sixty-three] when a man can be idle with impunity."

Lengthy Material. Lengthy quotations of two sentences or more should be indented four or five spaces, single spaced, and introduced by a colon. Indenting and single spacing signal your reader that you are quoting, so you omit quotation marks. For example, consider the following excerpt from a student paper:

Traditional approaches to farming were often based on principles that we now know are counterproductive. As Troeh, Hobbs, and Donahue point out:

> Years ago young persons learning to handle horses were instructed "Don't look back!" because a tug on the reins would turn the horses and make a crooked row. Straight rows are appealing but they also cause erosion. Straight rows on hilly land provide cultivated channels for runoff water to erode. Contour tillage is often the solution, but it must overcome tradition.

> Troeh, Frederick, Arthur Hobbs, and Roy Donahue. *Soil and Water Conservation: For Productivity and Environmental Protection.* Englewood Cliffs, N.J.: Prentice-Hall, 1980. 9.

Quotation Within a Quotation. Throughout the introduction to this section, we cautioned you to reproduce exactly the material that you quote. Ninety-nine percent of the time you will follow this advice; however, there is one exception. When the source already contains quoted material, change the double quotation marks around the existing quotation to single quotation marks. For example:

> According to James Boswell's account in *The Life of Samuel Johnson LL.D.,* the author Samuel Johnson kept his misery as a college student to himself and did not share his difficulties with his college associates. As Boswell observed, "Dr. Adams told me that Johnson, while he was at Pembroke College, 'was caressed and loved by all about him, was a gay and frolicsome fellow, and passed there the happiest part of his life.' "

EXERCISE 29

Following is the first draft of a paragraph from a student's paper followed by four quotations that could be used in the paragraph. Rewrite the paragraph to weave in the four quotations according to the instructions given with each quotation. You may change the sentences in the original as long as you preserve the overall meaning. All quotations are fictitious, as are their sources.

We often hear that studying history helps us learn from the successes and failures of others. However, it is easy to misunderstand the significance of events in the past. There are three reasons that can prevent us from learning the true lessons of history. First, situations from the past are rarely identical to present circumstances. Attempting to force a comparison between past and present events often leads to false conclusions. Second, many people pay attention only to the historical events that support their preconceived notions and ignore contradictory information. History's scope is so vast that evidence can be found to support any point of view. Third, any historical event is subject to a variety of interpretations. It is difficult indeed to use information about the past to make decisions about the present.

Use interpolation and ellipsis to weave in this quotation:

Veterans, politicians, and news reporters, all of whom were directly affected by the war, often had contrasting views on the significance of the war to the future of America's military involvement in foreign countries. (Journalist John Hayes in *Dateline Vietnam*)

Use ellipses to weave in this quotation:

History is our tutor, our wise, patient and yet strict teacher, that stands ready to guide us in our attempts to understand the present. (Historian Mary Stone in "History's Lessons")

Use techniques for handling lengthy material and quotations within a quotation to weave in this information:

Many commentators use Chamberlain's pact with Hitler prior to World War II as an example of the inherent problems with the politics of "appeasement." The failure of this pact is often used as evidence to argue that efforts to develop better relations with the Russians are dangerous to our country. In fact, Chamberlain's failure to achieve what he called "peace in our times" has little to do with current relations between the United States and the Soviet Union. (Senator Bill O'Connell in the *Congressional Record*)

Weave in only part of this quotation:

A basic characteristic of human behavior is selective neglect. (Psychologist George Samuelson in *An Introduction to Psychology*)

List the Sources

As you weave a quotation into your paper, you provide your audience with some identification of the source, usually the author and page number and sometimes the title. The reason for including this information is so that your audience can readily locate the complete reference in the list of sources at the end of the paper.

The way you will arrange the list depends on the documentation style you are using. As you were postreading/prewriting, you should have checked with your professor about the preferred style. Usually professors in the humanities require the MLA style, whereas professors in the social sciences prefer the APA style. In addition to the following guidelines for APA and MLA styles, see Appendix A.

First of all, compile your list of sources. It will contain entries for *every* source you used in your paper. *Remember you must cite and document source material that is paraphrased and summarized as well as that which is quoted.* You should assemble the index cards containing the documentary information you recorded during the postreading/prewriting stage and alphabetize them according to the authors' last names. Now you can type your list.

MLA Style. Title your list Works Cited. Do not underline or put quotation marks around this title. Rearrange the documentary information as shown in Figure 1. You will find it useful to refer to the examples in Appendix A.

Begin the first line of each entry at the left-hand margin. Indent subsequent lines. When you type your paper, double-space between entries.

Works Cited

Booth, Wayne C. "The Limits of Pluralism." Critical Inquiry 3 (1977): 407–23.

Donaldson, E. Talbot. "Briseis, Brieseida, Criseyde, Cresseid, Cressid: Progress of a Heroine." In Chaucerian Problems and Perspectives. Ed. Edward Vasta and Zacharias P. Thunday. Notre Dame, Ind.: Notre Dame Univ. Press, 1979. 3–12.

Gardner, John. The Poetry of Chaucer. Carbondale, Ill.: Southern Illinois Univ. Press, 1977.

Iser, Wolfgang. The Act of Reading. Baltimore: Johns Hopkins Univ. Press, 1978.

———. "The Reading Process: A Phenomenological Approach." In The Implied Reader. Baltimore: Johns Hopkins Univ. Press, 1974.

McAlpine, Monica E. "The Pardoner's Homosexuality and How It Matters." PMLA 95 (1980): 8–22.

For books   **Figure 1**

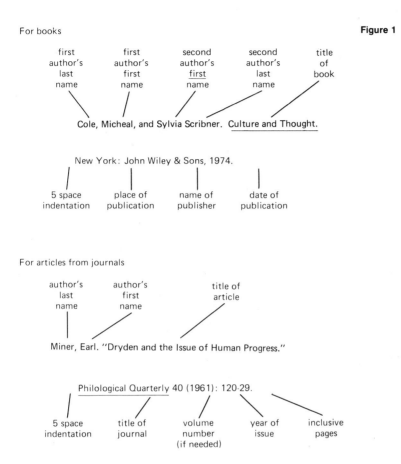

Cole, Micheal, and Sylvia Scribner. Culture and Thought.

New York: John Wiley & Sons, 1974.

| 5 space indentation | place of publication | name of publisher | date of publication |

For articles from journals

Miner, Earl. "Dryden and the Issue of Human Progress."

Philological Quarterly 40 (1961): 120-29.

| 5 space indentation | title of journal | volume number (if needed) | year of issue | inclusive pages |

Content Endnotes.   In addition to a "Works Cited" list, the MLA style makes provision for a list of comments, explanations, or facts that relate to the ideas discussed in the paper but do not fit into the actual text. You may occasionally need these *content endnotes* to provide information that is useful but must for some reason be separated from the rest of the paper. Some of the most common uses of endnotes are listed below:

> Providing additional references that go beyond the scope of the paper but could help the reader understand issues in more depth
> Discussing a source of information in more detail than is possible in a "Works Cited" list

Acknowledging special assistance in preparing a paper

Giving a personal opinion that does not fit into the text smoothly

Explaining ideas more fully than is possible in the text

Mentioning concerns that are not directly related to the content of the paper

Providing additional details that are relevant but would clutter up the text

Mentioning contradictory information that goes against the general trend discussed in the paper

Evaluating ideas that are explained in the paper

In the MLA style, endnotes are listed on a separate page(s) just before the "Works Cited" list. The first page of the endnote list is entitled "Notes." Each note is numbered sequentially (1, 2, 3, . . .), and a corresponding number is included in the text of the paper, typed halfway between the lines, to indicate the material to which the endnote refers. The following excerpts from the text of a paper and its list of endnotes illustrate the MLA endnote format:

Text of Paper
For hundreds of years, scientists thought that the sun's energy came from the combustion of a solid fuel such as coal.[1] However, work in the early twentieth century convinced researchers that the sun sustains a continuous nuclear fusion reaction.[2] The sun's nuclear furnace maintains a temperature. . . .

Notes

Endnote Page
[1] Detailed accounts of pretwentieth-century views of solar energy can be found in Banks and Rosen (141–55) and Burger (15–21).

[2] In very recent years, some scientists have questioned whether or not the sun does sustain a fusion reaction at all times. Experiments described by Salen (68–93) have failed to detect the neutrinos that should be the byproducts of the sun's fusion. This raises the possibility that the sun turns off and on periodically.

Notice that the reference numerals are placed in the text of the paper immediately after the material to which they refer. In most cases, the reference numerals will appear at the end of a sentence. No space is left between the reference numeral and the word or punctuation mark that it follows. However, in the "Notes" list, one space is left between the numeral and the first letter of the note. The first line of each endnote is indented five spaces. Notes are numbered according to the order in which they occur in the paper.

Any source that you mention in an endnote must be fully documented in the "Works Cited" list. Do not include this complete documentation in the endnote itself. Never use endnotes as a substitute for the "Works Cited" list.

Do not overuse endnotes. If possible, include all information in the text of your paper. For most of the papers you write, no endnotes will be necessary.

EXERCISE 30

Choose five books and two articles from recent periodicals. Use all seven sources to construct a "Works Cited" list using the MLA format.

APA Style.   The APA Style is comparable to the revised MLA style in many ways. Both styles require writers first to acknowledge the author of the source in the paper and then to give complete documentation in the list of sources at the end of the paper. The chief differences between the MLA and the APA styles are presented in Appendix A.

The following model is done in APA format.

References

Bartlett, F. C. (1932). <u>Remembering: A study in experimental and social psychology.</u> Cambridge: Cambridge University Press.

Frederiksen, C. H. (1975). Representing logical and semantic structure of knowledge acquired from discourse. <u>Cognitive Psychology</u> 7, 371–458.

Gauld, A., & Stephenson, G. M. (1967). Some experiments relating to Bartlett's theory of remembering. <u>British Journal of Psychology,</u> 58, 39–49.

Gomulicki, B. R. (1956). Recall as an abstractive process. <u>Acta Psychologica, 12,</u> 77–94.

Grimes, J. (1975). <u>The thread of discourse.</u> The Hague: The Mouton Press.

Kay, H. (1955). Learning and retaining verbal material. <u>British Journal of Psychology,</u> 44, 81–100.

Meyer, B. J. F. (1975) <u>The organization of prose and its effects on memory.</u> New York: Oxford American Elsevier.

EXERCISE 31

Review the "Works Cited" list that you compiled in Exercise 30. Rewrite this list using APA format.

AN EXPLANATION OF PLAGIARISM

We mentioned earlier that improper paraphrasing or summarizing can lead to plagiarism. Specifically, we stressed that your paraphrases and summaries must be written in your own words. We explained how to change both sentence structure and vocabulary to avoid plagiarism when you reword authors' ideas. However, plagiarism involves issues of academic honesty beyond those we have discussed so far. Since most of these issues are related to documenting sources, this chapter is an appropriate place to discuss the broader issue of plagiarism.

In general, *plagiarism* is the act of benefiting directly from someone else's writing or ideas without giving proper credit. Depending on its precise interpretation, plagiarism may refer to a wide range of academically dishonest behavior. Students are often amazed at the variety of activities that their professors consider dishonest. Some of the most common types of plagiarism are listed below:

Handing in a paper written by someone else

Copying directly from sources without either using quotation marks or providing complete documentation

Changing only slightly the author's word choice and sentence structure

Failing to Document a Paraphrase or Summary

Rewording a source does not give you any claim on the ideas it contains. If you borrow any information, you must credit the source. Students often find this rule hard to accept. In particular, they sometimes worry that documenting all borrowed information will clutter their papers with references. However, papers that rely heavily on sources will necessarily contain many references. Your reader will assume that any undocumented ideas are your own, so failing to reference a paraphrase or summary means that you are taking credit for someone else's thoughts.

Getting Help with Your Writing from Other People

We encourage our students to get help *as* they write. Students learn from the feedback they get while they are working on a paper as well as from comments on the final product. Your professors, the staff of your campus writing or learning laboratory, and your knowledgeable friends are all valuable and legitimate sources of help when you are working on a paper. However, there is a difference between asking specific questions about writing and getting someone else to do your work for you.

Plagiarizing Your Own Work

Can you plagiarize your own papers? In a sense, you can. In most cases, a new paper must be written for each assignment you are given. It is academically dishonest to submit the same paper twice or to borrow extensively from your earlier work without acknowledgment. Consult your professor if you think you have a legitimate reason to use for a new assignment part of a paper you wrote in the past.

We are not exaggerating when we say that a single case of plagiarism, intentional or unintentional, can destroy your academic career. If you have any questions concerning plagiarism, make sure you consult your professors or your college writing center.

CASE IN POINT 33

You are now ready to write the first draft of the essay you worked on in cases 30, 31, and 32. Refer again to the assignment in Case 30 and reread Anabel Dean's "How Animals Communicate" in the appendix. Write the first draft of your essay. Make sure you weave in the quotations you selected in Case 30. Use MLA documentation style.

REVISING

As we mentioned in earlier chapters you should revise *as* you write as well as *after* you have completed your first draft.

Revising Direct Quotations as You Write

Comparing the Quotation to the Original Source. After you have copied a quotation from the source, compare it to the source to be sure you have made an *exact* reproduction of the author's words and have acknowledged the source. The following repeating pitfalls should serve as your guide:

1. Changing the author's words
2. Failing to give sufficient background information
3. Failing to acknowledge the source
4. Failing to acknowledge correctly

Comparing the Quotations to the Topic and Assignment. As you write the first draft of your paper, you may decide to make a change in the direction your paper is taking. If this is the case, evaluate the material you have quoted directly. Be sure the quotations still help to develop your topic. Do not repeat authors' ideas simply for the sake of including direct quotations.

Comparing the Quotations to Audience Needs. When you incorporate direct quotations into your paper, your primary concern is that your audience have sufficient background information to understand how the quotation fits into your line of thought. Anticipate your audience's need. Do not leave your reader guessing about the source.

Revising After the First Draft Is Complete

Comparing the Quotations to the Overall Plan. Be sure that you have used quotations at appropriate places in your paper. Check that you have discussed one idea at a time, not one source at a time. You need not group together quotations from one source. Bring in information from different sources when appropriate.

Editing for Grammar, Usage, and Mechanics. As you revise, consult a *style manual* to answer questions about grammar, usage, and mechanics. The process of quoting can give rise to problems you need to be aware of as you edit. One of the biggest problems is maintaining a proper "grammatical fit" between the quotation and the rest of the paper. In other words, the use of quotation(s) should not result in grammatical errors, particularly errors in agreement between subjects and verbs and pronouns and antecedents. Consider this student example.

Mehrabian states that nonverbal actions "reinforces or contradicts feelings that are being communicated verbally" (245).

The word *actions* requires a plural verb. When the student edits the paper, he or she should change *actions* to the singular.

Other problems that arise as you quote are with punctuation and capitalization. Be sure to consult the rules given in this chapter.

CHECKLIST FOR REVISION

A. Does your paper have clear organizational divisions?
  1. Introduction?
  2. Body?
  3. Conclusion?
B. Does each paragraph include the necessary elements?
  1. Introduction: thesis sentence?
  2. Body Paragraphs: topic sentences? supporting information? transitions?
C. At the places where you have included direct quotations, have you:
  1. Provided sufficient background information so that your audience will understand the quotation?
  2. Acknowledged the author of the quotation?
  3. Provided proper documentation?
D. Have you avoided the repeat pitfalls of:
  1. Changing the author's words?
  2. Failing to give sufficient background information?
  3. Failing to acknowledge the source?
  4. Failing to acknowledge correctly?
E. Are there any problems with grammar, usage, or mechanics?

CASE IN POINT 34

Use the Checklist for Revision as you write the final draft of the paper you produced in Case 33. Carefully check your documentation of quotations for both completeness and accuracy.

WRAP-UP EXERCISE FOR REPEATING

The following exercise will help to clarify when you should quote and when you should paraphrase an academic source.

1. Divide the class into groups of three.
2. All students read the essay on Gandhi that appears in the introduction to this book.
3. As a group, go over the sections of the essay that the margin notes indicate were either paraphrased or quoted from Gene Sharp's book *Gandhi as a Political Strategist.* In each case, decide why the writer chose to quote rather than paraphrase and vice versa, and write down the reason. If you disagree with the writer's choice, write this down also.
4. Each group reads its list of reasons to the entire class.
5. The class discusses the lists and attempts to resolve any differences of opinion.

Reading
to Research

WHAT IS RESEARCHING?

The Random House Dictionary of the English Language tells us that research is "diligent and systematic inquiry or investigation into a subject to discover or revise facts, theories, applications, etc." Often we associate research with scientific and medical discoveries, for example, the research done by Copernicus that disproved the theory that the earth was the center of the universe; the research done by Galileo that affirmed Copernicus's position by calculating the position of the other planets; the research done by Salk that led to the discovery of the first polio vaccine; and the research done by Marie Curie that led to the discovery of radium. In those famous cases the research involved laboratory experiments, observation of events in nature, and mathematical calculations. There are also research activities that call for a systematic investigation of all that has been written about a subject. The researcher analyzes the written information, draws insights from it, and applies it to new situations. For example, in *Das Kapital* Marx set forth a new view of societal structure by drawing on the views of economists, philosophers, and historians. *Das Kapital* is the product of his research. At the beginning of your college career, teachers will expect you to do research of this second type. Later, depending on your major, you may engage in original-action research projects.

Purpose of the Research Paper

The reason professors assign research papers is to make you an active, independent scholar who is able, first, to locate other people's ideas and, second, to analyze and synthesize these ideas and come to a conclusion. In high school and in many college classes, the instructor serves as the storehouse of academic knowledge. He or she provides you with new information, concepts, and ideas by lecturing, facilitating discussion, and assigning readings. As you progress into upper-level courses, the professor will allow and expect you to work on your own. Truly educated people have learned how to learn; they know how to locate information independently and use it by themselves.

As we pointed out earlier, learning to work with other people's ideas is a difficult task. Having to locate these ideas is an added complication. As a result, professors often give students the ideas they expect them to use in papers by providing reading lists and other bibliographic sources. Yet many professors do ask even first-year students to conduct independent library research. The ultimate undergraduate task in locating source material is given to some students in the form of the senior or honors thesis assignment. It is a long journey from the review of a single source to a senior thesis in which you cover exhaustively all the literature in a particular field. Along the way, you will learn a great deal about academic writing. The information on researching contained in this book will help you progress along this path.

THE PROCESS OF RESEARCHING

The research process is the same as that of the other five Rs; just as in rephrasing, reducing, reacting, reviewing, and repeating, you will engage in periods of planning, writing, and revising. The amount of time that you spend on each of these activities, however, will increase. You will do more planning because you have to go to the library, locate sources, read them, and take notes on their contents. During writing you will have to organize and connect ideas from multiple sources as well as weave into your paper different academic writing forms including paraphrases, summaries, and quotations. Furthermore, the need for thoughtful revision, careful editing, and accurate typing may make revising a time-consuming activity. Researching involves more than just finding and recording information. A list of facts on a given subject may convey little to an audience without explanation, organization, and commentary. You may even find it difficult to locate appropriate sources in the library unless you understand the overall purpose of the research process. Good research requires careful thought. The clerical work of compiling a list of facts is only a small part of the overall process.

Although research begins with examining other people's ideas, it can develop into a highly creative activity. Bringing together information from different sources can help you come to new conclusions that are entirely your own. In Chapter 14 we will present a sample research paper in which the student comes to unique conclusions by discovering a connection between two separate bodies of scholarly research. In fact, most independent thought in academics begins with a careful examination of earlier work in the field.

> *Definition:* Researching is gathering information, usually from multiple sources, and then acting on this information by doing some or all of the following activities: organizing, analyzing, synthesizing, generalizing, and applying.

This definition makes two important points:

1. Research involves locating a number of different sources of information about a subject. For beginning academic writers who are not assigned original research projects, most of the sources will be reading materials, and they will be located in the college library.
2. Writing based on research involves one or several of the following processes: organization (fitting the information into a structured pattern), analysis (critically examining the information), synthesis (combining information from different sources), generalization (locating general trends in the information), and application (using the information in new ways).

Researching vs. the Other Five Rs

The research paper gives you a chance to use all the academic writing strategies you have learned in this book. After you locate, preview, and read the sources, you will present them to your audience by paraphrasing parts of them, summarizing them, quoting them, answering analysis questions about them, and occasionally reacting to them. The five Rs are the tools you use to interpret and reflect upon the information you gather through research. By using these techniques effectively, you are able to make your paper more than just a catalogue of facts. Thus, as we discuss writing research papers, we will refer frequently to the skills covered earlier in this book.

SUMMARY

What researching is:

A writing process as well as a search for information
An activity that draws on rephrasing, reducing, reacting, reviewing, and repeating

A means of discovery

A way of expressing independent and creative thought

What researching is not:

A mere collection of facts

HOW RESEARCHING FITS INTO THE STAGES OF THE ACADEMIC WRITING PROCESS

Planning
  Prereading
    1. Clarify the assignment and topic.
         Decide on general approach to the topic.
    2. Consider audience's needs.
    3. Preview the source.
         Locate sources and get an overview of topic.
         Narrow topic and form preliminary thesis.
    4. Set goals for reading.
  Close reading
    1. Use the five Rs and take notes accordingly.
    2. Record bibliographic information
  Postreading/Prewriting
    1. Recast preliminary thesis.
    2. Reconsider your audience's needs.
Writing
  Outline your ideas
    1. Reconsider your preliminary thesis.
    2. Group your note cards according to an organizational plan.
    3. Look for connections between ideas.
    4. Pick an appropriate outline form that represents the structure of your paper.
  Write the rough draft
    1. Weave paraphrases, summaries, reactions, reviews, and quotations into your paper.
Revising
  Revising as you write
    1. Check for researching pitfalls.
  Revising after you write
    1. Compare your paper to the assignment.
    2. Check for relative proportions of paraphrases, summaries, quotations, reactions, and analyses.
    3. Check paraphrases, summaries, quotations, and works cited listings for accuracy.
    4. Edit for grammar, mechanics, and usage.
    5. Check final draft for proper format.
    6. Proofread the finished paper.

chapter 13

Planning the Research Paper

The amount of planning you do before you sit down to compose your paper will depend on the specificity of your assignment. If your professor gives you an open-ended, broad subject area, such as poetry, to research, you must plan how you will focus on and narrow it. You will have to do a lot of prereading, and you may overview many sources before you get a firm enough grasp on the subject so that you can form a preliminary thesis. The amount of time you spend on close reading and postreading/prewriting depends on the number and length of the sources you consult. A short report based on three articles will obviously require much less time than a twenty-page paper based on a thorough investigation of fifteen to thirty sources.

PREREADING

Clarify the Assignment and Narrow the Topic

When professors assign papers that require research, they often have certain objectives in mind; they want students to learn specific techniques in using academic sources. Some of the most common of these specific learning objectives are listed in the following chart:

TYPICAL RESEARCH PAPERS

	Assignment (for a course on poetry)	Professor's Learning Objective for Students	Student's Decision About the Type of Paper to Write	Student's Narrowing of Topic and Formulation of Preliminary Thesis
#1	Discuss the cultural role of the oral poetry produced in a particular traditional society	Student will learn how to focus a broad topic area, narrow a topic, and form a thesis by locating library sources and synthesizing information	Report	Oral Poetry → African oral poetry → Oral poetry plays an important role in traditional African societies. → African oral poetry serves as a means of preserving important historical and cultural information, as an art form, and as a popular source of entertainment.
#2	Analyze Albert Lord's theory about the nature of traditional oral poetry	Student will engage in the activities for assignment #1. In addition, student will state a firm position or argue a point.	Review	Lord's characterization of traditional oral poetry → Comparison of Lord's evidence from Yugoslavian poets to evidence from another traditional culture. → Comparison of Lord's evidence to that from African cultures. →

#3 Write a paper on any aspect of oral poetic traditions.

Student will engage in the activities for assignments #1 and #2. In addition, this assignment gives the student leeway to introduce new ideas and apply source information to new situations.

Application

Lord's characterization of traditional oral poetry is supported by evidence from African cultures.

(student narrows topic to preliminary thesis of assignment #1.) →

In traditional African societies, poetry plays an important social role, but in modern Western culture, poetry has little impact. →

Modern popular culture in the West is oriented around solitary activities such as TV watching in sharp contrast to group cultural activities of traditional society. →

Modern society would be enriched by group cultural activities similar to those found in traditional societies.

Notice that the wording of the assignment is the key to the intended learning outcome and the guide to the type of paper that the student must write. Too often students respond only to the general topic area and do not notice a specific type of paper. For example, notice that a report that summarizes Lord's theory about oral poetry would not be sufficient for assignment #2, which asks for analysis. Typically, professors will either ask for rewrites or assign low grades when research papers do not speak directly to the assignment. Consult with your professor if you have any questions concerning what type of paper the assignment requires.

In many of your college courses, you will receive assignments that are fairly specific like assignment #2 above. Professors may provide you with a broad subject, however, in order to force you to break down the subject and focus on a narrow topic. If you try to write a research paper without achieving this focus, your paper may have no clear purpose or may deal only with generalities. Thus it is important that you learn how to identify a specific topic within a broad subject area.

If you have an assignment that requires narrowing, you must achieve some focus before you even begin to look at sources. A good first step is to create a list of topics that fall within the broad subject area. You can generate a list of possible topics by using the writer's plans you learned in our discussion of summarizing.

Recall that writers organize their ideas about a subject in five major ways: (1) antecedent/consequent, (2) comparison, (3) description, (4) response, and (5) time order. Apply each of these plans to the broad subject of your assignment by asking yourself a series of questions. Let us illustrate with oral poetry, the subject of the preceding examples.

Plan	*Sample Questions*
Antecedent/ Consequent	How do the constraints of oral composition (cause) determine the structure of oral poetry (effect)? How does the introduction of literacy affect an oral poetic tradition?
Comparison	How does the structure of oral poetry compare to that of written poetry? How do the attitudes of oral poets toward their work compare to those of literate poets?
Description	What are the characteristics of traditional oral poetry? How do people who cannot read and write go about producing poetry?
Response	Based on his study of Yugoslavian oral poetry, Albert Lord described what he felt were the general characteristics of orally composed

Plan	*Sample Questions*
	verse. Are the characteristics Lord identified typical of other traditions? Is Lord correct that oral poets value tradition over originality?
Time Order	Have oral poetic traditions disappeared in modern times? Does an oral poetic tradition change with time?

EXERCISE 32

Below is a list of broad subject areas for research. Use the five writer's plans—(1) antecedent/consequent, (2) comparison, (3) description, (4) response, and (5) time order—to focus the broad subject areas. Apply each plan to the subject by asking yourself a series of questions based on the writer's plan.

EXAMPLE: FOSSILS (BROAD SUBJECT AREA)

Antecedent/ Consequent	What do fossils tell us about life when the rocks were formed? What conditions caused the fossil to be preserved?
Comparison	What is the difference between paleontology (the study of fossils) and archaeology? How is the study of fossils like crime investigation?
Description	What are the different types of fossils? What are the features of each type? How do paleontologists remove fossils from rocks?
Response	How can fossils give clues to the diets and habits of prehistoric animals? How do paleontologists piece together fossils that are not intact?
Time Order	What do fossils tell us about the rates of plant and animal evolution?

Broad Subject Areas

Olympics	Feminism and women's rights	Hollywood
Censorship	Crime prevention	Adolescence
Marketing	Latin America in the twentieth century	Diet
Computers	Chemical engineering	Printing
Modern novels	Nuclear, chemical, & biological warfare	Organized sports
Myths & rituals	Prehistoric cave art	Jazz & rock music

From the list of questions you need to choose one that you will concentrate on. In making this choice, consider how strong your interest is in each question and how readily you will be able to research it. When you narrow the choice to two or three questions, try to list potential sources of information for each of the questions. If you are unable to think where you would first turn for information on one of the questions, it would be best to eliminate this choice.

When you have decided on a particular question to work with, you can use free writing, a technique you learned in Chapter 8, to help you further narrow your topic. Put the topic in a context you already understand by using your preexisting knowledge and experience. First, in an expressive free-writing style, write down your thoughts and understanding of the topic. Second, sift through your free writing looking for ideas that can help you further refine your topic. For example, assume you initially chose the question, Have oral poetic traditions disappeared in modern times? An excerpt from your free writing reads as follows:

> The Yugoslavian oral poets are widely known because literary scholars studied their work carefully. But they are not the only oral poets in the world. For one thing, there are blind poets who have never known how to read or write. Also, Professor Meyer mentioned that certain African tribes have a tradition of oral poetry. I read in *Shogun* that Japanese samurai composed short poems in their heads. Did the Japanese have an oral poetic tradition?

In your free writing you make reference to the professors's remarks on African poems during the lectures on oral poetry. Since you know that at least in the past there was a tradition of oral poetry in Africa, you decide to focus your research on determining the extent to which this tradition still exists. As your focus sharpens, you have a better idea of what sources you will look for when you reach the library stage of the research process.

Note that at this stage you have narrowed a preliminary topic that is still subject to change. After you collect information on the subject, you may need, or want, to change or refine your topic. Your library research may suggest new aspects of the topic that had not occurred to you earlier. You may also find that you are not able to locate enough sources on the subject you have chosen. Thus, you must remain flexible about your topic choice until after you have found and read sources. If you commit yourself too early to a specific topic, you may find yourself in the uncomfortable position of working on a topic that cannot be handled successfully no matter how hard you work.

Consider Your Audience's Needs

After you have arrived at a preliminary topic, turn your attention to your prospective readers. Considering what *you* know about the topic, what do you think *they* know about it? In light of the writer's-plan questions you posed for yourself, what questions do you think they will have as they read your paper? Take time before you begin your research to think about the potential needs of your audience, and write these thoughts down. As you gain more knowledge of your topic through research, you may well refine the questions you had initially.

When you write a research paper, you have to assume that your audience will be educated readers who have some knowledge of the topic—as you yourself did before you began to work on the paper—and who are open to learning more about it. At the same time, remember to aim your writing at your audience and not at yourself. Your readers will need background information because most likely they will not have read all the sources you used in your paper. The advice about attending to your audience's needs that we gave in earlier chapters still applies here. You may want to review that information.

CASE IN POINT 35

Choose a broad subject area. Narrow a research paper topic within this broad area by (1) asking questions based on the five writer's plans, (2) choosing a topic suggested by your answers to the questions, (3) free writing on the topic, and (4) focusing on one element of your free writing.

Stop here, unless your instructor tells you otherwise. You will have a chance to come back to this assignment later.

Preview Sources

There are two categories of information sources for research papers: *print* sources and *nonprint* sources. Sources that convey information through the medium of print, including books, magazines and journals, documents, microfiche and microfilm, and computer displays, are available in libraries. Nonprint sources, including films, tapes, and records, are either obtained from libraries or collected directly from the source of information. In this book our concern is helping you locate print sources in your college library.

The broad topic of print sources can be narrowed further to *primary* sources and *secondary* sources. Primary sources are writers' original creations, such as novels, poems, speeches, and government documents. Secondary sources are books and articles *about* primary sources—writings by recognized authorities about other people's work. For example, "Leda and the Swan" and "The Second Coming," two poems by the Irish poet William Butler Yeats, are primary sources. A. Norman Jeffare's *A Commentary on the Collected Poems of W. B. Yeats* and John Unterecker's *A Reader's Guide to William Butler Yeats* are secondary sources because in these books, Jeffare and Unterecker write about Yeats's poems. Most textbooks are also secondary sources since they consist largely of summaries of the work and discoveries of people other than the textbooks' authors. Some academic assignments call for the use of primary sources. For example, to write a comparison of two presidents' inauguration speeches, you would have to use primary sources, the two speeches themselves. But many research papers will be based chiefly on secondary sources. Notice that in researching African poetry, you would be limited to secondary sources unless you have access to tapes of the poets reciting their works, and you understand the languages they speak. It would be wrong to assume that primary sources are always superior to secondary sources. Inaccuracy, distortion, and error can appear in both primary and secondary sources. However, you should be careful to include primary sources if they are required by the assignment.

Familiarize yourself with the library. Knowing where to obtain an overview of your topic and locate the titles of useful sources gives you a good start on your research. General reference books, indexes, and the card catalogue are among the resources you can consult. You also have to know where to locate the sources themselves: on open shelves, in the stacks, at the reserve desk, in the periodicals room, or on microfiche and microfilm.

Reference Books.   Often the best place to begin your library search for sources is in the reference section. References are books you refer to for background information, including general overviews of a subject, definitions, geographical information, and dates. Start first with general reference books and then proceed to more specialized sources. General reference books include encyclopedias, dictionaries, almanacs, and atlases. You will find a degree of specialization even among these general references. For example, the *Encyclopedia of Educational Research* is an excellent general resource for students working on papers for education courses but less useful for work in other disciplines. Look over the full range of general references before you decide which ones to use. Do not rely on the first usable reference you find. A few minutes of searching may uncover general sources that will simplify tremendously your later research. A selection of these general references is listed below:

Encyclopedia Americana
Encyclopaedia Britannica
Collier's Encyclopedia
Facts on File Yearbook
The World Almanac and Book of Facts
International Encyclopedia of the Social Sciences
McGraw-Hill Encyclopedia of Science and Technology
Encyclopedia of Educational Research
Webster's Biographical Dictionary
Current Biography Yearbooks
Editorial Research Reports
Webster's New Collegiate Dictionary
Oxford English Dictionary
The Times Atlas of the World

General references are good starting places for research because they often indicate where you could look for more detailed information. For example, as you begin to search for information on the subject of African oral poetry, an encyclopedia article on African cultures will quickly show you that Africa contains many separate tribal groups, each of which has its own traditions and art forms. Thus, it might help to search for more detailed information under the names of the separate tribes as well as the general heading of African poetry. An encyclopedia will provide you with a list of the most important African tribes. Armed with general information on your subject, you will be able to make better use of other library resources.

CASE IN POINT 36

Go to your college library and use general references to obtain an overview of the topic you narrowed in Case 35. Write down any information that will help you in your search for detailed sources.

Stop here, unless your instructor tells you otherwise. You will have a chance to come back to this assignment later.

After you have obtained an overview of your topic, you next begin to list sources that may contain more detailed information. At this point, your search divides into two distinct branches: investigation of books and investigation of periodicals. This division is necessary because indexes, the references that catalogue sources of information, usually list either books or periodicals but not both. Depending upon the topic you are researching, you may decide to focus on either books or periodicals. For example, if you are writing about recent experimental work on gene splicing, you will probably find that current periodicals have the most up to date information. However, many topics will require you to research both books and periodicals. We will first discuss the indexes that help you locate information in books.

The Card Catalog.   The card catalog is the alphabetized listing of most of the materials the library contains. Although card catalogs may contain information on print and nonprint sources and on periodicals as well as books, we will focus in this section on the most common use of the catalog, locating books on specific subjects. Each source will have at least three different cards in the catalog: a subject card, a title card, and an author card. In some libraries there are three separate sets of card-catalog cabinets, one for each type of cards. Other libraries file all three types of cards together. These cards include a complete identification of the book and the *call number,* which indicates the book's location in the library. Imagine you are working on the African oral-poetry paper. On the basis of your overview of general references, you decide that the Bahima tribe may well have a strong oral tradition. Thus you look for information in the *subject index* under "Bahima." Your professor suggested a book entitled *Oral Literature in Africa,* so you look in the *title index* for this book. In addition, your course textbook quotes a man named Oyekan Owomoyela and refers to him as an expert on African literature. You look up Owomoyela's name in the *author index*. These three preliminary references lead you to three entries in the card catalog (see Figure 2).

Each catalog card contains the *call number* you will need to locate the book in the stacks. Call numbers are assigned according to one of two organizational schemes: the *Library of Congress* system and the *Dewey Decimal* system. Both of these systems group together books that deal with similar subjects. The catalog cards on the previous page have Library of Congress call numbers consisting of letters and numerals. Dewey Decimal call numbers have only numerals. When you locate a book in the card catalog, carefully copy the call number along with the title and author. Accurate work will help you avoid frustrating searches in the stacks for the wrong call number.

Even when you have the correct call number, you may find that the book you are looking for is not on the shelves. In most libraries, books circulate; students and professors may check them out. An individual may even check out the bulk of the library's collection on a given subject. Also, your library may loan books to other libraries, so the book you are searching for may be miles away,

---

Oral literature in Africa.

PL
8010
F5

Finnegan, Ruth H
 Oral literature in Africa, by, Ruth Finnegan. London, Clarendon P., 1970.

 xix, 558 p., fold. plate. map. 23 cm. index. (Oxford library of African literature) £5/-/-
                                                                                         B70-29902

 Bibliography: p. 552–536.
 I.–Folk literature. African–Africa. Sub-Saharan–History and criticism.   I.–Title.
PL–8010.F5   389'.0967   70-596309
 ISBN 0 19-815131-4
                                                                                         MARC

PL
8010
O97

Owomoyela, Oyekan.
 African literatures: an introduction
   /by Oyekan Owomoyela.—Waltham, Mass.:Crossroads Press, 1979.
   48 p.; 24 cm.—(The basic Africana library.)
 /Bibliography: p. 139–143.
 Includes index.

   1.–African literature—History and criticism.   2. Authors, African.   I.–Title

NII   25 APR 80 LRR   XIMMnc

Bahima (African People)

PL
8594
N3
M6

Morris, Henry Francis, *ed.*
  The heroic recitations of the Bahima of Ankole, by H. F. Morris. With a foreword by
A. T. Hatto, Oxford, Clarendon Press, 1964.
  xii, 142, 1, p. illus., geneal. table, maps. 23 cm. (Oxford library of African literature)
  Based on thesis, University of London in 1957, with title: The heroic recitations of the Ban-
yankore.
  In part, English or Runyankore.
  Bibliography: p. 143
  1.–Nyankole poetry 2.–Bahima (African people) 3.–Nyankole language.   I.–Title.
  PL8594.N3M6   896.3   64-5119 rev

Figure 2

even in another town. Near the end of the semester, books may be particularly hard to find since many students are trying to do research at the same time. Obviously, it pays to begin your research as early as possible. An early start ensures that you will find the books you need on the shelves and gives you time to recall books that have been borrowed or to arrange to use other libraries. Never count on using a source until you have it in your hands. The catalog only reflects a library's potential, not what it can actually deliver at a given time.

Since both the Library of Congress and the Dewey Decimal systems arrange books according to subject matter, you can often find a number of books on a given subject grouped together on the shelves. For example, all three books on African poetry described on the sample catalog cards are located within a few feet of each other in our college library. By tracking down just one of these books, our students can find the other two simply by browsing through the nearby shelves. Of course, this technique will not necessarily guide you to all of the books on African poetry. The separate sections of the library devoted to literature, history, and sociology may each have books that discuss African poetry, and these separate collections may be shelved far apart from each other. Never assume that one section of the library will have all the books on a given subject.

Your library will have a listing of the range of call numbers for particular topic areas. The *Library of Congress Subject Headings* contains hundreds of pages of very specific topic areas and their related call numbers. Figure 3 shows one section of the Library of Congress index containing entries related to African poetry.

Periodicals. In addition to locating full-length books for your paper, you will also want to search for information in periodicals. Periodicals, which are published at regular intervals (daily, weekly, monthly) offer more recent, more up to date information than you will find in books. The major periodicals you will use for college papers are general-interest magazines, specialized and scholarly journals, and newspapers. The most efficient way to find articles on your topic is to consult *periodical indexes*. These indexes are of two major types: indexes to general-interest publications such as the *New York Times* and *Newsweek* and indexes to special-interest publications such as *Quarterly Journal of Experimental Psychology*. We have listed a sampling of indexes below. Your reference librarian will help you locate others.

Indexes to General Interest Publications

Reader's Guide to Periodical Literature	*General Science Index*
Popular Periodical Index	*Humanities Index*
New York Times Index	*Social Science Index*
Wall Street Journal Index	*Business Periodicals Index*
Washington Post Index	*Psychological Abstracts*

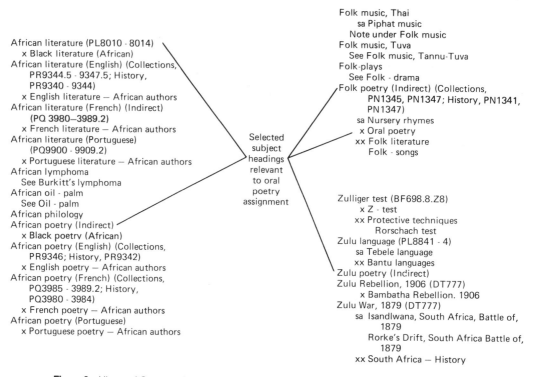

African literature (PL8010 - 8014)
    x Black literature (African)
African literature (English) (Collections,
    PR9344.5 - 9347.5; History,
    PR9340 - 9344)
    x English literature — African authors
African literature (French) (Indirect)
    (PQ 3980–3989.2)
    x French literature — African authors
African literature (Portuguese)
    (PQ9900 - 9909.2)
    x Portuguese literature — African authors
African lymphoma
    See Burkitt's lymphoma
African oil - palm
    See Oil - palm
African philology
African poetry (Indirect)
    x Black poetry (African)
African poetry (English) (Collections,
    PR9346; History, PR9342)
    x English poetry — African authors
African poetry (French) (Collections,
    PQ3985 - 3989.2; History,
    PQ3980 - 3984)
    x French poetry — African authors
African poetry (Portuguese)
    x Portuguese poetry — African authors

Selected
subject
headings
relevant
to oral
poetry
assignment

Folk music, Thai
    sa Piphat music
    Note under Folk music
Folk music, Tuva
    See Folk music, Tannu-Tuva
Folk-plays
    See Folk - drama
Folk poetry (Indirect) (Collections,
    PN1345, PN1347; History, PN1341,
    PN1347)
    sa Nursery rhymes
    x Oral poetry
    xx Folk literature
    Folk - songs

Zulliger test (BF698.8.Z8)
    x Z - test
    xx Protective techniques
    Rorschach test
Zulu language (PL8841 - 4)
    sa Tebele language
    xx Bantu languages
Zulu poetry (Indirect)
Zulu Rebellion, 1906 (DT777)
    x Bambatha Rebellion. 1906
Zulu War, 1879 (DT777)
    sa Isandlwana, South Africa, Battle of,
        1879
    Rorke's Drift, South Africa Battle of,
        1879
    xx South Africa — History

Figure 3 *Library of Congress Subject Headings.*
(From Library of Congress. *Library of Congress Subject Headings.* 9th ed. Washington, D.C.:
Government Printing Office 1980.)

In general, these indexes list articles from periodicals by subject area.
For instance, under the heading "African Poetry," the *Reader's Guide to Periodical Literature* for March 1968 to February 1969 lists an article with the title "Poetry Without Letters" that sounds like a promising source for the paper assignment discussed earlier. The *Reader's Guide* provides you with information on this article (see Figure 4).

In addition to listing article titles, some indexes include *abstracts,* short summaries of the articles. The *New York Times Index* contains abstracts of newspaper articles along with titles and authors. Specialized indexes contain articles on given subject areas. Consult your reference librarian for suggestions as to which indexes can help you the most with a particular assignment.

After you gather titles of articles concerning your topic, your next step is to locate these sources in your library. Before you look up magazines, journals, or newspapers in your card catalog, use your library's listing of periodical holdings. In some libraries this listing is called the *serials catalog.* Either the serials catalog or the card catalog will give you the call number of the periodical you

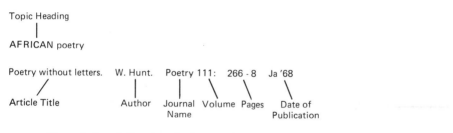

Figure 4 *Sample Entry from the Reader's Guide to Periodical Literature.*
(From the *Reader's Guide to Periodical Literature.* New York: H.W. Wilson, 1969.)

are trying to find. Often recent issues of journals and newspapers are displayed on open shelves whereas older issues are either bound in book form or stored on microfilm or microfiche.

Other Resources. In addition to reference books, card catalogs, and indexes, there are numerous other resources you can use when you are looking for sources. Listed below is a sampling of these resources. Be sure to ask your reference librarian to help you locate these and additional aids.

Editorials on File
American Statistics Index
Book Review Digest
ERIC (Articles related to education)
Pamphlet indexes
Government documents (*Congressional Record,* etc.)
Computer databases (automated searches of a number of computerized indexes)

EXERCISE 33

This exercise will give you practice locating source materials for a research topic. Choose one of the topics listed below and perform your library search as follows:

1. Start in the reference section of the library. Locate a general reference book that contains information about your topic. Record the page numbers and facts of publication (Review Chapter 12, pp. 176–77 if necessary).

2. Proceed to the card catalog. Locate entries for two books related to your topic. Record bibliographic information.

3. Consult a periodical index. Locate two entries for articles on your topic. Record bibliographic information.

TOPICS

Swahili	Silent films
Boston Massacre	Cybernetics
Criminal law	Woody Allen
American dialects	Hallucination
Jewish literature	Civil rights
Surrealism	Stonehenge
Musical comedy	American working women
Photojournalism	Choreography
The New Deal	Folklore
Harlem Renaissance	Aerodynamics
Atlantis	Genetic codes

CASE IN POINT 37

Use the information you obtained from general references in Case 36 to decide on subject headings and names of specific books and authors that are relevant to the topic you narrowed in Case 35. With this information go to the card catalog, indexes, and other resources and produce a list of potential sources for your research paper. Make sure you record the call number for books and the dates and page numbers for journal and magazine articles.

Stop here, unless your instructor tells you otherwise. You will have a chance to come back to this assignment later.

Once you have done an overview of your topic, obtained the titles of books and articles, and located the source materials in your library, review your narrowed topic. Does the material you have located seem relevant to your topic? Mark the sources that appear most useful and look for these first. If the majority of the sources you collected do not seem directly relevant to your narrowed topic, you will have to either search for additional sources or rethink your topic choice. If you decide to revise your topic, look carefully through the titles of the sources you have found. Often this procedure will suggest new ways to narrow the topic so that you can take advantage of the sources you have already located. Take care that there is a close correspondence between the content of your sources and the narrowed topic. It is easy to fall into the trap of trying to use information that is interesting but not directly relevant.

The next step is to preview each of the sources that you marked as clearly related to your topic. Ask the same general preview questions you have used throughout this book:

1. What is the title?
2. Who is (are) the author(s)?
3. What are the major subdivisions?
4. If there are study aids, what do they tell you about the content?
5. Can you make connections between the topic and the ideas in the source?

Set Goals for Reading

Last, before you begin your close reading, decide what you want to accomplish. Ask yourself the same goal-directed questions you have used throughout this book:

1. What do you expect to learn from the source?
2. What clues will help you to find the information you want?
3. Will you read all of the source or only the parts of the source that are relevant to your topic?

In addition, ask:

1. How will you present relevant source material to your audience—as paraphrases, summaries, or direct quotations?
2. Which parts of the source will you react to, and which parts will you review analytically?

CLOSE READING

Use the Academic Writing Strategies

Depending on the nature of the source material, you will paraphrase, summarize, react, review, or quote and take notes accordingly. Thus, as you read through the sources, you will be employing all of the academic reading and writing strategies you have practiced in this book. You may find it efficient to write your notes on cards or separate sheets of paper. To refresh your memory, let us recapitulate the close-reading, note-taking strategies.

Paraphrase

1. Jot down a loose paraphrase.
2. Substitute synonyms for words in the original source.
3. Change the sentence structure.
4. Change the order of ideas.
5. Break long sentences into shorter ones.
6. Make abstract ideas concrete.
7. Compare your final paraphrase to your loose paraphrase and to the original.

Creativity of African poets — from Finnegan   page 21

The creativity of the individual artist is important in African oral poetry even though the poetry is based on a tradition.

paraphrase

Summarize

1. Formulate the gist (sentence kernel and writer's purpose) of sentences you will summarize and the gist (topic sentence and writer's plan) of paragraphs you will summarize.

Why oral poetry differs from written poetry   — from Ong — thesis of entire book

Literacy has changed the thought processes of human beings in important ways. Thus the artistic products, including poetry, of preliterate cultures are different in fundamental ways from those of literate cultures.

summary

2. Determine the thesis and organizational format of longer passages.

3. Formulate summary-synthesis sentences of paragraphs, and connect the sentences with organizational signals to form a precis.

React

1. Combine the source ideas with preexisting ideas from your store of knowledge and experience. Carry on a dialogue with the author; agree or disagree; recall a previous association; ask or answer a question; express satisfaction or dissatisfaction; approve or disapprove.

2. Expand or speculate on the source ideas: recall a personal vicarious, or hypothetical incident or dramatized scenario; provide additional details, examples, and elaborations; ask questions about the direct consequence of the source ideas; draw personal implications from the ideas; assume a role and apply the ideas to a new situation.

```
Common example of                    - from Lord,
oral tradition                              pages 3-29


        The Yugoslavian oral poets Lord
    describes seem like the medieval
    minstrels I read about in high school.
    Both sing long stories as a source of
    entertainment for an illiterate audience.

                                        reaction
```

Review

1. What is the author's intended audience?

2. What are the author's objectives?

3. What assumptions does the author make?

4. Which particular aspects of the topic does the author emphasize?

5. What do the ideas, evidence, or explanations in the source suggest or prove?

6. How do the ideas in the source interact with those in other sources?

7. How can the author's ideas be used or applied?

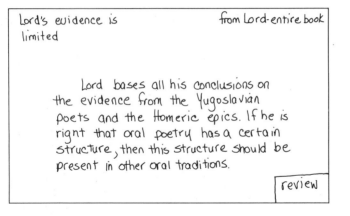

Lord's evidence is   from Lord-entire book
limited

         Lord bases all his conclusions on
the evidence from the Yugoslavian
poets and the Homeric epics. If he is
right that oral poetry has a certain
structure, then this structure should be
present in other oral traditions.

                                     review

Quote

1. Copy direct quotations accurately and punctuate them properly.
2. Write down sufficient background information to provide context for quotations.

illustration of praise-   -from Morris,
names in African poetry   Page 23

         "He Who Does Not Turn His Back
         On the Cattle".

shows that praise-names describe a
single personality characteristic.

                                  quotation

Record Necessary Bibliographic Information

For each source that you read and respond to using one or several close-reading strategies, copy the facts of publication in the order your document style specifies. (Consult Chapter 12 for explanations of the MLA style and the APA style). You will need this information for the works-cited or references page at the end of your paper.

EXERCISE 34

This exercise will enable you to review the 5 Rs and to practice writing note cards and identifying other writers' uses of the five academic writing strategies.

1. Reread Mehrabian's article "Communication without Words" in Appendix B and make ten note cards on the information in the article. Be sure to include at least one note card of each academic writing type. Write the type of academic writing strategy you use on the back of the note card.
2. Shuffle your cards and exchange them with another student. Read each card and identify the academic writing strategy used (without turning over the cards). You may want to match the card against the article.
3. Check your identifications by reading the notation on the back of each card.

CASE IN POINT 38

In Case 37 you wrote out a list of sources (books, magazines, journals, newspapers) that appeared relevant to your research-paper topic. Locate these sources in your library starting with the ones that seem most significant. Preview each source and set your goals for reading. As you read closely, write note cards for all information that you think you can use in your paper. Pattern your note cards after the samples in this chapter.

Stop here, unless your instructor tells you otherwise. You will have a chance to come back to this assignment later.

POSTREADING/PREWRITING

Reread the Assignment and Develop a Preliminary Thesis

After you have collected information on your narrowed topic, you are ready to come up with a preliminary thesis or main idea for your paper. There are three steps in this process:

Write down a generalization that sums up your research findings.

Read over your research note cards.

Refine the generalization so it fits more closely with the specific information you have collected.

For example, assume that you have narrowed the assignment discussed earlier to a comparison between the characteristics of oral and written poetry. In class your professor mentioned some of the unique qualities of Yugoslavian oral poetry that are mentioned in Albert Lord's *The Singer of Tales.* You refer to Lord's book first to get a precise idea of how he compares oral and written poetry. Then you explore general references for information on oral poetic traditions other than the one studied by Lord. These references guide you to a number of sources, which you then preview. You select some of these sources for close reading. When your close reading is complete, you reread the assignment and work on your preliminary thesis. First, you note that the sources you read on specific oral traditions mentioned characteristics similar to those Lord identified in Yugoslavian poetry. Thus you *generalize* that oral poetry does differ significantly from written poetry. Second, you *read over your note cards.* You notice that although you were able to collect information on oral traditions from several parts of the world, the bulk of your information is on African oral traditions. Finally, you decide to focus on how the information on African oral traditions supports Lord's theory. You write down the following *preliminary thesis:*

> A variety of African poetic traditions have characteristics similar to those found in Yugoslavian oral poetry suggesting that the differences between oral and written poetry are universal.

Note that this is a *preliminary* thesis. As you engage in writing the paper, new thoughts may occur to you that will cause you to revise the thesis. Writing assists your thinking, and you should take advantage of the ideas generated as you write rather than clinging to your initial thoughts.

Reconsider Your Audience

After you arrive at a preliminary thesis, read through your note cards once again to see if you have enough facts to provide your audience with sufficient background to understand your thesis. Since you have read or at least skimmed the original sources, you understand the overall *context* into which the preliminary thesis fits. Now ask yourself whether the information in your notes will give your audience an adequate understanding of this context. If you have not recorded enough information to make your audience understand your thesis, you may need to go back to the original sources and take more notes or even locate entirely new sources. You can write additional background information on the back of your note cards.

CASE IN POINT 39

Read over your narrowed research-paper topic and the original paper assignment. Then work through the three steps for developing a preliminary thesis.

Write down a generalization that sums up your research findings.

Read over your research note cards.

Refine the generalization so it fits more closely with the specific information you collected.

Check your notecards to make sure that you have enough facts to provide your audience with sufficient background to understand your thesis.

Stop here, unless your instructor tells you otherwise. You will have a chance to come back to this assignment later.

chapter 14

Writing and Revising the Research Paper

WRITING: OUTLINE YOUR IDEAS

When you are composing three-to-five-page essays, you can often decide on a specific writer's plan and then write a first draft directly from your notes and source annotations. However, you cannot write a research paper directly from your note cards. You need an *outline* to guide your writing. The outline provides the pattern you will overlay on the paraphrases, summaries, quotations, reactions, and analyses that you recorded on note cards. In writing an outline, you are forming the master plan for your paper.

Unfortunately, some students think of an outline only as a finished product and ignore the value of the process of outlining. Students concentrate so much on the form of the outline that the content becomes secondary. In extreme cases the students who are required to turn in outlines with their research papers actually produce the outline after the paper is completed. Constructing an outline should help you to clarify thinking, see relationships between ideas, and organize information. The first draft of your paper grows out of the organizational pattern that you establish as you work on your outline. In short, outlining should be thinking on paper rather than forcing your ideas into a rigid structure.

To outline your paper, use the procedure described on the following pages.

1. Reread your preliminary thesis and write it at the top of your outline page.
2. Group your note cards according to an organizational plan.
3. Look for connections between the ideas on individual note cards and the general categories in which they are grouped.
4. Pick an appropriate outline form and represent graphically the structure of your paper.

Reread Your Preliminary Thesis and Write It at the Top of Your Outline Page

The thesis provides the focus for the entire paper. Thus you must periodically refer back to the thesis as you organize the material you collected. If you find that you are beginning to develop a plan that does not fit with your thesis, you must either alter the plan or revise the preliminary thesis. By the time you complete your outline, the thesis and your organizational plan must work together.

As an example, we will return to the assignment on oral poetry that we discussed in Chapter 13. Recall the preliminary thesis that we arrived at near the end of the chapter:

A variety of African poetic traditions have characteristics similar to those found in Yugoslavian oral poetry suggesting that the differences between oral and written poetry are universal.

As you work to develop your outline, you must keep this thesis in mind.

Group your Note Cards According to an Organizational Plan

As we discussed in Chapter 13, evidence from several different African tribes supports Lord's theory. You could organize this information according to the name of the particular cultures or according to the separate differences between oral and written poetry that Lord mentions. These two organizational schemes are represented in figures 5 and 6.

The second diagram is a better pattern for the paper since it centers on the differences between oral and written poetry, the same issue raised in the thesis. After choosing this pattern, you next group the note cards according to the differences between oral and written poetry that Lord mentions. You have one pile for the social role of poetry, another pile for structure of poetry, and so on. If during this process you find that a lot of your note cards do not fit into

Thesis
|
Characteristics of modern written poetry
|
Characteristics of Yugoslavian oral poetry
|
Characteristics of Bahima oral poetry
|
Characteristics of Zulu oral poetry
|
Characteristics of Sotho oral poetry
|
Characteristics of Bantu oral poetry
|
Characteristics of Tswana oral poetry
|
Characteristics of Dinka oral poetry
|
Characteristics of Hausa oral poetry
|
Characteristics of Basotho oral poetry
|
Characteristics of Swahili oral poetry
|
Characteristics of Ethiopian oral poetry
|
Characteristics of oral traditions in general

Figure 5 An organizational scheme for research data.

the categories you established, you will need to try out another organizational pattern.

When there is no obvious way to sort the information on the note cards, try to use patterns based on the writer's plans we discussed earlier in this book. Recall that these writer's plans include the following: antecendent/consequent, comparison, response, description, and time order.

Notice that the organizational pattern selected for the African poetry paper is a comparison plan. The characteristics Lord identified in Yugoslavian poetry are compared to the characteristics of African oral poetry. Often the pattern that fits best with the information on your note cards will be one of these writer's plans.

Look for Connections Between the Ideas on Individual Note Cards and the General Categories in Which They Are Grouped

Next you look for connections between the ideas on note cards and the general category in which they are grouped. Figure 7 shows the types of connections you will often find.

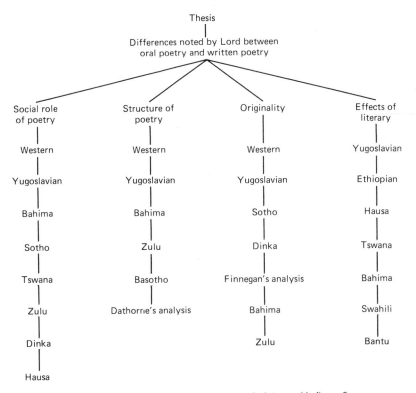

Figure 6 Another organizational scheme for the research data used in figure 5.

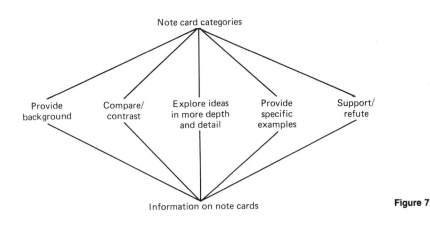

Figure 7

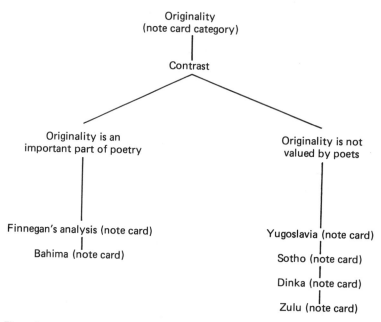

Figure 8

Figure 8 shows connections you were able to make between the ideas on your note cards and the category that concerns attitudes toward poetic originality.

Pick an Appropriate Outline Form That Represents the Structure of Your Paper

Finally, you construct an outline on paper that reflects your plan. Your professor may require that you use the traditional outline format. This format uses a set sequence of numerals and letters to show the relative importance of ideas and the relationships between ideas. The most important issues or the broadest generalizations in your paper are labeled with capitalized Roman numerals. The next most important pieces of information are grouped underneath the upper-level items and are labeled with capitalized letters. All the levels of embedding are shown below:

I.
  A.
    1.
      a.
        i.

Your professor may ask for a brief outline without much detail or may require an outline that contains all of the major pieces of information you intend to present. Examples of both a general and a detailed outline of the paper on African poetry follow.

GENERAL OUTLINE

Thesis: A variety of African poetic traditions have characteristics similar to those found in Yugoslavian oral poetry suggesting that the differences between oral and written poetry are universal.

I. Oral vs. written poetry
   A. Defining an oral poetic tradition
   B. Albert Lord's comparison of oral and written poetry
II. Role of poetry in society
   A. Poetry more prevalent in Yugoslavia than in Western culture
   B. Poetry widespread in African cultures
III. Structure of poems
   A. Yugoslavian poetry has a non-Western formulaic structure
   B. African poetry has formulaic structure
IV. Attitudes toward originality
   A. Yugoslavian poets do not value creativity as do Western poets
   B. African attitudes toward originality vary
V. Effects of literacy on oral poetry
   A. Literacy destroys abilities of Yugoslavian poets
   B. African evidence contradictory
VI. Further study of oral traditions needed
   A. There are universal differences between oral and written poetry
   B. Cause for differences is unclear

DETAILED OUTLINE

Thesis: A variety of African poetic traditions have characteristics similar to those found in Yugoslavian oral poetry suggesting that the differences between oral and written poetry are universal.

I. Oral vs. written poetry
   A. Defining an oral poetic tradition
   B. Albert Lord's comparison of oral and written poetry
II. Role of poetry in society
   A. Poetry more prevalent in Yugoslavia than in Western culture
   B. Poetry widespread in African cultures
     1. Bahima: all men composed and delivered poems
     2. Sotho: all men composed and delivered poems
     3. Tswana: all men memorized and composed poems
     4. Zulu: performance common by professional and amateur poets
     5. Dinka: each individual owns personal poetry
     6. Hausa: individuals own personal poetry

III. Structure of poems
    A. Yugoslavian poetry has a non-Western formulaic structure
    B. African poetry has formulaic structure
        1. Bahima: stereotyped phrases
        2. Zulu: formulaic praise names
        3. Basotho: formulae used for historical information
        4. Dathorne's analysis of African poetry
IV. Attitudes toward originality
    A. Yugoslavian poets do not value creativity as do Western poets
    B. African attitudes toward originality vary
        1. Originality important
            a. Finnegan's analysis of African poetry
            b. Bahima: novelty of poetry valued
        2. Non-Western attitudes toward originality
            a. Sotho: great poets quickly forgotten
            b. Dinka: poetry not owned by composer
            c. Zulu: praise name outlasts the composer
V. Effects of literacy on oral poetry
    A. Literacy destroys abilities of Yugoslavian poets
    B. African evidence contradictory
        1. Literacy destroys oral poetic ability
            a. Bahima: education interferes with oral poetry
            b. Tswana: schooling destroys poetic abilities
            c. Bantu: literacy discourages oral tradition
        2. Oral poetry and literacy coexist
            a. Swahili: Coexistence for centuries
            b. Ethiopian religious poetry coexists with literacy
            c. Hausa: writing preserves oral tradition
VI. Further study of oral traditions needed
    A. There are universal differences between oral and written poetry
    B. Cause for differences is unclear

If your professor does not specifically request traditional outline format, you should use whichever graphic representation best shows your organizational plan. Remember that the purpose of the outline is to help you think about your topic systematically and to guide you as you write the first draft. Do not force your paper into an outline format that is not suitable. For the paper on oral poetry, your outline could just as well be a tree structure similar to the one presented during the discussion of organizing note cards. If you have no formal requirements, use the outline format that helps you get the best overview of your writing. You may even try several different forms of outlining if the subject matter is particularly confusing.

CASE IN POINT 40

Using the note cards you wrote in Case 38 and the thesis you developed in Case 39, produce an outline for your paper by following the steps just described:

    1. Reread your preliminary thesis and write it at the top of your outline page.

2. Group your note cards according to an organizational plan.

3. Look for connections between the ideas on individual note cards and the general categories in which they are grouped.

4. Pick an appropriate outline form that represents the structure of your paper.

Stop here, unless your instructor tells you otherwise. You will have a chance to come back to this assignment later.

WRITING THE ROUGH DRAFT

As you begin to write your paper, you will find yourself juggling a number of materials: five different types of source notes (paraphrases, summaries, reactions, reviews, and quotations), an outline, works-cited cards, and in some cases the individual sources themselves. Although this process sounds complicated, your work in earlier parts of this book has prepared you for the task. As you write the rough draft of your paper, you will draw on all your academic writing skills and may need to refer back to earlier sections of this book.

Weaving Paraphrases, Summaries, Reactions, Reviews, and Quotations into your Paper

Rephrased and Repeated Information.   Provide your audience with sufficient background information and context for your paraphrases and quotations. Remember to put the author's name in parentheses or include it as part of the sentence. As we discussed in Chapter 12, you may cite the author's name *before, during,* or *after* the paraphrase or quotation.

As we pointed out in Chapter 12, it is important to provide transitions between your ideas and ideas from sources. If you have difficulty thinking of ways to lead in to a source and acknowledge an author, be sure to refer to the *lead-ins* suggested in Chapter 12.

Reduced Information.   The summaries you will incorporate into your research paper are the *component* type. You will rarely use freestanding summaries or lengthy précis in research papers. Remember to write a summary that is audience based rather than writer based. If your paper relies heavily on summaries, you may want to refresh your memory by rereading chapters 4, 5, and 6.

Reactions to Source Information.   Recall that reactions are not acceptable in all academic assignments. Check with your professor about the appropriateness of including reactions in the type of research paper you are writing. If you do include reactions to sources, be sure to avoid giving uninformed opinions and expressing unfair bias. Also be aware of the limits of your experience.

Reviews of Sources. Your critical analysis of the sources, that is, your answers to the seven analysis questions used in writing reviews, will figure highly in your research paper. Recall that you should not merely list the various parts of your analysis but rather should establish a pattern of relationships among them so that they will work together. You may find it useful to review the methods of connecting and ordering analytical thoughts that we presented in Chapter 10.

A Word About Titles, Introductions, Conclusions, References, and Content Notes

Titles. A research paper should have a title appropriate to its content. A title should be as descriptive as possible but very brief. As a rule of thumb, shorten titles that run over ten words. Make the title interesting, but don't disguise the subject of the paper in an effort to have an unusual title.

Introductions and Conclusions. Chapter 8 contains a series of suggestions for paper openers and conclusions you can use as you work on your research paper. Since a research paper is lengthy and complex, it is important to develop your introduction and conclusion in a way that will help your audience understand the overall point of your discussion. It is easy to get lost in the details of a research paper if the main point is not highlighted. The thesis must be clearly stated in the introduction, and the main points developed in the paper should be reviewed in the conclusion. Make sure that the introduction and conclusion are in harmony with each other and with the ideas in the body of the paper. The introduction of a research paper is a promise of what you intend to deliver in the paper, and you must make good on the commitment.

References and Content Notes. Closely follow the directions given in Chapter 12 for handling references and content notes. Make sure you ask your professor what documentation style is required for the paper. Do not assume that the MLA style can be used in all situations. The APA style or another style specific to a particular field of study may be required for your course.

CASE IN POINT 41

Write a rough draft of the paper you outlined in Case 40. Make sure that you use the appropriate methods for weaving paraphrases, summaries, quotations, reactions, and reviews into your paper. Provide an introduction, conclusion, and title.

Stop here, unless your instructor tells you otherwise. You will have a chance to come back to this assignment later.

On the following pages is a completed draft of the paper on oral poetry. Notice how the student has used all the various aspects of academic writing that have been covered in this book.

Differences Between Oral and Written Poetry:
Evidence from African Cultures

by
Samuel Jones

Foundations of Writing
Dr. Meyer
April 18, 1984

In modern Western culture, we think of poetry as written verse. We experience poetry by reading it to ourselves or occasionally by hearing someone else read it out loud. However, certain poetic traditions do not depend on reading or writing. A familiar example is the wandering minstrel of the Middle Ages who entertained his largely illiterate audiences with verse he composed orally or learned from the performances of other minstrels. Societies still exist in which poets who do not read and write compose and perform oral poetry (Owomoyela 1–21). Certain scholars claim that the form of this orally produced poetry distinguishes it from poetry created through writing (Havelock; McLuhan; Ong). Studies done of traditional poetic forms do show that oral poetry differs significantly from written poetry. These differences have been well documented in the case of Yugoslavian oral poetry (Lord). A variety of African poetic traditions have characteristics similar to those found in Yugoslavian poetry suggesting that the differences between oral and written poetry are universal.

The best-known study and analysis of traditional oral poetry was conducted by Albert Lord and Milman Perry. During the 1930s Perry studied and recorded the poetic songs of illiterate Moslems in rural Yugoslavia. In his book *The Singer of Tales,* Lord summarizes Perry's collection of songs and notes similarities between these songs and *The Iliad* and *The Odyssey.* Lord maintains that these ancient Greek epics were the products of an oral tradition rather than the independent work of the poet Homer. Lord concludes that verse from an oral culture has characteristics that will distinguish it from poetry written in a literate culture. Although Lord considers only Yugoslavian and Greek poetry, these are not the only oral poetic traditions. The distinctive features Lord identifies can also be found in African verse.

One of the most obvious differences between oral and written poetry involves their respective roles in society. In modern Western society relatively few people write or read poetry. However, Lord explains that recitation of long epic poems was a common form of entertainment in the Moslem Yugoslavian culture (11–17). The poems were usually sung, often to the accompaniment of a musical instrument. Although special attention was given to poetry during festivals and holidays, poems were performed regularly in coffee houses and in gatherings at homes.

There are a number of African cultures in which the performance of oral poetry is as widespread as it was among the Moslems of Yugoslavia. In the Bahima tribe of Uganda, all respectable men were expected to be able to compose and deliver praise-poems, which typically ran close to 100 lines in length (Morris 13). A similar tradition existed among the Sotho of South Africa (Damane and Saunders 18–33). The Tswana of South Africa assumed that every man would be familiar with the art of memorizing and composing poetry (Schapera 2). Although the Zulus maintained professional poets, performances by nonprofessionals were common (Cope 27–28). In the Dinka tribe of the Sudan, every individual owned a personal poetic song that only he or she could perform (Deng 78). All Hausa owned personal songs (Scharfe and Aliyu 34). Although there were few African cultures in which poems as long as the Yugoslavian epics were performed, poetic performances were more common than they are now in literate societies. Oral poetry was as integral a part of life in Africa as it was in rural Yugoslavia.

The structure of written poetry is determined largely by the poet. Although there are set structural forms, such as the sonnet, the modern poet has freedom to use any organizational or rhythmic scheme. Lord claims that oral poetry always had a "formulaic" structure (30–67). By this he means that the verse was shaped around a set structure, the story line, that was filled in largely with readymade expressions, the formulae. Each formula conveyed a specific idea and fit into a particular rhythmic pattern. Lord maintains that the formulaic structure eliminated the necessity of memorizing long poems word for word. If a poet knew a general story line and had a stock of poetic formulae with meanings appropriate to the story, he could fit the formulae into the structure of the story as he sang. Thus, he could perform a poem without learning the exact words of a prior version. An experienced poet was able to perform for hours without any prompt or memory aid. Naturally, each version of the poem varied somewhat since several different formulae could fit into the same slot in a given poem. Lord sees the use of the formula as the characteristic that is most typical of oral poetry and that clearly distinguishes it from written poetry.

Formulae similar to those described by Lord were found in African poetry. As Dathorne points out in his characterization of the African oral poet, "His repertoire was composed of archetypes that suited a variety of situations and experiences" (64). The formulaic structure was most obvious in praise poems. In this once common African poetic form, certain stock phrases reappeared again and again. Morris notes that among the Bahima, the praise poems were composed of little else but these stereotyped phrases (25). Each male Bahima had one or more of these phrases or praise names, which were used to refer to him in all tribal poems (22). These praise names usually described a single personality characteristic such as "He Who Does Not Turn His Back On the Cattle" or "He Who Is of Iron" (23). The Bahima poets also used stock poetic phrases as substitutes for common nouns. Guns were referred to as "the strikers of elephants" (26). Cope reports that Zulu court poets remembered long lists of past rulers' praise names and wove these praise names into the story lines of long poems (25–27). Kunene notes that formulaic praise names were used in the Basotho oral tradition to help recall specific deeds of individuals who lived in the past (13–20). Thus, African poets used formulaic structures similar to those found in the Yugoslavian oral tradition.

In modern Western society, the quality and value of poetry is determined largely by its originality. According to Lord, Yugoslavian singers report that they always tried to reproduce traditional songs exactly as they learned them (28). Although a singer created a new version of a song for each performance, from the singer's point of view the song never changed from version to version (99). Lord feels that the idea of originality makes sense only to those who have lived in a culture where writing and reading are widespread. Unlike our Western notion of the poet as a lone creative artist, the Yugoslavian oral poet saw himself as the means for conveying a tradition that existed before he was born. Although he might take pride in his ability to perform the poems well, he would not claim authorship (28). The singers always learned songs from other artists and did not acknowledge their own creative contributions to this tradition (13–29).

African attitudes toward originality are not as clear-cut as those among the Yugoslavian oral poets. There is at least some evidence that originality is a very important part of African poetic traditions. In her survey of African oral literature, Finnegan points out that even though African poetry was based on tradition, the creativity of the individual artist was very important (21). Morris states that the chief criterion by which the Bahima judged praise poems was the novelty of the formulaic phrases that the poets devised (25). The Bahima searched for unusual metaphors to use in their poetry. For example, the phrase "He Who Has Not Got Elephantiasis" was used to signify agility (25). Even in Bahima poems that described battles, the actual plot was considered of less importance than the uniqueness of the praise names (13). But still, in some African tribes, attitudes toward originality were very different from what they are in modern Western society. Often, a formulaic praise name was thought to be the property not of the composer but rather of the person it described. According to Deng, each of the Dinka owned a personal song, which only he or she could perform in public. But these personal songs could be composed by a song specialist as well as by the owner of the song. Employing an expert to do the job did not make the song any less the sole possession of the person it described (78). Clearly, this attitude diminishes the importance of the poet's creativity. Damane and Sanders note the speed with which the names of highly regarded poets were forgotten among the Sotho (23). In his discussion of how quickly the Zulu forgot the names of professional poets, Cope remarks, "It is significant that the remembrance of the praise long outlasts that of the praiser" (24). Thus, although the African poets did compose creatively, there is some evidence that they had a non-Western attitude toward originality. However, the African traditions did seem to value unique composition more than the Yugoslavian tradition did.

Lord argues that oral and written poetry not only are different but cannot coexist within a single culture. He maintains that learning to read and write will necessarily destroy the abilities of an oral poet. According to his analysis, literacy virtually wiped out the Yugoslavian oral tradition (124–38). If the introduction of literacy does indeed wipe out a culture's oral tradition, then this would indicate some very basic differences between the two forms.

While there is some evidence that literacy has disrupted African oral traditions, there were also situations in which both oral and written art forms existed. Morris reports that educated members of the Bahima tribe were usually unable to understand the traditional praise poems even though the unschooled Bahima continued to enjoy this oral poetry. Morris feels that the educated Bahima lost contact with the traditional vocabulary of praise poems and also developed Western patterns of thought that interfered with the traditional imagery (26). According to

Schapera, westernized Tswana had similar problems understanding the praise poems in their own oral tradition (1–42). Lestrade suggests that contact with Western culture dramatically reduced interest among the Bantu in their oral tradition (122–24). However, the Swahili oral tradition coexisted with literacy for centuries (Harries). Although an alphabet was used in Ethiopia as early as the fourth century A.D., a tradition of oral religious poetry continued into the twentieth century (Gerard 273–75). Scharfe and Aliyu in their analysis of the relationship between the oral and written poetry of the Hausa maintain that the principal effect of literacy was actually to preserve the oral tradition. They describe the literate Hausa poet as "an oral poet who has learned to write" (36). These data suggest that literacy may affect oral traditions but does not necessarily destroy them.

The Yugoslavian and the African oral poetic traditions do share common differences with modern Western poetry. The social role of poetry in Yugoslavia and Africa and the formulaic structure of the verse clearly distinguish these traditions from written poetry. Lord's theory that oral poets do not value originality is not fully supported by the African evidence, but traditional African attitudes toward originality are non-Western in several respects. If we accept that oral and written poetry are fundamentally different, it is logical to ask why these differences exist. We have seen that the formulaic structure is useful to oral poets because it helps them recall information. McLuhan and Ong suggest that literacy has profound effects upon the way that people think about the world, their culture, and their art forms. The distinct characteristics of oral poetry may reflect the form of an efficient memory system, the type of thought processes produced by an oral culture, or both of these factors. Lord's contention that literacy destroys oral poetic ability supports the notion that basic thought processes change with the introduction of literacy. However, the African evidence does not clearly show how literacy affects oral traditions. It is undoubtedly hard to separate the effects of literacy from those of other cultural changes that result from contact between traditional and modern societies. Thus, even though it does seem that oral and traditional societies are fundamentally different, the reason for this difference still needs further investigation.

Works Cited

Cope, Trevor. <u>Izibongo: Zulu Praise-Poems.</u> London: University Press, 1968.

Damane, M., and P. B. Saunders. <u>Lithoko Sotho Praise-Poems.</u> London: Oxford University Press, 1974.

Dathorne, O. R. <u>The Black Mind.</u> Minneapolis: University of Minnesota Press, 1974.

Deng, F. M. <u>The Dinka and Their Songs.</u> London: Oxford University Press, 1973.

Finnegan, Ruth. <u>Oral Literature in Africa.</u> London: Oxford University Press, 1970.

Gerard, Albert S. <u>Four African Literatures.</u> Berkeley: University of California Press, 1971.

Harries, Lyndon. <u>Swahili Poetry.</u> London: Oxford University Press, 1962.

Havelock, Eric. <u>Preface to Plato.</u> Cambridge, Mass.: Harvard University Press, 1962.

Kunene, Daniel P. <u>Heroic Poetry of the Basotho.</u> London: Oxford University Press, 1971.

Lestrade, G. P. "European Influences Upon the Development of Bantu Language and Literature." In <u>Western Civilization and the Natives of South Africa: Studies in Culture Contact.</u> Ed. I. Schapera. New York: Humanities Press, 1967. 105–27.

Lord, Albert B. <u>The Singer of Tales.</u> New York: Atheneum, 1974.

McLuhan, Marshall. <u>The Gutenberg Galaxy.</u> Toronto: University of Toronto Press, 1962.

Morris, H. F. <u>The Heroic Recitations of the Bahima of Ankole.</u> London: Oxford University Press, 1964.

Ong, Walter J. <u>The Presence of the Word.</u> New Haven, Conn.: Yale University Press, 1967.

Owomoyela, Oyekan. <u>African Literatures: An Introduction.</u> Waltham, Mass.: African Studies Association, 1979.

Schapera, I. <u>Praise-Poems of Tswana Chiefs.</u> London: Oxford University Press, 1965.

Scharfe, Don, and Yahaya Aliyu. "Hausa Poetry." In <u>Introduction to African Literature.</u> Ed. Ulli Beier. London: Longmans, Green, and Co., 1967.

EXERCISE 35

Reread the sample student paper. As you read, annotate the paper as follows:

1. Note the places where the student is using an academic writing strategy (rephrase, reduce, react, repeat, review) and identify the strategy in the margin.

2. Make note of the different ways the student writer has acknowledged the authors of the sources (either in the text or in parentheses).

REVISING: AS YOU WRITE

As you write the first draft of your paper, be aware of the following research-paper pitfalls:

1. Failing to narrow the topic
2. Failing to state a clear-cut thesis
3. Failing to develop an organizational plan for the paper
4. Stringing one source after another instead of integrating sources around ideas that support and develop your thesis
5. Using information from sources without acknowledging their authors or without documenting fully
6. Plunging into paraphrases, summaries, direct quotations, reactions, or reviews without providing sufficient background or context for your audience
7. Failing to tell your audience at all points in your paper what the source is for the ideas you are discussing
8. Losing coherence
9. Failing to develop a well-organized listing of sources

REVISING: AFTER YOU WRITE

Compare your Paper to the Assignment

If your assignment was narrow in scope, check that your paper speaks to the specific topic and hasn't distorted it in any way. If your assignment presented a broad topic and allowed for general discussion, be sure that your limited topic and thesis statement still relate to the original topic.

Check for Relative Proportions of Paraphrases, Summaries, Quotations, Reaction, and Analysis

Your audience should be able to distinguish between these different forms of academic writing. Also, you should check that you have devoted appropriate portions of your paper to each form of writing. Even though one form of writing may dominate—analysis, for example—it should not be used exclusively; your paper should also contain paraphrases, summaries, and quotations.

Check Paraphrases, Summaries, Quotations, and the Works-cited Listing for Accuracy

Review the procedures for editing paraphrases, summaries, and quotations. Be sure you have indicated clearly the places where paraphrase, summary, and quotation begin and end and have documented the sources accurately.

Edit for Grammar, Mechanics, and Usage

Review the checklist that we presented at the end of Chapter 12.

Type your Final Draft in the Proper Format

Refer to the sample paper presented earlier in this chapter and use the list below to check your finished work.

CHECKLIST FOR TYPING FINAL DRAFT

1. Does your title page contain the *title,* your *name,* the title and section of your *course,* your *professor's name,* and the *date?*
2. Is your manuscript double-spaced (except for extended quotations) throughout?
3. If you have included content endnotes, do they appear at the end of the paper on a separate page labeled "Notes?"
4. Have you included a properly organized works-cited page?

Proofread your Finished Paper

Typos count against you. Read each line of the paper, left to right. Correct in pen if you have to.

CASE IN POINT 42

Using the list of research-paper pitfalls, revise the rough draft of a research paper that you produced in Case 41. Type a final version and proofread it carefully.

RESEARCH: ADDITIONAL CASES AND ASSIGNMENTS

A. Consult a newspaper index of your choice: *New York Times, Wall Street Journal, Christian Science Monitor,* or the *Washington Post.* Look up two dates, the date either your mother or your father was born and your own birth date. Focus on three areas: news stories, sports stories, and entertainment (films, plays, television). Use the comparison plan to write an essay about the major events that took place on these two days.

B. Consult general and specific reference books, the card catalog, indexes, books, periodicals, and other sources to obtain information about each of the following events. Use the time-order plan to write an essay on the information you find.

(1) July 16, 1945: U.S. detonates first atomic bomb in New Mexico.

(2) August 6 & 9: U.S. drops atomic bombs on Hiroshima and Nagasaki.

(3) 1946: U.S. navy tests atomic bomb at Bikini.

(4) 1949: USSR tests first atomic bomb.

(5) 1951: Atomic energy used to produce electric power in Idaho.

(6) 1952: Britain conducts first atomic tests in Australia. U.S. explodes first hydrogen bomb in Pacific.

(7) 1953: USSR explodes hydrogen bomb.

(8) 1954: U.S. tests hydrogen bomb at Bikini. U.S. submarine *Nautilus* converts to nuclear power.

(9) 1955: Atomic power used to generate electricity in Schenectady, N.Y.

(10) 1959: U.S. nuclear-powered merchant vessel *Savannah* launched.

(11) 1960: U.S. *Triton* nuclear submarine launched.

(12) 1962: U.S. has 200 atomic reactors.

(13) 1967: People's Republic of China explodes hydrogen bomb.

(14) 1968: U.S. explodes hydrogen bomb underground near Las Vegas.

(15) 1971: U.S. explodes hydrogen bomb beneath island in Alaska.

(16) 1974: India explodes nuclear bomb.

(17) 1977: U.S. tests neutron bomb.

C. Can human babies be conceived outside the body of a woman? Research this topic and use the response plan to write a report on the information you find.

appendix a

Documentation Formats

EXAMPLES OF MLA STYLE

Book with one author:

Kennedy, William J. <u>Rhetorical Norms in Renaissance Literature.</u> New Haven: Yale University Press, 1978.

Book with two authors:

Lambert, William W., and Wallace E. Lambert. <u>Social Psychology.</u> Englewood Cliffs, N.J.: Prentice-Hall, 1964.

Book written by an organization:

Boston Women's Health Book Collective. <u>Our Bodies, Ourselves: A Book by and for Women.</u> New York: Simon & Schuster, 1971.

Book with an editor instead of an author:

Brofenbrenner, Urie, ed. <u>Influences on Human Development.</u> Hinsdale, Ill.: Dryden Press, 1972.

Book with a translator:

de Beauvoir, Simone. <u>Force of Circumstance.</u> Trans. Richard Howard. Harmondsworth, Middlesex, England: Penguin, 1968.

Section, chapter, or essay in a book or anthology:

Chomsky, Noam. "Psychology and Ideology." <u>For Reasons of State.</u>
    New York: Vintage, 1973.

Specific pages in a book:

Leggett, Glenn C., David Mead, and William Charvat. <u>Prentice-Hall</u>
    <u>Handbook for Writers.</u> 8th ed. Englewood Cliffs, N.J.: Prentice-
    Hall, 1982. 69–76.

Book with more than one edition:

Burgess, Ann Wolbert, and Aaron Lazare. <u>Psychiatric Nursing in the</u>
    <u>Hospital and the Community.</u> 2nd ed. Englewood Cliffs, N.J.:
    Prentice-Hall, 1976.

Encyclopedia:

Goris, Jan-Albert. "Belgian Literature." <u>Collier's Encyclopedia.</u> 1983 ed.

Play:

Miller, Arthur. <u>The Price.</u> New York: Bantam, 1969.

Poem:

Cornish, Sam. "To a Single Shadow Without Pity." In <u>The New Black</u>
    <u>Poetry.</u> Ed. Clarence Major. New York: International Publishers,
    1969. 39.

Pamphlet:

Hopper, Peggy, and Steve Soldz. <u>I Don't Want to Change My</u>
    <u>Lifestyle—I Want to Change My Life.</u> Cambridge, Mass.: Root and
    Branch, 1971.

Article in a scholarly or professional journal:
    Each issue has separately numbered pages:

Maimon, Elaine P. "Cinderella to Hercules: Demythologizing Writing
    Across the Curriculum." <u>Journal of Basic Writing</u> 2.4 (1980): 3–11.

    Entire volume has continuous page numbers:

Slack, Warner V., and Douglas Porter. "The Scholastic Aptitude Test: A
    Critical Appraisal." <u>Harvard Educational Review</u> 50 (1980): 154–75.

Article in a weekly or monthly magazine:
    Author's name given:

Golden, Frederic. "Heat over Wood Burning: Pollution from Home
    Stoves Is Nearing Crisis Proportions." <u>Time</u> 16 Jan. 1984: 67.

    No author's name given:

"Planning Ahead: Proposals for Democratic Control of Investment."
    <u>Dollars and Sense</u> Feb. 1983: 3–5.

Article in a newspaper:
  With byline:

Wald, Matthew L. "Coal Plants Held Cheaper Than Nuclear." <u>The New York Times</u> 11 Dec. 1983: 3.

  No byline:

"Breast Cancer Study to Begin on Long Island." <u>The Ithaca Journal</u> Ithaca, N.Y. 14 Jan. 1984: 2.

  Special feature:

"Breaking the Medicare Taboo." Editorial. <u>The New York Times</u> 8 Jan. 1984: E24, cols. 1–2.

Article reprinted in a book:

Nimkoff, Meyer F., and Russell Middleton. "Type of Family and Type of Enemy." <u>American Journal of Sociology</u> 66 (1960): 215–24. Rpt. in <u>Man in Adaptation: The Cultural Present.</u> Ed. Yehudi A. Cohen. Chicago: Aldine, 1968. 384–93.

Government publications:

U.S. Dept. of Energy. <u>Winter Survival: A Consumer's Guide to Winter Preparedness.</u> Washington, D.C.: GPO, 1980.

Congressional Record:

U.S. Cong. <u>Cong. Rec.</u> 13 April 1967, S5054-7.

Film:

<u>Duck Soup.</u> Paramount, 1933.

Television or radio program:

<u>The Day After.</u> New York: ABC-TV, 20 Nov. 1983.

Personal letter:

Siegele, Steven. Letter to author. 25 Nov. 1983.

Personal interview:

Erlich, Howard, asst. dean, Ithaca College. Personal interview. Ithaca, N.Y., 13 Jan. 1984.

Musical composition:

Bach, Johann Sebastian. <u>Mass in B Minor.</u>

Record:

Cooney, Michael. "Medley of Real Kids' Songs." In his <u>Pure Unsweetened: Live Family Concert.</u> Alliance, M4T2P4, 1982.

COMPARISON OF MLA AND APA STYLES

Parenthetical Documentation

<u>MLA</u>	<u>APA</u>

1. Give <u>last name of author</u> and the page number if you are citing a specific part of the source.

   e.g.:
   a. The question has been answered before (Sagan).
   b. Sagan has already answered the question (140–43).

1. Give <u>last name of author, publication date,</u> and the page number if you are citing a specific part of the source.
   e.g.:
   a. The question has been answered before (Sagan, 1980).
   b. Sagan (1980) has already answered the question (pp. 140–43).

2. Omit abbreviation for page.

   e.g.:
   Walsh dicusses this "game theory" (212–47).

2. Use "p." or "pp." to indicate pagination.
   e.g.:
   Walsh (1979) discusses this "game theory" (pp. 212–47).

3. Omit commas in parenthetical references.
   e.g.:
   The question has been answered before (Sagan 140–43).

3. Use commas within parentheses.

   e.g.:
   The question has been answered before (Sagan, 1980, pp. 140–43).

4. Use shortened form book title to distinguish between different works by the author.

   e.g.:
   Jones originally supported the single-factor theory (<u>Investigations</u>) but later realized that the phenomenon was more complex (<u>Theory</u>).

4. Use publication date (plus lowercase letters, if necessary) to distinguish between different works by the same author.
   e.g.:
   Jones originally supported the single-factor theory (1972) but later realized that the phenomenon was more complex (1979).

List of Sources

1. Title list of sources
   Works Cited

1. Title list of sources
   References

2. Use author's <u>full</u> name.

   e.g.:
   Sagan, Carl.

2. Use only the initials of author's first and middle names.
   e.g.:
   Sagan, C.

MLA

3. When there are two or more authors, invert the first author's name, insert a comma and the word <u>and,</u> and give second author's first name followed by surname.

e.g.:
Kennedy, Mary Lynch, and Hadley Mayo Smith

4. Capitalize all major words in all titles.

e.g.:
<u>The Beginner's Guide to Academic Writing and Reading</u>

5. List book data in the following sequence: author – title of book – place of publication – colon – publisher – date of publication.

e.g.:
Fries, Charles C. <u>Linguistics and Reading.</u> New York: Holt, Rinehart & Winston, 1962.

6. List journal article data in the following sequence: author – title of article – title of journal – volume number – date of publication in parentheses – colon – inclusive pages.

e.g.:
Booth, Wayne C. "The Limits of Pluralism." <u>Critical Inquiry</u> 3 (1977): 407–23.

7. List the data for an article in an edited book as follows: author of article – title of article – In – title of book – Ed. – editor's name – place of publication – colon – publisher – date – pages.

APA

3. When there are two or more authors, invert all of the names. After the first name, insert a comma and the abbreviation &.

e.g.:
Kennedy, M. L., & Smith, H. M.

4. Capitalize only the first word of the titles except for journals

e.g.:
a. <u>The Beginner's guide to academic writing and reading</u>
b. <u>Reading Research Quarterly</u>

5. List book data in the following sequence: author – date of publication in parentheses – title of book – place of publication – colon – publisher.

e.g.:
Fries, C. C. (1962). <u>Linguistics and reading.</u> New York: Holt, Rinehart & Winston.

6. List journal article data as follows:

author – date of publication – title of article – title of journal – volume number underlined – inclusive pages.

e.g.:
Booth, W. C. (1977). The limits of pluralism. <u>Critical Inquiry, 3,</u> 407–23.

7. List the data for an article in an edited book as follows: author of article – date – title of article – In – name of editor – (Ed.) – title of book– (pages) – place of publication – publisher.

MLA	APA
e.g.: Donaldson, E. Talbot. "Briseis, Criseyde, Cresseid, Cressid: Progress of a Heroine." In <u>Chaucerian Problems and Perspectives.</u> Ed. Edward Vasta and Zacharias P. Thundy. Notre Dame, Ind.: Notre Dame Univ. Press, 1979. 3–12.	e.g.: Donaldson, E. T. (1979). Briseis, Criseyde, Cresseid, Cressid: Progress of a heroine. In E. Vasta & Z. P. Thundy (Eds.), <u>Chaucerian problems and perspectives</u> (pp. 3–12). Notre Dame, Ind.: Notre Dame Univ. Press. Note: The proper names in the article title are capitalized as is the word following the colon.

Content Endnotes

MLA	APA
1. Title for endnote list: Notes	1. Title for endnote list: Footnotes
2. Place endnote list immediately <u>before</u> list of references.	2. Place endnote list immediately <u>after</u> list of references.
3. Skip one space between reference numeral and endnote. e.g.: [1] For more information, see Jones and Brown.	3. Do not skip any space between reference numeral and endnote. e.g.: [1]For more information, see Jones (1983) and Brown (1981).

appendix b

Readings

Communication Without Words

by Albert Mehrabian

Suppose you are sitting in my office listening to me describe some research I have done on communication. <u>I tell you that feelings are communicated less by the words a person uses than by certain nonverbal means—that, for example, the verbal part of a spoken message has considerably less effect on whether a listener feels liked or disliked than a speaker's facial expression or tone of voice.</u>

So far so good. But suppose I add, "In fact, we've worked out a formula that shows exactly how much each of these components contributes to the effect of the message as a whole. It goes like this: Total impact = .07 verbal + .38 vocal + .55 facial."

What would you say to that? Perhaps you would smile good-naturedly and say, with some feeling, "Baloney!" Or perhaps you would frown and remark acidly, "Isn't science grand." My own response to the first answer would probably be to smile back: the facial part of your message, at least, was positive (55 percent of the total). The second answer might make me uncomfortable: only the verbal part was positive (seven per cent).

Mehrabian, Albert. "Communication Without Words." *Psychology Today* 2.4 (1968): 53–55.

The point here is not only that my reactions would lend credence to the formula but that most listeners would have mixed feelings about my statement. People like to see science march on, but they tend to resent its intrusion into an "art" like the communication of feelings, just as they find analytical and quantitative approaches to the study of personality cold, mechanistic and unacceptable.

The psychologist himself is sometimes plagued by the feeling that he is trying to put a rainbow into a bottle. Fascinated by a complicated and emotionally rich human situation, he begins to study it, only to find in the course of his research that he has destroyed part of the mystique that originally intrigued and involved him. But despite a certain nostalgia for earlier, more intuitive approaches, one must acknowledge that concrete experimental data have added a great deal to our understanding of how feelings are communicated. In fact, as I hope to show, analytical and intuitive findings do not so much conflict as complement each other.

It is indeed difficult to know what another person really feels. He says one thing and does another; he seems to mean something but we have an uneasy feeling it isn't true. The early psychoanalysts, facing this problem of inconsistencies and ambiguities in a person's communications, attempted to resolve it through the concepts of the conscious and the unconscious. They assumed that contradictory messages meant a conflict between superficial, deceitful, or erroneous feelings on the one hand and true attitudes and feelings on the other. Their role, then, was to help the client separate the wheat from the chaff.

The question was, how could this be done? Some analysts insisted that inferring the client's unconscious wishes was a completely intuitive process. Others thought that some nonverbal behavior, such as posture, position and movement, could be used in a more objective way to discover the client's feelings. A favorite technique of Frieda Fromm-Reichmann, for example, was to imitate a client's posture herself in order to obtain some feeling for what he was experiencing.

Thus began the gradual shift away from the idea that communication is primarily verbal, and that the verbal message includes distortions or ambiguities due to unobservable motives that only experts can discover. Language, though, can be used to communicate almost anything. By comparison, nonverbal behavior is very limited in range. Usually, it is used to communicate feelings, likings and preferences, and it customarily reinforces or contradicts the feelings that are communicated verbally. Less often, it adds a new dimension of sorts to a verbal message, as when a salesman describes his product to a client and simultaneously conveys, nonverbally, the impression that he likes the client.

A great many forms of nonverbal behavior can communicate feelings: touching, facial expression, tone of voice, spacial distance from the addressee, relaxation of posture, rate of speech, number of errors in speech.

Some of these are generally recognized as informative. Untrained adults and children easily infer that they are liked or disliked from certain facial expressions, from whether (and how) someone touches them, and from a speaker's tone of voice. Other behavior, such as posture, has a more subtle effect. A listener may sense how someone feels about him from the way the person sits while talking to him, but he may have trouble identifying precisely what his impression comes from.

Correct intuitive judgments of the feelings or attitudes of others are especially difficult when different degrees of feeling, or contradictory kinds of feeling, are expressed simultaneously through different forms of behavior. As I have pointed out, there is a distinction between verbal and vocal information (vocal information being what is lost when speech is written down—intonation, tone, stress, length and frequency of pauses, and so on), and the two kinds of information do not always communicate the same feeling. This distinction, which has been recognized for some time, has shed new light on certain types of communication. Sarcasm, for example, can be defined as a message in which the information transmitted vocally contradicts the information transmitted verbally. Usually the verbal information is positive and the vocal is negative, as in "Isn't science grand."

Through the use of an electronic filter, it is possible to measure the degree of liking communicated vocally. What the filter does is eliminate the higher frequencies of recorded speech, so that words are unintelligible but most vocal qualities remain. (For women's speech, we eliminate frequencies higher than about 200 cycles per second; for men, frequencies over about 100 cycles per second.) When people are asked to judge the degree of liking conveyed by the filtered speech, they perform the task rather easily with a significant amount of agreement.

This method allows us to find out, in a given message, just how inconsistent the information communicated in words and the information communicated vocally really are. We ask one group to judge the amount of liking conveyed by a transcript of what was said, the verbal part of the message. A second group judges the vocal component, and a third group judges the impact of the complete recorded message. In one study of this sort we found that, when the verbal and vocal components of a message agree (both positive or both negative), the message as a whole is judged a little more positive or a little more negative than either component by itself. But when vocal information contradicts verbal, vocal wins out. If someone calls you "honey" in a nasty tone of voice, you are likely to feel disliked; it is also possible to say "I hate you" in a way that conveys exactly the opposite feeling.

Besides the verbal and vocal characteristics of speech, there are other, more subtle, signals of meaning in a spoken message. For example, everyone makes mistakes when he talks—unnecessary repetitions, stutterings, the omission of parts of words, incomplete sentences, "ums" and "ahs." In a number of studies of speech errors, George Mahl of Yale University has found that errors become more frequent as the speaker's discomfort or anxiety increases. It might be interesting to apply this index in an attempt to detect deceit (though on some occasions it might be risky: confidence men are notoriously smooth talkers).

Timing is also highly informative. How long does a speaker allow silent periods to last, and how long does he wait before he answers his partner? How long do his utterances tend to be? How often does he interrupt his partner, or wait an inappropriately long time before speaking? Joseph Matarazzo and his colleagues at the University of Oregon have found that each of these speech habits is stable from person to person, and each tells something about the speaker's personality and about his feelings toward and status in relation to his partner.

Utterance duration, for example, is a very stable quality in a person's speech; about 30 seconds long on the average. But when someone talks to a partner whose status is higher than his own, the more the high-status person nods his head the longer the speaker's utterances become. If the high-status person changes his own customary speech pattern toward longer or shorter utterances, the lower-status person will change his own speech in the same direction. If the high-status person often interrupts the speaker, or creates long silences, the speaker is likely to become quite uncomfortable. These are things that can be observed outside the laboratory as well as under experimental conditions. If you have an employee who makes you uneasy and seems not to respect you, watch him the next time you talk to him—perhaps he is failing to follow the customary low-status pattern.

Immediacy or directness is another good source of information about feelings. We use more distant forms of communication when the act of communicating is undesirable or uncomfortable. For example, some people would rather transmit discontent with an employee's work through a third party than do it themselves, and some find it easier to communicate negative feelings in writing than by telephone or face to face.

Distance can show a negative attitude toward the message itself, as well as toward the act of delivering it. Certain forms of speech are more distant than others, and they show fewer positive feelings for the subject referred to. A speaker might say "Those people need help," which is more distant than "These people need help," which is in turn even more distant than "These people need our help." Or he might say "Sam and I have been having dinner," which has less immediacy than "Sam and I are having dinner."

Facial expression, touching, gestures, self-manipulation (such as scratching), changes in body position, and head movements—all these express a person's positive and negative attitudes, both at the moment and in general, and many reflect status relationships as well. Movements of the limbs and head, for example, not only indicate one's attitude toward a specific set of circumstances but relate to how dominant, and how anxious, one generally tends to be in social situations. Gross changes in body position, such as shifting in the chair, may show negative feelings toward the person who is talking. They may also be cues: "It's your turn to talk," or "I'm about to get out of here, so finish what you are saying."

Posture is used to indicate both liking and status. The more a person leans toward his addressee, the more positively he feels about him. Relaxation of posture is a good indicator of both attitude and status, and one that we have been able to measure quite precisely. Three categories have been established for relaxation in a seated position: least relaxation is indicated by muscular tension in the hands and rigidity of posture; moderate relaxation is indicated by a forward lean of about 20 degrees and a sideways lean of less than 10 degrees, a curved back, and, for women, an open arm position; and extreme relaxation is indicated by a reclining angle greater than 20 degrees and a sideways lean greater than 10 degrees.

Our findings suggest that a speaker relaxes either very little or a great deal when he dislikes the person he is talking to, and to a moderate degree when he likes his companion. It seems that extreme tension occurs with threatening addresses, and extreme relaxation with non-threatening, disliked addresses. In particular, men tend to become tense when talking to other men whom they dislike; on the other hand, women talking to men or women and men talking to women show dislike through extreme relaxation. As for status, people relax most with a low-status addressee, second-most with a peer, and least with someone of higher status than their own. Body orientation also shows status: in both sexes, it is least direct toward women with low status and most direct toward disliked men of high status. In part, body orientation seems to be determined by whether one regards one's partner as threatening.

The more you like a person, the more time you are likely to spend looking into his eyes as you talk to him. Standing close to your partner and facing him directly (which makes eye contact easier) also indicate positive feelings. And you are likely to stand or sit closer to your peers than you do to addressees whose status is either lower or higher than yours.

What I have said so far has been based on research studies performed, for the most part, with college students from the middle and upper-middle classes. One interesting question about communication, however, concerns young children from lower socioeconomic levels. Are these children, as some have suggested, more responsive to implicit channels of communication than middle- and upper-class children are?

Morton Wiener and his colleagues at Clark University had a group of middle- and lower-class children play learning games in which the reward for learning was praise. The child's responsiveness to the verbal and vocal parts of the praise-reward was measured by how much he learned. Praise came in two forms: the objective words "right" and "correct," and the more affective or evaluative words, "good" and "fine." All four words were spoken sometimes in a positive tone of voice and sometimes neutrally.

Positive intonation proved to have a dramatic effect on the learning rate of the lower-class group. They learned much faster when the vocal part of the message was positive than when it was neutral. Positive intonation affected the middle-class group as well, but not nearly as much.

If children of lower socioeconomic groups are more responsive to facial expression, posture and touch as well as to vocal communication, that fact could have interesting applications to elementary education. For example, teachers could be explicitly trained to be aware of, and to use, the form of praise (non-verbal or verbal) that would be likely to have the greatest effect on their particular students.

Another application of experimental data on communication is to the interpretation and treatment of schizophrenia. The literature on schizophrenia has for some time emphasized that parents of schizophrenic children give off contradictory signals simultaneously. Perhaps the parent tells the child in words that he loves him, but his posture conveys a negative attitude. According to the "double-bind" theory of schizophrenia, the child who perceives simultaneous contradictory feelings in his parent does not know how to react: should he respond to the positive part of the message, or to the negative? If he is frequently placed in this paralyzing situation, he may learn to respond with contradictory communications of his own. The boy who sends a birthday card to his mother and signs it "Napoleon" says that he likes his mother and yet denies that he is the one who likes her.

In an attempt to determine whether parents of disturbed children really do emit more inconsistent messages about their feelings than other parents do, my colleagues and I have compared what these parents communicate verbally and vocally with what they show through posture. We interviewed parents of moderately and quite severely disturbed children, in the presence of the child, about the child's problem. The interview was video-recorded without the parents' knowledge, so that we could analyze their behavior later on. Our measurements supplied both the amount of inconsistency between the parents' verbal-vocal and postural communications, and the total amount of liking that the parents communicated.

According to the double-bind theory, the parents of the more disturbed children should have behaved more inconsistently than the parents of the less disturbed children. This was not confirmed: there was no significant difference between the two groups. However, the total amount of positive feeling communicated by parents of the more disturbed children was less than that communicated by the other group.

This suggests that (1) negative communications toward disturbed children occur because the child is a problem and therefore elicits them, or (2) the negative attitude precedes the child's disturbance. It may also be that both factors operate together, in a vicious circle.

If so, one way to break the cycle is for the therapist to create situations in which the parent can have better feelings toward the child. A more positive attitude from the parent may make the child more responsive to his directives, and the spiral may begin to move up instead of down. In our own work with disturbed children, this kind of procedure has been used to good effect.

If one puts one's mind to it, one can think of a great many other applications for the findings I have described, though not all of them concern serious problems. Politicians, for example, are careful to maintain eye contact with the television camera when they speak, but they are not always careful about how they sit when they debate another candidate of, presumably, equal status.

Public relations men might find a use for some of the subtler signals of feeling. So might Don Juans. And so might ordinary people, who could try watching other people's signals and changing their own, for fun at a party or in a spirit of experimentation at home. I trust that does not strike you as a cold, manipulative suggestion, indicating a dislike for the human race. I assure you that, if you had more than a transcription of words to judge from (seven per cent of total message), it would not.

Human Communication

by John F. Wilson and Carroll C. Arnold

There are two good reasons for studying how we communicate. First communication is necessary to human beings' healthy development. Solitary confinement is severe punishment just because it ends association and communication with others. Experiments have shown that people even begin to have hallucinations when deprived of the company of other humans. Second, understanding how we communicate reveals a great deal that is widely useful for understanding all social behavior, as we suggested in the previous section.

Wilson, John F., and Carroll C. Arnold. *Dimensions of Public Communication*. Boston: Allyn and Bacon, 1976, 9–10.

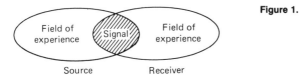

Figure 1.

Scholars have represented how we communicate in a number of ways, but Figure 1 is a graphic representation we like because it is simple and shows some basic features of all of our satisfying relationships with one another. The major points made by this figure, which we have adapted from one originally drawn by Wilbur Schramm, are:

1. Each human being engaged in communication lives within his or her *own* "field of experience." You and everyone else know what experience has taught. You understand soccer, but I don't, so you must teach me about soccer—put it into my experience—before we can communicate about it as equals. So it is in all communication and in most other social relationships; for understanding, there must be *shared* experience. But it is not possible for us to sense and know everything exactly alike. Some of our awarenesses and understandings are always different from those our partners have. In the figure these unshared aspects of our experiences are represented by the unshaded portions of the two ellipses. For most people there is more unshared than shared experience.

2. We communicate by signaling one another. The source chooses one kind of signal or another (speech, writing, waving flags, dressing in certain ways, etc.). Our signals represent our meanings, but they are not meanings in themselves. In communication we signal with *symbols*—behaviors that *stand for* specific meanings.

3. For us to understand each other, the signals of a source must fall within the experience of the receiver; the signals must be *mutually* understood. That we can only communicate through commonly understood symbols is represented in the figure by placing the "signal" within the shaded area of overlapping experience.

4. All you and I can really know about one another is what we can communicate to one another through experiences we have or can share. Each of us will remain ignorant of most of the others' experiences.

5. The most important point of the figure is this: the problem we face in making communication work is the problem of creating signals that (a) are understood by those we try to communicate with, and (b) have meanings that relate to experiences shared by both of us. Put differently, the problem is to keep communicative efforts constantly within the overlapping portion of our partners' and our own experience.

We shall not go further into the subject of general communication theory because our concern is with a special kind of communication: rhetorically speaking—any speaking intended to get someone else to understand or agree to an idea or set of ideas. Obviously this kind of speaking will involve us in a close study of the *ideas* speakers and listeners share or can be helped to share. Indeed, the basic task of public speakers is to discover the true natures of their listeners, as they listen in a situation shared with the speaker.

Everyone Communicates

by Anabel Dean

When you talk with a friend, that is communication. But you do not have to talk to communicate. You can shake your head when you mean "no," put your fingers to your lips when you mean "quiet." Your arm around a friend who has been hurt shows you are sorry. *Communication takes place any time a message is sent and received.*

From human beings down to the smallest insect, every animal has some way of communicating. For animals to survive as a *species*—a group with characteristics in common—they must have a food supply, a safe place to live, a mate and young. To get these things, they must communicate.

People communicate. What would you do if you were to bang your head on a branch while traveling through the jungles of Zambia? You would probably say "Ow!" and rub your head. If a Zambian hit his head on the same branch, he would do the same thing. A cry of fear, joy, or pain is the same no matter what the language. Gestures, also, often mean the same thing to many different peoples. People communicated with cries and gestures long before they developed languages.

But cries and gestures do not give exact information. It would be hard to grunt an order for a sundae with three scoops of chocolate fudge ice-cream, strawberries and nuts, and have it come out right!

Words probably came into use one by one. One small group of people might have started to use a certain sound for some object—let's say a rock. After a long time, everyone from that tribe used the same sound for rock. It took thousands of years for a spoken language to develop.

For many centuries, spoken language was the only way to pass on knowledge. Over distances and years, much information was lost forever. Then people began to keep records by making marks in the dirt or scratching and painting pictures on cave walls or rocks, and, much later, on clay tablets. It took hundreds of years more for groups of people to develop an alphabet, with a letter to represent each sound they used. Then the letters could be put together to form any words. This is the method we use with our alphabet of 26 letters.

Writing made it possible to communicate over distances, and time. We read books written by people who died long before we were born. We communicate with letters and newspapers and radio and television pictures. Pictures and words can be sent around the world and to and from the moon—and Mars.

Humans and animals communicate. People and animals communicate by learning each other's signals. The hunter's scent carried downwind warns the deer to run. The shepherd steers his sheep dog with a motion of his arm. Many dogs have been able to follow the scent trail left by a human after smelling an article of clothing.

A dog brings a ball and lays it at someone's feet to show it wants to play. We snap our fingers for the dog, or whistle. We call, "Here, kitty, kitty," and the cat comes to us. Other types of sounds can also carry messages. The sound of the can opener may bring the dog or cat into the kitchen. The jingle of the car keys may send the dog running to the door.

Messages are passed between animals and humans by touch. A cat rubs against a person's legs when it wants something. You pat your dog to show approval.

Experiments are being made to see if an animal can be taught to communicate with a human language. Keith and Cathy Hayes took Viki, a six-week-old chimpanzee, and raised her as if she were a child. In six years, Viki learned many directions, so she understood many words. But speaking them was too difficult—she only learned to say three words.

In 1966 Allan and Bea Gardner took a chimp, Washoe, into their home to teach her the sign language used by the deaf. When Washoe was four, she could use more than sixty words in sign language. She made the sign for "please" by drawing an open hand across her chest. She could say "I want more" by putting her fingertips together.

After Washoe learned the word for "open" when she wanted the door to her room opened, she was able to understand that she could use the word for anything she wanted opened. She also learned to put words together to make sentences.

Will humans and any of the animals ever be able to talk together using human language? The answer to that question still remains to be answered.

How Communication Works

by Wilbur Schramm

Communication comes from the Latin *Communis,* common. When we communicate we are trying to establish a "commonness" with someone. That is, we are trying to share information, an idea, or an attitude. At this moment I am trying to communicate to you the idea that the essence of communication is getting the receiver and the sender "tuned" together for a particular message. At this same moment, someone somewhere is excitedly phoning the fire department that the house is on fire. Somewhere else a young man in a parked automobile is trying to convey the understanding that he is mooneyed because he loves the young lady. Somewhere else a newspaper is trying to persuade its readers to believe as it does about the Republican Party. All these are forms of communication, and the process in each case is essentially the same.

Communication always requires at least three elements—the source, the message, and the destination. A source may be an individual (speaking, writing, drawing, gesturing) or a communication organization (like a newspaper, publishing house, television station, or motion picture studio). The message may be in the form of ink on paper, sound waves in the air, impulses in an electric current, a wave of the hand, a flag in the air, or any other signal capable of being interpreted meaningfully. The destination may be an individual listening, watching, or reading; or a member of a group, such as a discussion group, a lecture audience, a football crowd, or a mob; or an individual member of the particular group we call the mass audience, such as the reader of a newspaper or a viewer of television.

Now what happens when the source tries to build up this "commonness" with his intended receiver? First, the source encodes his message. That is, he takes the information or feeling he wants to share and puts it into a form that can be transmitted. The "pictures in our heads" can't be transmitted until they are coded. When they are coded into spoken words, they can be transmitted easily and effectively, but they can't travel very far unless radio carries them. If they are coded into written words,

Schramm, Wilbur, ed. *The Process and Effects of Mass Communication.* Champaign, Ill.: University of Illinois Press, 1954, 3–4.

they go more slowly than spoken words, but they go farther and last longer. Indeed, some messages long outlive their senders—the *Illiad*, for instance; the Gettysburg address, Chartres cathedral. Once coded and sent, a message is quite free of its sender, and what it does is beyond the power of the sender to change. Every writer feels a sense of helplessness when he finally commits his story or his poem to print; you doubtless feel the same way when you mail an important letter. Will it reach the right person? Will he understand it as you intend him to? Will he respond as you want him to? For in order to complete the act of communication the message must be decoded. And there is good reason, as we shall see, for the sender to wonder whether his receiver will really be in tune with him, whether the message will be interpreted without distortion, whether the "picture in the head" of the receiver will bear any resemblance to that in the head of the sender.

We are talking about something very like a radio or telephone circuit. In fact, it is perfectly possible to draw a picture of the human communication system that way:

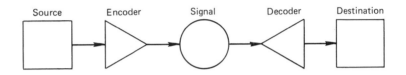

Substitute "microphone" for encoder and "earphone" for decoder and you are talking about electronic communication. Consider that the "source" and "encoder" are one person, "decoder" and "destination" are another, and the signal is language, and you are talking about human communication.

Now it is perfectly possible by looking at those diagrams to predict how such a system will work. For one thing, such a system can be no stronger than its weakest link. In engineering terms, if the source does not have adequate or clear information; if the message is not encoded fully, accurately, effectively in transmittable signs; if these are not transmitted fast enough and accurately enough, despite interference and competition, to the desired receiver; if the message is not decoded in a pattern that corresponds to the encoding; and finally, if the destination is unable to handle the decoded meessage so as to produce the desired response—then, obviously, the system is working at less than top efficiency. When we realize that all these steps must be accomplished with relatively high efficiency if any communication is to be successful, the everyday act of explaining something to a stranger, or writing a letter, seems a minor miracle.

Social Psychology

by William W. Lambert and Wallace E. Lambert

Recently, Stanley Schachter* boldly and profitably reopened an issue in the study of socialization that earlier researchers had found rather fruitless—that of birth order. He discovered (to his own surprise) in a study of some college students that a person's position in the birth order of his family is related to his choice of remaining alone or being with others when faced with a frightening situation. The preponderance of persons who were first-born or only children reported that in a frightening situation they chose to be with others, whereas the preponderance of those who were later-born chose to face their worry alone. Of course, the degree of fright may be of importance in this relationship, and first-born and only children tend to have, or at least to report, greater fear. But even when only highly anxious people are considered, the same results related to order of birth are found. This effect Schachter found shows up most clearly in an anxiety-producing or threatening situation. It is not related to family size, but it appears to be related to absolute order of birth in that a fourth-born person is even more likely to want to be alone than is a second born-one. These are clear and germinal findings, yet they were determined only after many other researchers had concluded that birth order was probably not a particularly significant source of differences in socialization.

Schachter was a good social psychological detective here, looking backward and forward, as well as carefully analyzing his findings. He looked back into the early period of personality formation to discover what there is about being first-born that might explain these differences. His best hunch, after reviewing past literature, is that dependency is highly developed in the first child by oversolicitous and inexperienced parents. He is given more care than later children and is more often breast-fed. Ratings of both boys and girls in a nursery school showed that first-borns tend to seek help, proximity, physical contact, attention, and recognition from adults more than do later-born children. Having developed these habits, the children may retain them and draw on them whenever they are anxious. This is a tentative interpretation, and there is need for further research here.

Schachter looked ahead to later behavior in which a difference in a dependency might show up. He found indications that first-borns are more prone to utilize psychotherapy than are later-borns, the latter pre-

Lambert, William W., and Wallace E. Lambert. *Social Psychology.* © 1964, pp 24,25. Reprinted by permission of Prentice-Hall, Inc. Englewood Cliffs, NJ.

*S. Schachter. The psychology of affiliation. Stanford: Stanford University Press, 1959.

ferring to solve problems on their own. And other differences were detected. More later-borns are found among alcoholics than would be expected solely from their number in the population. Fewer fighter pilots who are first-born children become aces (with five or more kills), perhaps because of their higher anxiety. Harold H. Kelley† has recently pushed matters still farther with evidence suggesting that first-borns may handle power struggles in a manner different from that of later-borns. The former try to get their own way through means that will not alienate others, whereas the latter are more prepared to throw down the gauntlet and demand their own way, hang the consequences. The first-born seem to like to leave their adversaries feeling subordinated. This difference may stem from power strategies learned in the home: The first-born, as we have seen, is dependent and anxious and learns first to deal with unbeatable adults; the later-born, less dependent and less scared, learns early to deal with a first-born who can be frightened by a straight power-play. Schachter's findings, like all good science, casts light on old questions and gives us the opportunity to raise new ones.

Schachter has two suggestions regarding the value to first-borns in facing trouble with others rather than alone. First, the presence of others directly reduces anxiety; second, he can satisfy his desire for self-evaluation by watching others and comparing his own response in the situation to theirs. "Know thyself" may be an admonition created by a first-born child.

A Red Light for Scofflaws

by Frank Trippett

Law-and-order is the longest-running and probably the best-loved political issue in U.S. history. Yet it is painfully apparent that millions of Americans who would never think of themselves as lawbreakers, let alone criminals, are taking increasing liberties with the legal codes that are designed to protect and nourish their society. Indeed, there are moments today—amid outlaw litter, tax cheating, illicit noise and motorized anarchy—when it seems as though the scofflaw represents the wave of the future. Harvard Sociologist David Riesman suspects that a majority of Americans have blithely taken to committing supposedly minor derelictions as a matter of course. Already, Riesman says, the

†H. H. Kelley, Report to NSF, Grant NSF-G553, 1961.

ethic of U.S. society is in danger of becoming this: "You're a
fool if you obey the rules."*

Nothing could be more obvious than the evidence supporting
Riesman. Scofflaws abound in amazing variety. The graffiti prone
turn public surfaces into visual rubbish. Bicyclists often ride as
though two-wheeled vehicles are exempt from all traffic laws.
Litterbugs convert their communities into trash dumps. Widespread flurries of ordinances have failed to clear public places
of high-decibel portable radios, just as earlier laws failed to wipe
out the beer-soaked hooliganism that plagues many parks. To-
bacco addicts remain hopelessly blind to signs that say NO
SMOKING. Respectably dressed pot smokers no longer bother
to duck out of public sight to pass around a joint. The flagrant
use of cocaine is a festering scandal in middle- and upper-class
life. And then there are (hello, Everybody!) the jaywalkers.*

The dangers of scofflawry vary wildly. The person who illegally spits on the sidewalk remains disgusting, but clearly poses
less risk to others than the company that illegally buries hazard-
ous chemical waste in an unauthorized location. The fare beater
on the subway presents less threat to life than the landlord who
ignores fire safety statutes. The most immediately and meas-
urably dangerous scofflawry, however, also happens to be the
most visible. The culprit is the American driver, whose lawless
activities today add up to a colossal public nuisance. The hazards
range from routine double parking that jams city streets to the
drunk driving that kills some 25,000 people and injures at least
650,000 others yearly. Illegal speeding on open highways? New
surveys show that on some interstate highways 83% of all drivers
are currently ignoring the federal 55 m.p.h. speed limit.*

The most flagrant scofflaw of them all is the red-light runner.
The flouting of stop signals has got so bad in Boston that resi-
dents tell an anecdote about a cabby who insists that red lights
are "just for decoration." The power of the stoplight to control
traffic seems to be waning everywhere. In Los Angeles, red-light
running has become perhaps the city's most common traffic violation. In New York City, going through an intersection is like
Russian roulette. Admits Police Commissioner Robert J. Mc-
Guire: "Today it's a 50–50 toss-up as to whether people will stop
for a red light." Meanwhile, his own police largely ignore the
lawbreaking.*

Red-light running has always been ranked as a minor wrong,
and so it may be in individual instances. When the violation
becomes habitual, widespread and incessant, however, a great
deal more than a traffic management problem is involved. The

flouting of basic rules of the road leaves deep dents in the social mood. Innocent drivers and pedestrians pay a repetitious price in frustration, inconvenience and outrage, not to mention a justified sense of mortal peril. The significance of red-light running is magnified by its high visibility. If hypocrisy is the tribute that vice pays to virtue, then furtiveness is the true outlaw's salute to the force of law-and-order. The red-light runner, however, shows no respect whatever for the social rules, and society cannot help being harmed by any repetitious and brazen display of contempt for the fundamentals of order.*

The scofflaw spirit is pervasive. It is not really surprising when schools find, as some do, that children frequently enter not knowing some of the basic rules of living together. For all their differences, today's scofflaws are of a piece as a symptom of elementary social demoralization—the loss by individuals of the capacity to govern their own behavior in the interest of others.*

The prospect of the collapse of public manners is not merely a matter of etiquette. Society's first concern will remain major crime (see Cover Story), but a foretaste of the seriousness of incivility is suggested by what has been happening in Houston. Drivers on Houston freeways have been showing an increasing tendency to replace the rules of the road with violent outbreaks. Items from the Houston police department's new statistical category—freeway traffic violence: 1) Driver flashes high-beam lights at car that cut in front of him, whose occupants then hurl a beer can at his windshield, kick out his tail lights, slug him eight stitches' worth. 2) Dump-truck driver annoyed by delay batters trunk of stalled car ahead and its driver with steel bolt. 3) Hurrying driver of 18-wheel truck deliberately rear-ends car whose driver was trying to stay within 55 m.p.h. limit. The Houston Freeway Syndrome has fortunately not spread everywhere. But the question is: Will it?*

Americans are used to thinking that law-and-order is threatened mainly by stereotypical violent crime. When the foundations of U.S. law have actually been shaken, however, it has always been because ordinary law-abiding citizens took to skirting the law. Major instance: Prohibition. Recalls Donald Barr Chidsey in *On and Off the Wagon:* "Lawbreaking proved to be not painful, not even uncomfortable, but, in a mild and perfectly safe way, exhilarating." People wiped out Prohibition at last not only because of the alcohol issue but because scofflawry was seriously undermining the authority and legitimacy of government. Ironically, today's scofflaw spirit, whatever its undetermined origins, is being encouraged unwittingly by government at many levels. The failure of police to enforce certain laws is only the surface of the problem; they take their mandate from the officials and constituents they serve. Worse, most state legislatures have helped subvert popular compliance with the federal 55 m.p.h. law, some of them by enacting puny fines that trivialize transgressions. On a higher level, the Administration in Washington has dramatized its wish to nullify civil rights laws simply by opposing instead of supporting certain court-ordered desegregation rulings. With considerable justification, environmental groups, in the words of *Wilderness* magazine, accuse the Administration of "destroying environmental laws by failing to enforce them, or by enforcing them in ways that deliberately encourage noncompliance." Translation: scofflawry at the top.*

The most disquieting thing about the scofflaw spirit is its extreme infectiousness. Only a terminally foolish society would sit still and allow it to spread indefinitely.*

Index

A

Abstract words, 34–35
Academic writing, definition, 1
Analysis questions, 130–43
Analyzing academic sources (*see* Reviewing academic sources)
APA style, 189
Arnold, Carroll C., 250–52
Assignments, academic writing, 1–2
Audience:
    for academic writing, 2–3
    for a paraphrase, 15–16
    for a quotation, 172
    for a reaction, 94
    for research, 204–5
    for a review, 126–28
    for a summary, 50–51
Author's plan (*see* Organizational plans for academic writing)

B

Body paragraphs, 70

C

Capitalization, for quotations, 181–82
Card Catalog, 207–9
Clauses, 30–33
Close reading (*see* Reading for academic writing)
"Communication Without Words" (Mehrabian), 244–50
Conclusions, 70
Concrete words, 34–35
Context clues to word meaning, 26–27

D

Dean, Anabel, 252–54

E

Ellipses, 183
"Everyone Communicates" (Dean), 252–54